INSTITUTE OF MODERN LANGUAGES RESEARCH
UNIVERSITY OF LONDON

BITHELL SERIES OF DISSERTATIONS
VOLUME 44

Society and its Outsiders in the Novels of Jakob Wassermann

INSTITUTE OF MODERN LANGUAGES RESEARCH

BITHELL SERIES OF DISSERTATIONS

Launched in 1978 by the then Institute of Germanic Studies, the Bithell Series of Dissertations is designed to help young scholars publish recent work of high quality which has been accepted for the award of a research degree by a University in the United Kingdom or the Republic of Ireland. Volumes 14 to 41 were published in conjunction with the Modern Humanities Research Association. From 2015 onwards, publication has been resumed by the Institute of Modern Languages Research (IMLR). For a list of previous volumes in the series, see http://modernlanguages.sas.ac.uk/publications/bithell-series-dissertations/.

Theses for possible inclusion in the series are considered by the Bithell Editorial Board twice annually, in May and November. Recommendations for theses to be considered should be made by the supervisor and/or examiner(s), should be accompanied by a copy of the Examiners' Report and Abstract, and sent to Dr Godela Weiss-Sussex at the Institute of Modern Languages Research, University of London, Senate House, Malet Street, London WC1E 7HU (email: godela.weiss-sussex@sas.ac.uk).

Society and its Outsiders in the Novels of Jakob Wassermann

by
Katharina Volckmer

Institute of Modern Languages Research
2016

Published by the

Institute of Modern Languages Research
School of Advanced Study, University of London
Senate House, Malet Street, London WC1E 7HU
http://modernlanguages.sas.ac.uk

Cover image: designed by Ute Kirkwood

First published 2016

ISBN 978 0 85457 250 2

ISSN 0266-7932

CONTENTS

ACKNOWLEDGEMENTS

I want to begin by thanking Ritchie Robertson for having been a wonderful supervisor. None of this would have been possible without his advice, his dedication and his friendship. The Queen's College has been a great network of universal support and I want to thank it for making me feel at home. I am grateful for the four years spent at this institution. Charlie Louth and Betiel Wasihun have given me the chance to gain some teaching experience, which I have greatly enjoyed. At the same time I want to thank the students of Queen's College and Lincoln College for having been a challenge and a source of inspiration. I wish them the best of luck for the future. I have greatly appreciated the advice of my previous examiners Tony Phelan, Tom Kuhn and Ben Morgan. I also want to thank Ben for organizing the reading group on Fridays which has been one of the highlights of my Oxford life. I hope it will continue for many years to come. Ben Morgan and David Midgely turned my viva into a great experience. Thank you. The staff at the Deutsches Literaturarchiv in Marbach were of great help when it came to unearthing Wassermann's correspondence. They also generously supported me for a one-week workshop there in 2012.

The staff at the Stadtbibliothek Nürnberg were also very helpful in giving me access to some of Wassermann's letters as well as his private library. Anne Simon has been a great editor and I would like to thank her for all her support and patience. Camillo de Vivanco and Matthew McCarthy-Rechowicz have been great DPhil colleagues, friends and agony aunts and together we have become experts in the art of moaning. Without their support this project would have been much more difficult. Monica Merlin has been a continuous source of advice and without her IT-support the aesthetic value of this piece could not have been guaranteed. Ute Kirkwood has been a loyal friend throughout this project and has been kind enough to reply to most of my numerous (mostly) dispirited text messages sent from the Taylorian. Research, it seems, is not such a lonely project after all. Conor O'Brien has listened to all my questions with saintly patience and has managed to explain to me the difference between fog and mist. Leonard Olschner, my former supervisor, has remained a friend and an advisor throughout this project, for which I would like to thank him. Shahin Zarinbal is a wonderful human being. My *Sitzungen* with Florian Strob have kept me sane and continue to do so. My father Karsten Volckmer has been a great proof-reader, patiently accepting my idiosyncratic approach to punctuation. My brother Jan has been my constant companion in what seemed like an endless battle against Microsoft Word and up to this point it remains uncertain who actually won. My partner Maurizio Zatti has accompanied me on this exciting journey and has never let me down. I feel humbled by your love. *Se non ci fossi dovrei inventarti.*

I dedicate this work to Karsten and Hannelore Volckmer because they are wonderful parents.

NOTES ON REFERENCING

References to Wassermann's primary works are given in brackets with the following abbreviations:

Caspar Hauser oder Die Trägheit des Herzens (Munich: DTV, 1983) [*CH*]
Christian Wahnschaffe (Berlin: Fischer, 1920) [*CW*]
Etzel Andergast (Munich: DTV, 1988) [*EA*]
Der Fall Maurizius (Munich: DTV, 2007) [*FM*]
Joseph Kerkhovens dritte Existenz (Munich: DTV, 1989) [*JK*]
Die Juden von Zirndorf (Munich: DTV, 1996) [*JZ*]
Die Geschichte der jungen Renate Fuchs (Berlin: Fischer, 1901) [*RF*]

Other abbreviations:
DLA Deutsches Literaturarchiv Marbach

INTRODUCTION

Critical Views

The case of Jakob Wassermann is most curious: a former international star of the literary world who, it seems, has been forgotten since his death in 1934. However, Wassermann's works are still in print today, pointing towards an aspect of his story that was already well-established during his lifetime: loved by an international readership, Wassermann found himself largely rejected by his critics. While the criticism during his lifetime, however, was partly and increasingly tainted by the rise of anti-Semitism, the post-war discourse seems to suggest a deliberate exclusion of Wassermann from the literary canon. Most notably among the early post-war critics, Marcel Reich-Ranicki and Hans Mayer spoke out against Wassermann, with Mayer openly rejecting a new edition of the author's collected works.[1] Reich-Ranicki, on the other hand, wrote: 'Niemals wurde die Leidenschaftlichkeit seines Engagements angezweifelt, niemals sein Ernst bestritten. Gleichwohl ist es schwer, seine Romane immer ernst zu nehmen'.[2] Apart from supporting the view of Wassermann as a mediocre writer, Ranicki, moreover, reinforced a trend in Wassermann scholarship that has continued until the present day: namely, the interest in the writer's biography. Beginning with the early biographies by Walter Goldmann,[3] Siegmund Bing[4] and Marta Karlweis,[5] this trend has found further expression in the works of Dierk Rodewald,[6] Rudolf Koester,[7] Beatrix Müller-Kampel[8] and Thomas Kraft.[9]

1 Hans Mayer, 'Der Fall Wassermann', in *Literatur der Übergangszeit* (Berlin: Volk und Welt, 1949), pp. 177–82.
2 Marcel Reich-Ranicki, 'Jakob Wassermann, der Bestsellerautor von gestern', in *Jüdische Wochenzeitung*, 34 (16 February 1979), 7.
3 Walter Goldmann, *Wassermann: Sein Kampf um Wahrheit* (Leipzig & Zurich: Grethlein, 1929).
4 Siegmund Bing, *Jakob Wassermann: Weg und Werk des Dichters* (Berlin: Fischer, 1933).
5 Marta Karlweis, *Jakob Wassermann: Bild, Kampf und Werk* (Amsterdam: Querido, 1935).
6 Dierk Rodewald (ed.), *Jakob Wassermann 1873–1934: Ein Weg als Deutscher und Jude* (Bonn: Bouvier, 1984).
7 Rudolf Koester, *Jakob Wassermann* (Berlin: Morgenbuch, 1996).
8 Beatrix Müller-Kampel, *Jakob Wasserman: Eine biographische Collage* (Vienna: Mandelbaum, 2007).
9 Thomas Kraft, *Jakob Wassermann: Biografie* (Munich: DTV, 2008).

In addition to an interest in Wassermann as a literary figure, this focus on biography is inextricably linked to the Jewish question and thus to one of the other main fields of scholarship. In fact, Karl Leydecker and Regina Schäfer are right to assume that it was this interest in Wassermann's engagement with his Jewish identity that led to a rediscovery of his works in the 1980s.[10] The outcome of this concern with Wassermann as a Jewish figure is manifold and often contradictory. While Christa Joeris has aimed to show how Wassermann's entire work is deeply influenced by rabbinic Judaism as well as the Kabbalah,[11] Hans Otto Horch has arrived at the altogether more convincing version that, as an assimilated Jew, Wassermann's knowledge about Judaism in terms of tradition and culture was very limited.[12] This view seems supported by the fact that Wassermann, according to Arthur Schnitzler, considered leaving the Jewish community once the Jewish question, or that of anti-Semitism, had been resolved.[13] Moreover, the son he had with his second wife Marta Karlweis was baptized. Nonetheless, with anti-Semitism on the rise Wassermann was increasingly forced to respond. Heike Lindemann-Luiken has shown how Wassermann was subject to anti-Semitic literary criticism and how, more generally, the impact of ongoing discrimination can be traced throughout his work.[14] Further analysis of Jewish aspects in Wassermann's life and writing can, be found, among others, in Ritchie Robertson[15] as well as in two collections of essays edited by Dirk Niefanger[16] and Rudolf Wolff.[17]

Ever since the publication of his *Caspar Hauser*, the concept of the 'Trägheit des Herzens' has become a convenient key to the understanding of

10 Karl Leydecker, 'The Case of Jakob Wassermann: Social, Legal, and Personal Crises in the Weimar Republic', in *German Novelists of the Weimar Republic: Intersections of Literature and Politics* (Rochester, N.Y.; Woodbridge: Camden House, 2006), pp. 85–101 (p. 88); and Regina Schäfer, *Plaidoyer für Ganna: Männer und Frauen in den Romanen Jakob Wassermanns* (Tübingen: Niemeyer, 1992), p. 7.

11 Christa Joeris, *Aspekte des Judentums im Werk Jakob Wassermanns* (Aachen: Shaker, 1996).

12 Hans Otto Horch, 'Deutschtum und Judentum: Eine unmögliche Synthese? Jakob Wassermann im Kontext der deutsch-jüdischen Literaturgeschichte', in *Jakob Wassermann: Deutscher – Jude – Literat*, ed. by Dirk Niefanger and others (Göttingen: Wallstein, 2007), pp. 69–91 (p. 77).

13 Arthur Schnitzler, *Tagebuch*, ed. by Peter Michael Braunwarth and Werner Welzig, 10 vols (Vienna: Verlag der Österreichischen Akademie der Wissenschaften, 1981–2000), v (1983), *20/09/1914*, p. 137.

14 Heike Lindemann-Luiken, *Die Auswirkungen des Antisemitismus im ausgehenden 19. und beginnenden 20. Jahrhundert auf Leben und Werk Jakob Wassermanns* (Frankfurt a. M.: Peter Lang, 2005).

15 See Ritchie Robertson, *The 'Jewish Question' in German Literature 1749–1939: Emancipation and its Discontents* (Oxford: Oxford University Press, 1999).

16 Niefanger (ed.), *Jakob Wassermann: Deutscher – Jude – Literat.*

17 Rudolf Wolff (ed.), *Jakob Wassermann: Werk und Wirkung* (Bonn: Bouvier, 1987).

Wassermann's work.[18] Moreover, this leitmotif has become significant in the context of the debate on the author's longing for justice, which he reiterates rather frequently. This question of justice pervades much of the criticism and has often been linked to Wassermann's understanding of Judaism as based on the idea of justice. The most significant scholarship on this aspect of Wassermann's work has been produced by Stephen Garrin[19] and, more recently, by Elisabeth Jütten.[20] While Garrin focuses on the different concepts of justice presented throughout the *Andergast* trilogy, Jütten's findings are more relevant in the context of this study, for Jütten relates the question of justice in *Der Fall Maurizius* and *Christian Wahnschaffe* to a wider philosophical framework, notably to Nietzsche, and thus demonstrates that Wassermann's concept of justice is relevant universally as well as specifically for the discourse of the early twentieth century.

The question of Wassermann's relevance has, unfortunately, become a topic in itself, which takes us to the realm of negative criticism. While some of the accusations against Wassermann by now serve as a source of entertainment, among them John C. Blankenagel's criticism of Wassermann for his 'insistence on sexual perversion,'[21] others ought to be taken more seriously. Critics have mostly taken offence at Wassermann's allegedly old-fashioned way of writing, his lack of any theoretical foundation, and thus the lack of any concrete solutions to social problems. Finally, some critics have come to consider him the author of trivial, sensationalist works that are of neither aesthetic nor artistic value.

The charge of being an old-fashioned narrator is among the commonest criticisms and has, for example, been put forward by Müller-Kampel: 'Im Grunde schöpft Wassermann aus einem Reservoir erzählerischer Verfahrensweisen, die sich spätestens seit den 1890er Jahren rapide banalisiert haben und seitdem einem verstärkten Vulgaritätsverdacht ausgesetzt waren.'[22] Admittedly, Wassermann might not have been the most radical or experimental writer of his time, yet it is problematic just to ignore the obvious developments that his writing underwent in the course of his lifetime. When he is being portrayed as traditional, the image of Wassermann as a stagnant author is easily conveyed, even though it clearly fails to do him justice. As this

18 See, for example, Walter Voegeli, *Jakob Wassermann und Die Trägheit des Herzens* (Winterthur: Keller, 1956).

19 Stephen H. Garrin, *The Concept of Justice in Wassermann's Trilogy* (Bern: Peter Lang, 1979).

20 Elisabeth Jütten, *Diskurse über Gerechtigkeit im Werk Jakob Wassermanns* (Tübingen: Niemeyer, 2007).

21 John C. Blankenagel, *The Writings of Jakob Wassermann* (Boston: Christopher, 1942), p. 322.

22 Beatrix Müller-Kampel, 'Jakob Wassermann und die Autoren Jung-Wiens,' in *Deutscher – Jude – Literat*, pp. 45–69 (p. 61).

book will show, Wassermann's narrative technique, especially with regards to the depiction of character, is not as traditional as is often portrayed. Most recently, Nicole Plöger has successfully demonstrated how Wassermann's early works can indeed be related to modern discourse and are not solely the products of a traditional author.[23]

The claim that Wassermann is a traditional author relying on old-fashioned narrative techniques stands in strange contrast to the frequently mentioned critique that his works lack any coherent structure. According to Theo Elm, Wassermann's work is characterized by 'Orientierungslosigkeit' and:

> in Wassermanns Romanen [bricht sich] eine 'orientalische', eine ebenso reiche wie ungezügelte Fabulierlust Bahn, die mit bizarren Zufällen, Weissagungen, dramatischen Auftritten, Flucht und schicksalhaften Verstrickungen die sozialhistorischen Konturen der Romane in den Hintergrund drängt – oft mehr Kolorit als Thema.[24]

In his interpretation Elm fails to see a connection that is vital for the understanding of Wassermann's work, namely the connection between form and content. What Elm here refers to as the 'sozialhistorische[n] Konturen' are, in particular in Wassermann's later work, brought to light precisely by this apparent lack of an overall structure. The crumbling of the outer form and the gradual resignation into shapelessness are of pivotal importance when it comes to analysing Wassermann's oeuvre in its entirety. The alleged lack of structure in his works can therefore be understood as a response to a world which no longer produces any clear structures and has become for the most part incoherent. Similarly, the view that Wassermann is guilty of 'sensationalism', as also put forward by Elm amongst others, overlooks some of Wassermann's more interesting reasons for employing those techniques. Instead of dismissing it as a cheap way of selling more copies, this study will attempt to link Wassermann's 'sensationalism' to a wider framework of social developments.

In his analysis, Elm touches on another issue that is often brought forward against Wassermann, that is, his failure to provide concrete solutions to social problems. Elm misses a 'gesellschaftliches Programm'[25] in Wassermann's novels, while Leydecker claims that Wassermann's 'novels are open to the accusation that they shy away from offering a concrete analysis of the specific political and

23 Nicole Plöger, *Ästhet – Ankläger – Verkünder: Jakob Wassermanns literarische Anfänge (1890–1900)* (Würzburg: Ergon, 2007).

24 Theo Elm, 'Kafkas Talmud, Wassermanns Kabbala: Gibt es ein "jüdisches" Erzählen?', in *Deutscher – Jude – Literat*, pp. 127–41 (p. 136).

25 Elm, 'Kafkas Talmud', p. 136.

social ills of the day'.[26] In a similar vein Mayer claims that Wassermann is only concerned with 'Scheinprobleme' and therefore fails to address the actual conflicts of his time.[27] Mayer's claim about the 'Scheinprobleme' is hard to maintain in the face of Wassermann's immense popularity with his readers, especially Germany's youth, who looked to him for guidance and advice in all areas of their lives. They therefore clearly felt that Wassermann was addressing their concerns. Leydecker's and Elm's claims will not be refuted here but merely confronted with the question of whether it is indeed a novelist's task to come up with a 'concrete analysis of specific political and social ills'. Moreover, given the complexity of the times in which Wassermann lived, especially the Weimar years, this is a great deal to require from a work of fiction. At the same time it seems that with his focus on people's everyday lives and their psychological or even spiritual concerns, Wassermann nevertheless presents very important portrayals of German society. Victor Zuckerkandl's approach is, therefore, more fruitful as he observes that Wassermann tackles the important topics of his day yet 'nicht vom Standpunkt des Fachmannes, sondern – wertvoller, weil unwiderlegbar – aus rein menschlicher Anschauung heraus'.[28]

The final point dealt with in the negative criticism is the question as to whether, in the case of Wassermann, we are dealing with an author who was successful due to his talent or simply the product of a clever marketing strategy. This point is closely linked to the question of how far he is, therefore, still relevant for today's readers and critics. According to Müller-Kampel, '[es] spricht alles dafür, daß Jakob Wassermann als Künstler wie Erfolgsautor in erster Linie kraft der sozialen Felder erschaffen wird, aus denen er kommt und in die er gelangt'.[29] This theory, according to Martin Neubauer's findings, was already advanced during the author's lifetime.[30] Wassermann's most recent biographer arrives at the conclusion that only some of the author's major works are, in fact, still relevant and worth reading today.[31] The question regarding the mechanisms at work in the making of Wassermann as an international success is, even though of socio-cultural interest, not important for the interpretation of his works. It is, therefore, one of the central aims of this monograph to make the author relevant outside a biographical framework. We shall thus seek to return to Wassermann's works while mostly leaving the biography behind; and in that way look for other ways of making them

26 Leydecker, 'Case', p. 87.

27 Mayer, 'Fall', p. 179.

28 Victor Zuckerkandl, 'Jakob Wassermanns Essaybuch', in *Die Neue Rundschau*, 40 (1929), pp. 719–20.

29 Müller-Kampel, 'Wassermann', p. 56.

30 Martin Neubauer, *Jakob Wassermann: Ein Schriftsteller im Urteil seiner Zeitgenossen* (Frankfurt a. M., Berlin: Lang, 1994), p. 171.

31 Kraft, *Wassermann*, p. 212.

worth reading. In this version relevance becomes a process that seeks actively to engage readers and make them see beyond the usual categories.

Central Thesis

One way of looking at Wassermann's oeuvre, and an aspect for which he has not yet been given full credit, would be to consider it as an ambitious attempt to portray German society at different historical stages; and thus to see Wassermann, as Goldmann did, as a 'Wegweiser durch die Zeit'.[32] Possibly due to Wassermann's indifference towards political matters, especially in his early life, his overall concern with (mostly) German society has not been acknowledged. Neubauer even identifies Wassermann's lack of political interest as one of the reasons for his being neglected for a considerable time after the Second World War.[33] Wassermann's project of offering critical analyses of society at different stages can therefore be understood as the basis of this monograph. It in turn influences the decision as to which of his many novels should be its focus, for it is necessary to offer a fair representation of his entire oeuvre. To begin with, it is essential to strike an equal balance between those works written during the Wilhelmine era and those written during the Weimar Republic, as well as to acknowledge the significance that the Great War had for Wassermann's writing. Accordingly, the first two chapters are concerned with Wassermann's earlier novels, namely *Die Juden von Zirndorf* (1897), *Die Geschichte der jungen Renate Fuchs* (1901) and *Caspar Hauser oder Die Trägheit des Herzens* (1908). Space does not allow a discussion of *Das Gänsemännchen* (1915), which forms part of Wassermann's critique of Wilhelmine Germany. In order to mark the Great War as an important moment in Wassermann's writing it is essential to look at *Christian Wahnschaffe* (1919), a novel that is a powerful expression of the wider changes taking place around him. Finally, an analysis of Wassermann's oeuvre could never be complete without taking into consideration the *Andergast* trilogy, especially since it can be understood as a summary, even the climax, of his entire life as a writer. Chapter 5 will deal exclusively with Wassermann's most famous novel *Der Fall Maurizius* (1928); this will be followed by a discussion of *Etzel Andergast* (1931) and *Joseph Kerkhovens dritte Existenz* (1934) in Chapter 6.

In order further to justify the choice of these novels it will be necessary to introduce the other two key elements in this project, namely the figure of the outsider and the question of character. As will become apparent in the

32 Goldmann, *Wassermann*, p. 9.

33 Neubauer, *Schriftsteller*, p. 30.

course of this study, these three elements become increasingly linked in Wassermann's writing and thought. In this context, the concept of character is understood as something that is in constant flux, that is, as something that Wassermann continuously developed and altered. Although he started with the intention of creating realistic characters, Wassermann increasingly lost faith in their depictability in a work of fiction. This problem inevitably became linked to the question of whether such a thing as character as a coherent unity exists at all, thus making it a problem that affects the fictional and the real in equal measure. In the course of Wassermann's life as a writer these two questions became more and more pressing, producing sometimes astounding results which taken together seem to refute the notion of him as a traditional writer. In fact, it is with regard to 'character' that the work Wassermann produced during and after the Great War may even be called experimental. For Wassermann, character therefore becomes not only a space in which to explore new narrative techniques, but also a key mode of expression. Moreover, we shall aim to show how these questions concerning character and Wassermann's depiction of society complement each other in most intriguing ways. Character, in Wassermann's version, falls apart alongside society.

The figure of the outsider is one of the starting points for this study and almost immediately leads to the discovery of Wassermann's concern with society. The outsider and society complement each other as they are mutually dependent categories: the outsider can only exist if excluded from a given society and, as we shall see later, society needs the outsider as a negative mirror image in order to define itself. In combination they also provide a good structural framework for the analysis of a large part of Wassermann's oeuvre. The concept of the outsider might at first seem like an obvious and not very revelatory choice, given how close Wassermann himself felt to this status in society; and yet, following the aim of leaving the biographical framework behind, the discussion of this figure can indeed be taken beyond the Jewish characters in his writing. To be more precise, it can be demonstrated how Wassermann starts with the outsider status of the Jew in *Zirndorf* in order to draw, in the course of his entire work, extensive parallels between the status of the Jews and that of the woman, the homosexual man and the child. The focus on these parallels offers a new, as well as revelatory, way of looking at these figures as well as allowing them to be connected to the depiction of society. While the concern with the woman and the child are very characteristic of Wassermann's early writing, the figure of the homosexual man, albeit already present in his pre-war work, is of great importance for the later works, in particular the *Andergast* trilogy. It is also in this trilogy that the three essential elements – character, outsider and society – are finally brought together and used connectively.

In order to highlight the parallel status of the woman and the Jew in Wassermann's writing, we must look at *Zirndorf* and *Renate Fuchs*. Concerning the status of the Jew in society, Wassermann here embarks on a complex journey for he aims to show how this figure is clearly affected by mechanisms of exclusion while at the same time being keen to negate Judaism as a marker of difference in a world of mass irreligion affecting the Gentile and the non-Gentile alike. This is closely tied to the question of whether it is indeed possible to leave outsider status behind and, as in the case of the protagonist Agathon Geyer, to cease being Jewish. Similarly to Wassermann's later concern with the depiction of character, the category of the outsider is, therefore, not a stable one but in constant flux. As a result, these outsider figures – with the exception of Warschauer in *Maurizius* – always contain an element of hope or the possibility of change. In their own way they tend to embody possible solutions to their situations even if in the end the solutions can hardly ever be realized. Moreover, since these outsiders do not occupy stable positions, their views on society are equally not to be thought of as black-and-white. Through the use of these complex outsider figures, Wassermann frequently arrives at damning portrayals of society, yet at the same time they are never without an element of understanding. In the case of Agathon, this element of hope is closely linked to the other outsider figure, namely the 'fallen' woman, Renate Fuchs. After many trials and tribulations these two figures dare to go beyond common categories and not only unite, but even attempt to found a race and thus a society of their own, away from the Gentile man. In response to the criticisms made regarding Wassermann's lack of concrete solutions, it needs to be pointed out that the ending of *Renate Fuchs* is not to be understood as a failure to provide useful answers to pressing social questions. Instead, it is more fruitful to read it as a thought-experiment revealing the broad range of possibilities which Wassermann actually considered. At the same time, the strong sense that it is an unrealistic ending speaks for itself. More than anything else it makes clear that Wassermann was still writing from a point in history at which the idea of an emancipated woman, as well as that of the Jews' equality, were beyond most people's imagination. Through the use of these outsider figures Wassermann thus not only challenges the society depicted in these two novels, but also his readers' way of looking at the world.

The next significant outsider figure in Wassermann's writing is the child and thus the protagonist of his *Caspar Hauser*. The parallels Wassermann draws here between the status of the Jew and that of the child are subtler than those in the above-mentioned novels, for in *Caspar* there is not a single Jewish character and yet Davide Stimilli has shown how the figure of Caspar can nevertheless be understood as a Jewish figure.[34] Tellingly, his interpretation is based partly on the fact that Kafka came to think of the foundling's story as a version of the history of the Jewish people. Bearing this in mind, Wassermann's concern with the figure of the child acquires an even wider significance, for just as the foundling is given a double identity, so too is the society depicted in the novel. With the help of the Biedermeier setting, Wassermann arrives at an important depiction of his contemporary Wilhelmine world. Alert to people's suffering due to an oppressive political system, Wassermann creates insightful portraits of life in Germany just after the turn of the century.

Following the appearance of the 'Märchenkönig' Ludwig II of Bavaria at the end of *Zirndorf*, *Caspar* contains a less subtle attempt to pick up the theme of the homosexual man's status in society. The character of Lord Stanhope is portrayed with a clear homoerotic tendency and thus further underlines Wassermann's growing concern with other outsider figures. At the same time, Stanhope is Wassermann's first figure to show signs of his creator's developing concern with the depiction of character as well as the question of identity. Wassermann's concept of identity is intrinsically linked to that of character as both need to be understood as something in constant flux, a process rather than a stable entity. Unlike character, identity here also means a person's introspection and thus their version of themselves. Character is, therefore, more of a narrative tool, the outside view of a fictional figure, whereas identity involves a figure's inner life and grants him a certain level of agency. Throughout this study we shall encounter numerous characters who are at odds with their own identity, who are no longer sure which version of their self is true, how much of it is conditioned by their environment and how much of it is their own choice. Identity, therefore, increasingly becomes something fluid, something that can seemingly be altered and performed, as opposed to the self, which, in Wassermann's version, cannot be changed. Despite their evident confusion when it comes to their identity, Wassermann's characters always circulate around a part of themselves they cannot escape and which is their self. Wassermann presents us with characters who experience the limit of their identities, voluntarily as well as involuntarily, and who find themselves confronted with a self they cannot leave behind. The character of Stanhope contains first traces of the kind of writing that became typical of Wassermann during and after the Great War. Thus he marks the beginning of an intricate relationship between the ways in which he creates his characters and the pictures of society which he draws. Increasingly with Wassermann, character becomes a mirror of the more

34 Davide Stimilli, 'Findlinge: Franz Kafka und Jakob Wassermann', in *Deutsche Vierteljahrsschrift*, 73 (1999), 478–500.

general developments he witnesses in society. Moreover, in *Caspar* there is once again, and for the last time, a union between two outsider figures, namely between Caspar and Stanhope. The idea of the union between outsiders is, therefore, characteristic of Wassermann's early writing, for when he allows this figure to return in *Maurizius* in the character of Warschauer, the latter's world is characterized by complete social isolation with even this last element of comfort taken away from him.

For this study as a whole, *Christian Wahnschaffe* (1919) has in some ways proven to be the most difficult as well as the most revelatory novel. Given its experimental form, it is challenging to find a productive way into the novel which leads to an altogether new way of looking at it. Writing this chapter was, therefore, partly about discovering the method to Wassermann's apparent madness. Written during the Great War, *Christian Wahnschaffe* clearly shifts Wassermann's attention away from the figure of the outsider in favour of a new approach to the question of character. The novel is thus significant because it functions as a line of separation between Wassermann's early and his later works, for not only has the concept of character acquired a new significance for him, but his analysis of society is now linked to the question of human perception, a concern that becomes an ongoing theme right up to the *Andergast* trilogy.

Wahnschaffe represents Wassermann's most significant engagement with modern life for it is here that he acknowledges the influence of the cinema, the metropolis and political upheaval, in particular the revolutionary forces sweeping across Europe from the East, on his own writing as well as on the way in which we perceive the world. As a result, a new way of reading *Wahnschaffe* would be to consider it as a response to the ways in which modern life has altered our perception. Wassermann shows himself to be highly aware of these changes, which have also been described by Georg Simmel, Sigmund Freud and Walter Benjamin. The eponymous protagonist undergoes a journey towards perception which, curiously, also ends with the disappearance of his character, a narrative technique that can hardly be referred to as traditional. The end of the self here becomes an expression of the radical changes Wassermann witnessed around himself. This development, even though it carries positive connotations of selflessness, nevertheless foreshadows the impossibility of a stable character, something Wassermann will portray in his trilogy. *Wahnschaffe* is therefore also his first work to be written in more of a 'Weimar spirit', revealing his previous writing to be part of a world to which he could no longer return.

Severely troubled by the events of the Great War, in *Wahnschaffe* Wassermann leaves the provincial setting of his early novels behind and attempts to portray German society in its entirety, but also that of Europe.

Tellingly, much of the novel is set in Berlin, the centre of this new world, which also features in the trilogy. All these characteristics create a rather curious sense of time in *Wahnschaffe*. Although it is set during the time immediately before the Great War, the novel, in particular its second volume entitled *Ruth*, has a more modern feel to it. In contrast to *Caspar*, in which this double identity in terms of time and setting is intentional, here it seems as if these boundaries have been unconsciously blurred as Wassermann felt himself cut off from his previous experiences. In the context of Wassermann's writing, 'modern' refers to his turning away from more traditional, in particular nineteenth-century, narrative techniques and his engaging with those that originated in the early twentieth century.

Since the development of Christian Wahnschaffe is modelled on that of St Francis of Assisi, the novel carries important religious connotations. However, following on from Agathon's search for meaning beyond religion in *Zirndorf*, Christian's development cannot be read as favouring one particular religious concept. Rather, it seems that Wassermann here takes his search for spiritual renewal a step further. While Agathon's visions remain altogether vague, the figure of Christian Wassermann clearly supports the idea of saintly behaviour in an everyday context. This need for spiritual renewal, which Wassermann perceived so strongly during and immediately after the Great War, can be understood as a major contribution towards the syncretic approach to spirituality he later takes in the trilogy.

Der Fall Maurizius (1928) is, even today, Wassermann's most successful and most widely discussed novel. Even though part of the *Andergast* trilogy, *Maurizius* will be discussed in a separate chapter. This is partly because of the substantial amount of critical attention it has received and partly because, unlike the other novels in the trilogy, it can stand on its own as a work of art. A major success during Wassermann's lifetime, the novel was widely discussed during the Weimar Republic as well as afterwards; and yet it is necessary to contest the notion of this work as a crime novel and thus as an affirmation of Wassermann as a traditional narrator. This view found support from, among others, Bertolt Brecht, who took offence with 'der üblichen stumpfsinnigen Form unseres Romans, dessen Prototyp etwa Wassermanns "Fall Maurizius" ist'.[35] Instead, analysis will show that the novel is not necessarily a piece of detective writing, as the story of the innocent prisoner Maurizius merely serves as the framework for a more significant portrayal of father-and-son relationships.

35 Bertolt Brecht, *Die Besten Autoren über die besten Bücher des Jahres*, in *Schriften 1*, Große kommentierte Berliner und Frankfurter Ausgabe, ed. by Werner Hecht and others, 30 vols (Berlin and Frankfurt a.M.: Aufbau und Suhrkamp, 1992), pp. 255–56 (p. 255). Quoted in Neubauer, *Schriftsteller*, p. 187.

The novel is characterized by a carefully constructed form, yet contains some significant further developments regarding Wassermann's approach to character. Combined with the return of the figure of the outsider in the character of Warschauer, *Maurizius* becomes the clearest expression of the link that Wassermann saw between the state of society and the fictional characters it produces. Tellingly, in his 'Rede über die Gestalt' (1924) Wassermann came to understand the 'Gestalt' as the most important mirror of its time: 'Nicht in den Zuständen spiegelt sich die Zeit, nicht die Ereignisse deuten das Schicksal: die Gestalt ist Spiegel und Deuter'.[36] Alongside a society that has stopped functioning and only produces individuals in a state of emotional isolation, Wassermann now also focuses on the disintegration of character. He does not achieve this through the depiction of characters overcoming themselves as in *Wahnschaffe*; instead, their identities collapse as the boundaries between them and other characters are blurred. In this bleak version of the later Weimar years people have lost control over their identities, something which is emphasized by the fact that all the main characters in the novel have a double identity forced onto them by the surrounding circumstances.

Hitherto the question of a double identity in relation to Wassermann and his work has led to discussion of his own situation as a German Jew, mostly inspired by his autobiography *Mein Weg als Deutscher und Jude* (1921).[37] However, as *Maurizius* shows, this question had a much wider significance for him because these double identities are the expression of a world that is beyond comprehension, where nothing is as it seems. Moreover, while in his earlier novels Wassermann is keen to depict the union between different outsider figures, he now presents his reader with a character combining two such identities, namely the homosexual Jew Georg Warschauer. So far Warschauer has largely been discussed as the product of Wassermann's own experience as a German Jew and the identity crisis resulting from it.[38] At the same time, the obvious homosexual aspects of his character have been neglected with the exception of a few negative remarks. However, given Wassermann's overall interest in the situation of homosexual men, the importance of Warschauer's double identity cannot be overestimated, for it is through this figure that the

36 Jakob Wassermann, 'Rede über die Gestalt', in *Lebensdienst: Gesammelte Studien. Erfahrungen und Reden aus drei Jahrzehnten* (Leipzig & Zurich: Grethlein,1928), pp. 347–83 (p. 382).

37 Jakob Wassermann, 'Mein Weg als Deutscher und Jude', in *Deutscher und Jude: Reden und Schriften 1904–1933*, ed. by Dierk Rodewald (Heidelberg: Lambert Schneider, 1984), pp. 35–132.

38 See, for example, Gershon Shaked, 'Der Fall Wassermann', in *Die Macht der Identität: Essays über jüdische Schriftsteller*, trans. by Ulrike Berger and others (Königstein: Athenäum, 1986), pp. 94–112; or Martina Landscheidt, 'Mutmaßungen über Waremme, Annäherung an Warschauer: Zu der jüdischen Doppelfigur Warschauer-Waremme in Jakob Wassermanns Roman Der Fall Maurizius', in *Jakob Wassermann: Werk und Wirkung*, pp. 14–33.

Jew and the homosexual man are finally given a parallel status of exclusion in Wassermann's version of society.

Wassermann's last two novels, *Etzel Andergast* (1931) and *Joseph Kerkhovens dritte Existenz* (1934), are highly complex and at times confusing pieces of writing that have not received much critical attention. This holds in particular for *Kerkhoven*, which was published posthumously and did not undergo a final editing process since Wassermann died before he could undertake it. One aim of this chapter is to show how, with their focus on male-male or symbolic father-and-son relationships, these two novels can be seen as a continuation of *Maurizius*, which is why the term trilogy, often debated, is appropriate. At the same time *Andergast* is Wassermann's most important examination of life in the later years of the Weimar Republic. Wassermann approaches this topic from two angles, yet always by means of a male-male relationship. However, these male-male relationships are not to be thought of as mere depictions of conflict between generations. Instead, they increasingly become an expression of a longing for reconciliation between the generations that cannot be fulfilled. In particular the relationship between Etzel Andergast and Joseph Kerkhoven is symptomatic of the rebellious son's longing for a father figure, while at the same time the 'father' is unable to develop a genuine emotional bond with his 'son', a situation which ends in catastrophe. Wassermann offers a sensitive and intelligent account of the reasons why the older and the younger generation are at odds with each other, despite a mutual longing for reconciliation. Wassermann's lengthy engagement with Weimar's troubled youth needs to be considered as an important contribution to this topic. First, he portrays the relationship between Johann Irlen, a representative of the Wilhelmine era and another homosexual outsider, and the young physician Kerkhoven. In this way Wassermann shows the Weimar Republic to be heavily influenced by the Wilhelmine era and this finds expression in another character experiment: the dying Irlen literally becomes a part of Kerkhoven's character. This experiment is the first hint at a theory, propounded throughout the two novels, according to which character can never be a stable identity since every human life is made up of several existences.

Even though the two novels are mostly set in the later years of the Weimar Republic, Wassermann is nevertheless keen to emphasize certain continuities. In *Kerkhoven* he adds a new layer of significance to the question of character by introducing himself, as the author Alexander Herzog, into the novel. Moreover, the novel also contains an only slightly fictionalized account of Wassermann's first marriage to Julie Speyer. However, instead of relating this account to Wassermann's biography, it is more fruitful to look at its consequences for the novel as a whole and in particular for Wassermann's approach to character. The result is that Wassermann not only allows himself to merge with his fictional creation Kerkhoven but, through the introduction of this biographical element, successfully plays with the reliability of human perception in relation to the question of human identity. Towards the end of the novel this question is extended towards a concern regarding the reliability of the text. The disappearance of Kerkhoven's precious manuscript, a lifetime's work, becomes Wassermann's strongest expression of the general collapse he had to witness around him. His writing therefore ends not just with the end of character but also with the end of the text.

CHAPTER 1

Looking for Pleasure – the Jew and the Woman in Wassermann's Early Novels *Die Juden von Zirndorf* (1897) and *Die Geschichte der jungen Renate Fuchs* (1901)

Introduction

In his two early novels, *Die Juden von Zirndorf* (1897) and *Die Geschichte der jungen Renate Fuchs* (1901), Wassermann sets out to tell the story of two figures who are outsiders in the world of the Gentile man and through their actions become outcasts within their own communities: the rebellious Jew and the 'fallen' woman. Across the two novels, which are linked thematically as well as through the reappearance of several characters, these two figures allow Wassermann to explore the general cultural malaise affecting society at the turn of the century and to arrive at some thought-provoking conclusions. Moreover, by introducing the figure of the 'Literat' Stefan Gudstikker into these novels, Wassermann gives a prominent place to the question of the role that art plays in this context. In Wassermann's version all people are without pleasure in their lives, regardless of their religious background or their status in society. *Die Juden von Zirndorf* can therefore be read as an angry young man's attack not only on the Jewish community but on society as a whole. Through the perspective of the outcast Agathon Geyer, Jews and Christians are shown to be equally unhappy since they are all stuck in an antiquated moral system and a by now meaningless religion that does not allow them to enjoy their lives freely.

At the same time Wassermann seems eager to demonstrate that to distinguish between Jews and Christians has become irrelevant as well as impossible. Everyday life is shown to be indifferent towards this distinction and Jewishness has almost become a mere character trait that can also be used to describe non-Jewish people. In a similar vein, in *Renate Fuchs,* Wassermann refuses to acknowledge the distinction between a 'good' and a 'fallen' woman and offers a sympathetic portrait of a woman's search for happiness, which, however, does not always coincide with a search for emancipation. At the end of the novel Wassermann carries out an exciting experiment: in one night of love, Agathon and Renate, the two outcasts, conceive a child that is referred to as the founder of a new race. Could the union of the two outcasts be the solution to their problems? Could the Jew and the woman together 'defeat' Gentile man? And where would that leave the Jewish woman?

The analysis of the depiction of Jewish and Christian characters in *Zirndorf* will show how, in Wassermann's view, the distinction between Jews and Christians is often an arbitrary one. By focusing on the portrayal of people's daily lives, Wassermann highlights how Jews and Christians are filled with the same hopes, dreams and desires and are not so different from one another after all. In this version the basis for much anti-Semitism is therefore simply unfounded. At the same time he launches a fierce attack not only on the Jewish community but on society as a whole and therefore includes Christian beliefs and values. As Nicole Plöger puts it: 'Dementsprechend finden sich in diesem Text all die Unzulänglichkeiten, all die Fehlentwicklungen und all das Beklagenswerte ebenso außerhalb der nichtjüdischen Welt'.[1]

If the novel is to be understood as an attack on society as a whole, then a new understanding of its structure becomes available. The prologue, which is otherwise only loosely connected to the rest of the novel, becomes Wassermann's means of illustrating the fact that in the course of two hundred years society has changed very little and certainly not for the better. Through the use of characters functioning as mirror images in the prologue and in the novel, Wassermann makes it clear that the general cultural malaise has, if anything, intensified. In this context it is important to establish that Christian characters do not function exclusively as representatives of an anti-Semitic world view but are shown to be equally affected by a general sense of crisis. The broad range of the critique expressed in the novel can therefore only be grasped fully if the Christian characters are also taken into account.

The protagonist Agathon Geyer, who turns out to be the son of a Christian father and a Jewish mother, stands at the centre of Wassermann's critique of society. In the course of the novel Agathon not only renounces the Jewish faith but also comes to think of Christianity as a younger yet equally obsolete religion. Towards the end of the novel he therefore declares:

> Den Menschen den Himmel nehmen und ihnen die Erde geben, [...] das ist alles, was ich will. [...] Sie müssen die reine Erde haben, ohne Kreuz, ohne Abfall, ohne Verzicht, ohne Abrechnung mit einem Droben.[2]

1 Plöger, *Ästhet*, p. 282.

2 Jakob Wassermann, *Die Juden von Zirndorf* (Munich: DTV, 1996), pp. 235–36. The text is based on the first edition, published by Albert Langen in 1897. The edition published by Fischer in 1906 has been changed considerably and will only be referred to when the

The reasons for his revolt are most intriguing and offer the key for a new reading of the novel. Through the lens of this outcast, Wassermann shows how people's actions are largely motivated by a longing for happiness and pleasure, something they have been systematically deprived of for at least two millennia. This basic yet telling insight prompts Agathon to go on a mission to bring people more joy that ends with a burning church and his fervent, if futile, support of the Bavarian 'Märchenkönig' Ludwig II, a king born for pleasure. The general emphasis on pleasure might seem trivial at first and yet corresponds well with Sigmund Freud's insight that life is essentially 'governed by a "Trieb"'.[3] A longing for pleasure therefore stands at the centre of all our actions.[4]

The figure of the 'Literat' Stefan Gudstikker deserves further analysis since he can also be understood as a mirror image of Wassermann himself. Gudstikker is present throughout the two novels, in the course of which he advances from a penniless poet to a well-established and commercially successful novelist. In the two novels Gudstikker is a predominantly negative, at times even ridiculous, figure and yet there are moments of ambiguity on the part of the narrator. Moreover, there are hints that Gudstikker is at least partly a portrayal of Wassermann himself. However, this is not to be understood as an autobiographical depiction of actual events but rather as an expression of Wassermann's personal concern with the role of the commercial 'Literat', the image of the 'uncreative' Jew and the function of art in the society he is depicting.

The important female characters from both novels will be discussed in the same section because of the striking parallels between them. At the same time it will become apparent that Wassermann makes a first attempt to structure the story of a male protagonist, in this case that of Agathon, around his encounters with different women, a technique he will return to in *Christian Wahnschaffe*. Moreover, this section will also serve to highlight the parallels between the depiction of the Jew and the woman as outsiders in *Zirndorf* and *Renate Fuchs*. As with Agathon, the female characters of Jeanette Löwengard and Renate Fuchs are driven by their search for pleasure. Both women run

argument requires it. Henceforth page references given in the text. See Notes on Referencing for the abbreviations of Wassermann's works.

3 Ritchie Robertson, 'Modernism and the Self 1890–1924', in *Philosophy and German Literature 1700–1990*, ed. by Nicholas Saul (Cambridge: Cambridge University Press, 2002), pp. 150–97 (p. 158). See also Sigmund Freud, 'Triebe und Triebschicksale', in *Gesammelte Werke, Werke aus den Jahren 1913–1917*, 18 vols (Frankfurt a.M.: Fischer, 1991), x, pp. 210–32.

4 More recently this has been confirmed by neuro-scientific research. See Morten L. Kringelbach, *The Pleasure Center: Trust your Animal Instincts* (New York: Oxford University Press, 2009).

away from a lucrative marriage that would have secured them a life of great riches and a high social status in favour of personal happiness and, in Jeanette's case, sexual liberation. In both cases this search proves to be a road of no return that inevitably leads to a life of degradation. By not allowing either of the two women to lead an independent life in which they are not forced to be either a housewife or to be involved in some form of prostitution, Wassermann seems to deny that such a life is indeed possible at the time.

As a Jewish woman, Jeanette finds a less favourable ending than Renate – while she returns to Munich as a jaded dancer desperate to become the mistress of the King, Renate becomes a happy mother who is reconciled with her father. The more problematic situation of the Jewish woman compared to that of the Gentile woman is underlined even further in the depiction of the minor characters of Monika Olifat and Gisa Schumann. The latter is reduced to being a sexual object with no voice of her own – in the opening scene of *Renate Fuchs* she finds herself naked and helpless on the streets of Munich – and eventually breaks down into insanity. As the mother of an illegitimate child, Monika is only prevented from a similar fate through her marriage to Agathon.

In terms of genre these two early novels can be considered *Zeitromane*, revealing the young author's ambition to present exhaustive panoramas of society. *Zirndorf* in particular helped to found the genre of the Jewish 'Zeitroman'.[5] According to Dirk Göttsche's definition, a *Zeitroman* deals with the depiction of a historical experience and social realities in connection with a critical reflection of the present in its historical framework.[6] In his youth, Wassermann enthusiastically read realistic novels presenting a panorama of society by such authors as Ivan Turgenev, William Makepeace Thackeray and Fyodor Dostoyevsky. Wassermann wrote to Hans Aufricht on 2 January 1932: 'Dieser Autor [Turgenev] ist ja, Sie wissen es, meine erste literarische Leidenschaft gewesen'.[7] He shared their ambition to draw wide pictures of society. Hence in his early novels Wassermann attempts to show members of all social classes as well as from Jewish and Christian backgrounds while focusing on the individual characters of his protagonists Renate Fuchs and Agathon Geyer.

5 Ritchie Robertson, 'Schnitzler and Wassermann', in *Confrontations / Accommodations: German-Jewish Literary and Cultural Relations from Heine to Wassermann*, ed. by Mark H. Gelber (Tübingen: Niemeyer, 2004), pp. 24–63 (p. 250).

6 Dirk Göttsche, *Zeit im Roman: Literarische Zeitreflexion und die Geschichte des Zeitromans im späten 18. und 19. Jahrhundert* (Munich: Fink, 2001), p. 21.

7 Jakob Wassermann to Hans Aufricht, 2.1.1932, Wassermann-Nachlass, Deutsches Literaturarchiv, Marbach, call number: 73.200/3.

Jews and Christians – Are Times Finally Changing?

To understand the relationship between Jews and Christians in *Zirndorf*, it is important to acknowledge that the novel can also be read as a critical 'Heimatroman', a reading which therefore stands in strong opposition to Fritz Martini's claim: 'Die Kombination von Geschichte und Heimat [in *Zirndorf*] hat nichts mit Heimatkunst zu tun'.[8] Wassermann here expresses his great concern with the concept of 'Heimat' by introducing his reader to the Jewish paradox of being attached to a hostile 'Heimat'. The rules of the conventional 'Heimatroman' are reversed as Wassermann focuses on those who usually only figure as outsiders and tells the story of 'Heimat' from their perspective. However, as we shall see, this does not result in a uniquely favourable depiction of Jewish life and characters but rather in a highly critical and searching portrayal.

The genre of the 'Heimatroman' belongs to the kind of art known as 'Heimatkunst', a term which began to be used in Germany in the 1890s and describes literature as well as other forms of art depicting rural and provincial life. It is, however, not to be understood as a glorification of the 'Heimat'. It can be seen as a response to the tensions between regional and national identity which marked the unification of Germany in 1871, as well as to urbanization and industrialization. In Germany and Austria many people thought that their countries were changing too quickly and felt that the rural population were being driven from their land by ruthless capitalists. Moreover, they resented being dominated by big urban centres such as Berlin. As can be seen with Gustav Frenssen's *Jörn Uhl* (1901) and Wilhelm von Polenz's *Der Büttnerbauer* (1895), two of the most famous examples of this genre, the 'Heimatroman' often depicts a 'Heimat' in decline with its inhabitants given to violence and alcoholism.[9] 'Heimatkunst' sometimes even makes use of Naturalist techniques, notably with its bleak depictions of domestic violence and rural poverty. Nonetheless, for all those 'modern' tendencies within the genre, the 'Heimat' discourse remained a predominantly conservative one.

According to Elizabeth Boa, within the 'Heimat' discourse, the Jew helped to sustain German identity by being the alien, non-German Other. At the same time the assimilated Jew fuelled anxiety about the dilution of identity through infiltration: he is a scary mimic who can never become German. 'Heimat' must, therefore, be defined through exclusion of the radically different and

8 Fritz Martini, 'Die Utopie eines Messias in der Moderne', in *Zeit der Moderne: Zur deutschen Literatur von der Jahrhundertwende bis zur Gegenwart*, ed. by Hans-Henrik Krummacher and others (Stuttgart: Kröner, 1984), pp. 461–85 (p. 465).

9 Gustav Frenssen, *Jörn Uhl* (Berlin: Grote, 1903); and Wilhem von Polenz, *Der Büttnerbauer* (Berlin: Fontane, 1895).

alien, as the integration of a stranger endangers boundaries: in other words, 'Heimat' needs the Other or the exotic to exist; what is 'Heimat' for the locals may be a place of loneliness and exile for the stranger.[10] A prime example of this use of the Jew in the 'Heimat' discourse can be found in von Polenz's portrayal of the malicious Jewish usurer Samuel Harrassowitz: it not only marks the Jew as an outsider but also as the enemy to the 'Heimat'. Mayer refes to this depiction as 'offenherzig antisemitisch'.[11] Plöger's notion of Wassermann's engagement with 'Heimatkunst' is problematic since it is predominantly informed by a negative understanding of this form of art. In her view, Wassermann shares with 'Heimatkunst' a reductive, black-and-white view of the world as well as an aversion to the masses, decadence, the city with its artists and intellectuals and brutal forms of capitalism.[12] Apart from being rather clichéd, this view does not address the relevant reasons for Wassermann's engagement with 'Heimatkunst'.

The paradox of being attached to a hostile 'Heimat' is central to the understanding of Wassermann's particular notion of 'Heimat'. He insists that Jews are not strangers in Germany, since they have lived there for many centuries and form an undeniable part of its history and culture. Tellingly, despite the hostility he encountered there, Wassermann considered Franconia, where *Die Juden von Zirndorf* is set, to be his 'Heimat'. By adopting this view he goes against pervading stereotypes of the Jews as a nomadic people; on the contrary, he claims that they are indeed attached to their homes and landscapes, a sentiment which means they could not simply live anywhere. Moreover, Plöger is certainly right in concluding that this love for his 'Heimat' is at the same time a clear rejection of Zionism.[13] Nevertheless, in *Der Judenstaat* (1896) Theodor Herzl makes a similar claim regarding the relationship between Jews and their hostile Heimat: 'In unseren Vaterländern, in denen wir ja auch schon seit Jahrhunderten wohnen, werden wir als Fremdlinge angeschrien; oft von solchen, deren Geschlechter noch nicht im Lande waren, als unsere Väter da schon seufzten'.[14] Wassermann's concept of 'Heimat' therefore helps to express his idea that Jews and Christians are attached to the same 'Heimat' and consequently not so different from each other. In this context the categories of 'Jew' and 'Christian' should long since have become irrelevant.

10 See Elizabeth Boa and Rachel Palfreyman, *Heimat – a German Dream: Regional Loyalties and National Identity in German Culture 1890–1990* (Oxford: Oxford Universtiy Press, 2000), pp. 28, 52.

11 Hans Mayer, *Außenseiter* (Frankfurt a.M: Suhrkamp, 1975), p. 391.

12 Plöger, *Ästhet*, p. 324.

13 Plöger, *Ästhet*, p. 291.

14 Theodor Herzl, *Der Judenstaat* (Zurich: Manesse, 1988), p. 15.

Zirndorf consists of two parts: a prologue and the actual novel. The prologue tells the story of the collective Jewish excitement aroused by the false Messiah Sabbatai Zevi in the seventeenth century. Sabbatai Zevi (1626–76) was a Sephardic Rabbi and cabalist. He appeared in Smyrna in 1666, electrifying Jewish communities all over Europe by declaring himself to be the Jewish Messiah. The Zevi movement came to a sudden end when the alleged Messiah was forced by the Ottoman Sultan to convert to Islam.[15] The main function of this prologue-novel construction is to highlight the fact that nothing much has changed in the course of two hundred years, in the sense that people still yearn for an unattainable happiness. Wassermann establishes a link between the two texts not only by re-naming various places and buildings that feature in the novel as well as the prologue but also by having characters mirror each other in those separate parts.[16] The structure of the two societies he depicts is therefore in many ways the same. Stagnation is the most suitable word to describe the state of a society in which the possibility of learning from history is apparently denied: as anti-Semitism is still violently present at the end of the nineteenth century and Judaism has not undergone any substantial reforms, it becomes apparent that non-Jews and Jews are equally stuck in the past. Nevertheless, people's daily lives prove the opposite, for it is here that non-Jews and Jews are blind to their apparent differences. A longing for pleasure, it seems, can easily overcome racial prejudice.

The first set of characters which function as mirror images are the figures of Maier Knöcker and Agathon's grandfather Enoch Karkau, who, being usurers, ruin many lives around them. Since Maier Knöcker is the father of Rahel, a distant ancestor of Agathon's family, he, too, is to be seen as an ancestor of Enoch, which makes the link between them even more interesting. Their lives are dominated by greed: 'Er [Enoch] kannte keine Sehnsucht als die nach dem Gold, und Gefühlen anderer Art war er gänzlich verschlossen' (*JZ*, p. 72). This description could also have been used for Maier Knöcker, whose love for his treasure is described in similar terms. Moreover, both men are shown to bury part of their possessions in their gardens rather than leaving it to their families. Enoch is eventually arrested and sentenced for usury, which, as the wise man Gedalja points out, has been equally detrimental for Jews and Christians: 'Sin user fufzig Leit im

15 The standard work on Sabbatai Zevi is Gershom Scholem, *Sabbatai Sevi: The Mystical Messiah* (Princeton: Princeton University Press, 1973). In fiction Sabbatai is mentioned, for example, in Lion Feuchtwanger, *Jud Süß* (Berlin: Aufbau, 1991).

16 Plöger mentions Wassermann's use of the mirroring technique but does not go into further detail regarding specific characters (Plöger, *Ästhet*, p. 284).

Dorf, die so um all ihr Geld kommen, Juden und Gojim' (*JZ*, p. 138).[17] Jews and Christians are thus not only united in their suffering from the unlawful practice of usury but, in a curious turn of events, the daughters of both men have an illegitimate child with a Christian man. Wassermann highlights how in matters of the heart Jette and Rahel, the two above-mentioned daughters, are indifferent towards the Jewish or non-Jewish question. As a consequence, the distinction between a Jew and a non-Jew becomes blurred and there are children growing up in the Jewish community who are actually, like Agathon, from a mixed background.

The combination of 'Jewish girl meets non-Jewish boy' is repeated several times throughout the novel – Zirle and Wagenseil, Jette Geyer and Gudstikker's father, Jeanette Löwengard and Bojesen, Sema's mother Thella Hellmut and the Bavarian King – yet it is only in the case of Monika Olifat and Stefan Gudstikker that the link to the prologue is made explicit. As with Rahel and the student Hummel, Gudstikker leaves Monika behind even though she is pregnant:

> Es zeigt sich, daß zweihundert Jahre das Gemüt der Menschen nicht verändern, daß dies nur eine winzige Phase ist im Prozeß der Umwandlungen. Es scheint, als ob Charaktere oder Seelen über Jahrhunderte hinweg in einer neuen Kette von Erscheinungen und Ereignissen zu neuem Dasein erwachen müssen. Es ist dann gleichgültig, ob dieser Wiedergekehrte Thomas Peter Hummel oder Stefan Gudstikker heißt (*JZ*, p. 246).

This can be understood as a first hint at Wassermann's growing interest in the concept of human character. Moreover, it also becomes apparent that he is more interested in the human side of things than in any questions of religious affiliation. Monika's Jewishness plays, if at all, a secondary role in her relationship with Gudstikker, who also has no moral qualms about breaking his engagement with the non-Jewish girl Käthe Estrich.

Religious affiliation only matters because it would forbid these couples to 'legalize' their relationship, that is, their communities would not allow them to marry. Rahel is therefore aware that she would have to cope with 'Heimatlosigkeit' (*JZ*, p. 27) if her pregnancy became known. In a similar vein Jette writes to her lover: 'Mein Liebster, das kann ich nicht, was du von mir forderst. Ich bin keine freie Frau, kein freies Mädchen' (*JZ*, p. 139). Jette signs the letter with her maiden name, something which indicates that her lack of freedom is not linked to another man but to the fact that she is Jewish and her lover is not. For Wassermann the idea of these mixed relationships

17 The omission of this form of Yiddish is one of the most significant changes Wassermann made to the 1906 edition of the novel. See also Bing, *Wassermann*, p. 104. Tellingly, this later edition was commercially more successful (Müller-Kampel, *Collage*, p. 83).

is of pivotal importance. Florian Krobb observes that, in the prologue, the encounters between Jewish women and non-Jewish men are decisive for their individual fates as well as that of their community.[18]

Further evidence for this can be deduced from the role Wassermann assigns to the offspring of these unions. The pregnant Rahel is described as follows: 'Sie trug die Zukunft im Schoß, ein neues Geschlecht, Kämpfer später Zeiten' (*JZ*, p. 55). Jette, on the other hand, gives birth to the messianic figure of Agathon, while little Sema also seems to be endowed with special gifts. Wassermann therefore seems to be clearly in favour of the idea of intermarriage, a topic that, as David Biale has shown, continues to be hotly debated within Jewish communities to this day.[19] However, this does not necessarily mean:

> daß für die moderne jüdische Geschichte eine autonome jüdische Entwicklung eine Illusion bleiben muß, da das Geschick der Juden untrennbar mit dem der nichtjüdischen Umgebung verknüpft ist, und daß Orientierungslosigkeit und Verführbarkeit bis in die Gegenwart hinein Kennzeichen einer jahrhundertealten jüdischen Sinnkrise geblieben sind.[20]

Rather, in Wassermann's view Judaism and Christianity have ceased to be a significant marker of difference since both religions died a long time ago, while at the same time he rejects the concept of race. Through the use of mirror images in the prologue and the novel Wassermann therefore not only establishes a connection between the two but also sets a clear focus, namely the everyday relationship between Jews and Christians.

In the novel this at times very paradoxical relationship between Jews and Christians is embodied in the figure of the teacher Bojesen. His general views could easily be described as anti-Semitic and yet it is his passionate love for Agathon's cousin Jeanette Löwengard that will ruin his life. Apart from highlighting this paradox, the figure of Bojesen is important because it is through him that Wassermann shows how non-Jews are equally affected by a general cultural malaise and an antiquated moral system: stuck in a sexless marriage, Bojesen is dismissed from his job as a teacher because he has been seen with the dancer Jeanette and is therefore considered morally unfit. In the following we shall look at the figure of Bojesen in relation to the assimilated, decadent Jewish figure of Edward Nieberding and to Jeanette.

In his relationship to Edward Nieberding, Bojesen is probably best described as a theoretical anti-Semite. Bojesen and Nieberding are, albeit in

18 Florian Krobb, *Die Schöne Jüdin: Jüdische Frauengestalten in der deutschsprachigen Erzählliteratur vom 17. Jahrhundert bis zum Ersten Weltkrieg* (Tübingen: Niemeyer, 1993), p. 221.

19 David Biale, *Eros and the Jews: From Biblical Israel to Contemporary America* (New York: Basic Books, 1992), p. 23.

20 Krobb, *Jüdin*, p. 223.

different ways, in love with the same woman, which leads to several nocturnal conversations. For Bojesen these conversations serve the purpose of expressing his anti-Semitic views, especially with regard to the figure of the Jewish artist (which will be discussed in connection with Gudstikker) and the question of Jewish assimilation. Bojesen considers the modern, assimilated Jew to be a great source of danger:

> Die Juden sind bis zu dem Punkt ungefährlich, als sie nicht an der Kultur eines Volkes teilnehmen. Sobald das kommt, sind alle prägnanten Linien verwischt, das Bild wird unruhig, die Gärung beginnt. Es ist, als ob diese Nation eine Art giftiger Sauerteig wäre (*JZ*, p. 181).

Bojesen thus expresses a stereotypical fear of the infiltration of society by the 'invisible Jew', yet his main point of critique seems to be that these modern Jews have, once again, given birth to Christianity by assimilating to a Gentile culture. A consistent anti-Semite would therefore also have to be an anti-Christian, as can be inferred from the words addressed to Nieberding: 'Geben Sie uns nur dies geistige Christentum wieder, endlich, das unsere starke, säftereiche Rasse ausgelöscht und vernichtet hat binnen sechzehnhundert oder weniger Jahren' (*JZ*, p. 179). This idea of Christianity as a direct continuation of repressive Jewish morals sounds familiar from Nietzsche's *Zur Genealogie der Moral*, where he writes:

> Dieser Jesus von Nazareth, als das leibhafte Evangelium der Liebe, dieser den Armen, den Kranken, den Sündern die Seligkeit und den Sieg bringende "Erlöser" – war er nicht gerade die Verführung in ihrer unheimlichsten und unwiderstehlichsten Form, die Verführung und der Umweg zu eben jenen jüdischen Werthen und Neuerungen des Ideals? Hat Israel nicht gerade auf dem Umwege dieses "Erlösers", dieses scheinbaren Widersachers und Auflösers Israel's, das letzte Ziel seiner sublimen Rachsucht erreicht?[21]

However, the most intriguing aspect of the relationship between the two men is not only that Nieberding agrees, in the sense that he refers to himself as having the soul of a Christian, but that Bojesen becomes attached to his 'enemy'. As his social isolation increases, Bojesen feels ever more drawn towards this representative of the modern Judaism that he despises, and seeks his company in moments of loneliness. Nieberding therefore seems justified in drawing the following conclusion: 'Aber daß wir hier sitzen und uns über Christentum und Judentum echauffieren, ist auch trivial' (*JZ*, p.182) The relationship between Nieberding and Bojesen is, therefore, further evidence of the triviality that the

21 Friedrich Nietzsche, *Zur Genealogie der Moral* (Stuttgart: Reclam, 1988), p. 24. For a more detailed discussion of Nietzsche's influence on Wassermann's early work, see Plöger, *Ästhet*.

difference between Jews and Christians has become in the face of everyday human relationships. Many years later, in 1923, when pressed to make a statement regarding the relationship between Jews and Germans, Wassermann would still arrive at the same conclusion: 'Es hat dieses ganze Gerede über "die" Juden, "die" Deutschen keinen Sinn und Zweck. Es sind angewandt auf soziale Erscheinungen, Hilfkonstruktionen und Ablenkungstheorien. Ich kenne nur Menschen.'[22]

In an attempt to escape his marriage to a woman who thinks that sexuality is essentially a filthy business, Bojesen starts to frequent a vaudeville show named 'Zum Siebenten Himmel' in which Jeanette works as a dancer. Jeanette uses the stage name 'Luisina' and Bojesen immediately falls for her and the air of sexual liberation that surrounds her. However, even after he finds out who she really is, he never makes any reference to her Jewishness and vice versa. This difference therefore seems to be of no consequence to their relationship. Their union is probably best understood as that of two outcasts seeking pleasure outside the realm of the society to which they initially belonged. After a brief affair Jeanette leaves for Paris, yet it seems that it is Bojesen's desperate love for her that eventually ruins his marriage and his life: 'Jeanettes Bild stieg auf. Nun wußte er sein ruheloses Forschen zu deuten [...]. Er ging im Zimmer umher und dachte an nichts anderes als daran, wie er sie wieder gewinnen könne' (*JZ*, p. 206). The man who had hitherto claimed there could be no link between a Jew and a Christian is thus proven wrong and once more revealed to be only a theoretical anti-Semite.

In the prologue as well as in the novel Wassermann therefore depicts a society that is from the outset divided into Jews and non-Jews by a wall of anti-Semitism, yet he seems keen to reveal the hypocrisy behind that divide by showing how Jews and non-Jews share many aspects of their daily lives. Lindemann-Luiken is therefore right to conclude that the Jews in the novel 'weder in nationaler noch in religiöser Hinsicht wesentliche Unterscheidungsmerkmale zu den Deutschen aufweisen.'[23] Just as they can be united by a longing for pleasure, they can also be united by fear, which Wassermann conveys by depicting how the people in the prologue react to strange signs in the night sky: 'Viel Volk sammelte sich schweigend an den Ufern der Regnitz und Pegnitz, und Christen und Juden standen in gleicher Furcht, in gleicher mystischer Andacht Schulter an Schulter' (*JZ*, p. 19). It is shoulder to shoulder that Wassermann, whom Peter Gay rightly refers to as a 'reconciler,'[24] would like to see the people that for him all share the same 'Heimat.'

22 Jakob Wassermann, 'Zwei Briefe an einen deutschen Philosophen,' in *Lebensdienst*, pp. 160–73 (p. 171).

23 Lindemann-Luiken, *Auswirkungen*, p. 123.

24 Peter Gay, *Freud, Jews and other Germans: Masters and Victims in Modernist Culture* (New York: Oxford University Press, 1978), p. 149.

Agathon's Vision – Is Pleasure Possible?

Another function of the prologue is to prepare the reader for Agathon's later quest for universal happiness and pleasure. In the prologue the main result of the news about Sabbatai Zevi is a form of sexual revolution that takes place within the Jewish community. Moritz Heimann, Wassermann's close friend and editor, praised the prologue as a successful depiction of how Sabbatai's message could excite the Jewish community in the way it did: 'Das vom Gesetz schlimmer noch als vom äußeren Druck niedergehaltene Leben bricht mit orgiastischer Raserei aus, in religiösen, wollüstigen und grausamen Taumeln sich entladend'.[25] Indeed, the prologue does not shy away from depicting orgies that even involve sexual intercourse with animals. Moreover, when Agathon later finds out about the false Messiah he seems reluctant to judge him but instead considers him a bringer of joy: '[E]r zweifelte nicht an der Ehrlichkeit des Propheten, der das Leben in so großen Linien gelebt und alle Mitlebenden beglückt hatte' (*JZ*, p. 167). Agathon will therefore start by renouncing Judaism and, after being briefly fascinated by Christianity, come to reject the idea of following one specific religion. Instead he will look for other, spiritual ways to make people happy, a quest which marks the beginning of Wassermann's lifelong search for a more syncretic approach to spirituality that will culminate in his final novel *Joseph Kerkhovens dritte Existenz* (1934).

Even though the novel focuses on society as a whole, it can nevertheless also be understood as a Jewish family novel. This version of the *Zeitroman* was a very popular way of exploring Jewish subcultures at the turn of the century. Other examples are Arthur Schnitzler's *Der Weg ins Freie* (1908) and Max Brod's *Jüdinnen* (1911).[26] With the family at the centre they all deal with conflicts between generations, often revolving around the question of assimilation and the materialism associated with the older generation. In *Zirndorf*, the family is the place in which the general unhappiness first becomes apparent, mainly because it has become dysfunctional. In the novel the reader is presented with the family of Agathon and that of his rich cousin Jeanette; in both cases generations live estranged from each other as they seem to live in different worlds. In Jeanette's case it is the vast fortune of her father that contributes to her unhappiness while Agathon has to witness the ever increasing poverty of his family. Moreover, the family is depicted as a space of oppression in which thoughts and desires are not allowed to roam freely. Neither Jeanette nor, as we

25 Moritz Heimann, 'Zwei Romane', *Die Neue Rundschau*, 9 (1898), 642–47 (p. 646).

26 More examples are listed in Robertson, *'Jewish Question'*, p. 274. See also Ehrhard Bahr, 'Max Brod as a novelist: from the Jewish Zeitroman to the Zionist novel', in Mark H. Gelber and others (eds.), *Von Franzos zu Canetti: Jüdische Autoren aus Österreich* (Tübingen: Niemeyer, 1996), pp. 25–36.

have seen, Agathon's mother Jette is allowed to marry for love since that would have interfered with their families' interests.

In a similar vein, the generation of Agathon's father is depicted as hostile towards, and potentially scared of, any Christian influence. Agathon is appalled by the fanatical religiosity of their visitor Joelsohn, a member of the older generation:

> [Er] redete sich in eine flammende Hitze gegen die Christen und wurde schließlich fanatisch in seinen Anklagen. Er ist um ein paar Jahrhunderte verspätet, dachte Agathon. Es gab viele solcher Juden [...]. Das Gebet ging ihnen über alles, über Gott selbst, und wer nicht betete, war der Feind, und der Christ (*JZ*, p. 111).

When Elkan finds Agathon reading the New Testament he is at first furious and tears the book apart; and is then overcome by fear: 'Elkan empfand plötzlich eine unerklärliche Furcht vor ihm [Agathon]' (*JZ*, p. 80). Elkan is thus scared of a son who dares to leave the old ways behind. At the same time, Agathon's rejection of his father's empty traditions and shallow religiosity strongly resembles Kafka's *Brief an den Vater* in which he reproaches his father for the 'Nichts von Judentum' that he had received from him.[27]

At the beginning of Agathon's mission to bring happiness to the world stands the murder of the innkeeper Sürich Sperling. This episode is rather obscure and probably best understood in terms of its symbolic value, especially since Sürich can hardly be considered an actual character. Gudstikker refers to him as 'personifizierte[s] Germanentum' (*JZ*, p. 90) and Sürich is indeed the village's most passionate anti-Semite. Nevertheless, the description of Sürich is not without sympathy:

> Er war ein Tier: wild, stolz, unbezähmbar, keinem Vernunftgrund der Welt zugänglich. [...] Er war ein Sohn dieser großen Natur rings umher [...]. Sein Vater soll eine Riese gewesen sein [...]. Sürich Sperling paßte nicht herein in diese Welt. "Das Urbild des Germanen" fand kein Bett, worin es bequem ruhen konnte (*JZ*, p. 77).

Sürich can, therefore, be considered an almost mythical figure or even a natural force as well as an outsider figure. When he dies unexpectedly it soon becomes apparent that it was most probably Agathon who murdered him. In conversation with Bojesen, Agathon later reveals the curious events that led to this murder:

> [Er] zog mich nackt aus, nahm Stricke und band mich an ein schwarzes Kreuz an der Wand, neben dem Jesus Christus hing. Dann schlug er mich und fügte

27 Franz Kafka, *Brief an den Vater* (Frankfurt a.M.: Fischer, 1999), p. 37.

> mir Wunden zu, daß ich fühlte, wie mein Blut floß. [...] Da sagte ich zu ihm: 'Sürich Sperling, das ist Ihr Tod.' Da lachte er und sagte: 'Sprich, du Aas, habt ihr nicht den Heiland gekreuzigt? Das ist eure Schuld. Deswegen sind wir lauter Schnapssäufer, weil er Mönche aus uns gemacht hat, Jesus von Nazareth. Er hat einen großen Sarg aus der Welt gemacht' (*JZ*, pp. 133–34).

The scene becomes even more obscure when the Jew Lämelche Erdmann suddenly arrives to curse Sürich: 'Der ewige Jud ist jetzt erlöst, und du, Sürich Sperling, wirst werden der Ewige Christ' (*JZ*, p. 134).

The following night Agathon murders Sürich, a deed that according to him will bring happiness to the world. One possible interpretation of this scene and the ensuing murder is that Agathon wants to break a vicious circle in the sense that he does not envision a world in which the Jews take revenge. The two religions are not supposed to reverse their roles but ought to disappear altogether. According to Agathon the murder of Sürich is therefore a good deed because with him the entire Christian religion seems to have died, 'oder vielleicht nur der christliche Geist in diesem Volk, durch den es hassen mußte und Blut vergießen mußte' (*JZ*, p. 194).

Soon afterwards Agathon publicly renounces the religion of his fathers and leaves the house of his parents behind in order to go on his mission. Tellingly, once he has renounced his Jewishness, Agathon is no longer perceived as a Jew by the people around him. Not only the peasants with whom he stays are unaware of his origins but even Jeanette doubts that he is actually a Jew: 'Wessen Blut steckt eigentlich in dir? [...] Ich kenne keinen von den Leuten, bei denen du aufgewachsen bist, der mit dir zu vergleichen wäre' (*JZ*, p. 234). In this version it therefore seems possible to cease being Jewish at one's own will, in the sense that a Jew is not recognizable from his outer appearance. This can be read as another refutation of the concept of race.

The essence of Agathon's vision becomes apparent in three key scenes: the burning of the church, the loss of his virginity to Jeanette, and the death of the King. The scene of the burning church takes place in the midst of a revolt that has been caused by a failed attempt to make people happy: the alchemist Baldewin Estrich has found a way to make gold and by giving it out freely to the poor has created an angry, greedy mob. In this scene materialist means are clearly rejected as insufficient to fill people's inner void. Soldiers try to contain the mob and people seek shelter in a church, which is suddenly set on fire by a flash of lightning. Initially, Agathon appears in a Christ-like manner, protecting the people in the church from the soldiers. However, he then has a vision:

> Er dachte, daß die Städte zerstört, niedergerissen werden, verlassen werden müßten, damit der Mensch wieder sich selbst finde, und je mehr Agathon sein

> ganzes Selbst aufgab in den beengenden Träumen, je mehr wurde ihm auch der Geist des Christentums zur lebenden Gestalt, die mit feindseligen Armen stand und ihm den Weg versperrte, und dahinter, einem Gespenst gleich, klein und zäh, heuchlerisch und gewandt, der Jude, jetzt mehr als je bereit, den alttestamentarischen Mantel abzuwerfen und in das neuere Kleid des ehedem geächteten Nazareners zu schlüpfen (*JZ*, p. 228).

Agathon's desire for the church in Nuremberg to burn down indicates that the problem of religion itself supersedes questions of Judaism and Christianity. In an era in which, as Jütten puts it, 'Glaubensverlust zum Massenschicksal [wird]',[28] Agathon is looking for a substitute which will make people happy and embrace life, which is why he longs to found a 'neues, gottloses Geschlecht' (*JZ*, p. 229).[29] The prestige of science, the scholarly criticism of the Bible and the impact of secular philosophies, such as those of Schopenhauer and Nietzsche, have made Christianity and traditional Judaism appear increasingly implausible. Nevertheless, this loss of religion has left people with an inner void. There was:

> a need to fashion out of spare and questionable post-Christian materials a self that would not be overwhelmed by the freedom secured to it by a liberal agenda, by the social coerciveness of democratic society and by the pressures and solicitations of modern urban life.[30]

Wassermann is alive to this dilemma, yet without trying to provide answers or solutions. Atheism is not an option for Agathon and it seems the only way of finding the universal happiness he envisions is, as we shall see in *Renate Fuchs,* to live a life outside society and away from the cities. Failure therefore becomes inevitable or, as Martini argues: 'Die Größe seiner [Agathon's] Bestimmung zieht ihrer Verwirklichung eine Grenze'.[31] In other words, Agathon's general vision of happiness has to remain an unfulfilled utopia in order for the novel to be at all realistic. The vision quoted above also contains a first hint of the spiritual overcoming of the self as a means to happiness, a theme that Wassermann will develop at length in his later novel *Christian Wahnschaffe* (1919).

The scene of Agathon's first and only sexual encounter with Jeanette makes it apparent that sexuality plays a key role in his vision of universal happiness,

28 Jütten, *Diskurse*, p. 84.

29 Gunnar Och has rightly observed that this type of ecstatic language can be seen as a foreboding of Expressionism (Gunnar Och, 'Ahasver oder das andere Ich: Eine mythische Chiffre im Werk Jakob Wassermanns', in *Deutscher – Jude – Literat*, pp. 109–27 (p. 115)).

30 J. W. Burrow, *The Crisis of Reason: European Thought, 1848–1914* (New Haven & London: Yale University Press, 2000), p. xii.

31 Martini, 'Utopie', p. 463.

one which justifies the use of the word pleasure in this context. His first reaction to the loss of his virginity is decidedly negative as he is affected by a 'grenzenlosen, vorher nie erfaßten noch geahnten Jammer' (*JZ*, p. 241). It does not take him long, however, to realize that a negative attitude towards sexuality stands at the centre of the unhappiness he witnesses every day: 'Ist es nicht vielleicht deswegen Schmutz, weil wir es so wollen? [...] weil Christus es gewollt hat?' (*JZ*, p. 242). Agathon is familiar with a world in which sexuality is not talked about at school, boys at the Jewish orphanage are punished severely for masturbating, and he perceives the awakening of his own sexuality as a threat. However, Jeanette's reaction to his vision of a new way of looking at sexuality immediately reveals it to be unfeasible:

> Du willst die Sinnlichkeit wieder auf den Thron setzen, den sie seit zweitausend Jahren verlassen hat. [...] Ja, eher kannst du dein Hirn verbrennen, oder du mußt neue Menschen formen. [...] Und dann bedenke, eine Religion, die nicht die Sinnlichkeit erstickt, schleudert die Könige vom Thron (*JZ*, p. 242).

Wassermann therefore sees a clear link between people's sexual repression and their overall freedom. This is already hinted at in the prologue, in which people enjoy their new and brief freedom in the form of sexual liberation. The topic will be explored further in connection with the depiction of the Bavarian King at the end of the novel.

Agathon's vision of universal happiness and sexual freedom comes to a sudden end when he has to accept that it is already a reality, albeit not in his idealized form. His counterpart Gudstikker reveals a certain level of hypocrisy behind Agathon's claims when he mocks the latter's outrage at Gudstikker's illegitimate affair with Monika Olifat: 'Sie kommen daher als Ritter eines kleinen Mädchens, das in leichter Stunde vom Piedestal der Tugend stieg. Was macht das? Leben wir etwa, um tugendhaft zu sein? He? Oder leben wir, um zu leben?' (*JZ*, p. 258). While this argument certainly serves as an excuse for leaving Monika behind with a child, it also shows the worldly limits of Agathon's vision.

However, Gudstikker does not stop there. He volunteers to be Agathon's Asmodeus, his demon of lust, for one evening and introduces Agathon to the city's nightlife. Tellingly, it is the false laughter of the prostitutes that is among the most shocking experiences for Agathon: '[S]ie hatten keine Aufgabe, als die zu lachen' (*JZ*, p. 260). It is this propagation of false happiness combined with a ubiquitous level of depravity that makes Agathon give up his vision and realize that true happiness has become an unrealistic aim:

> Und Agathon sah das Ziel in der Ferne zerstäuben zu nichts [...] und erkannte, daß er gegen die gigantische Masse des Elends nichts war als ein Kind, das mit seinen Händchen Gebirge abtragen will. Und Jude oder Christ, was bedeutete ihm das noch gegenüber diesem heimlichen und lautlosen Kampf, der hier

> zwischen schlafenden Mauern geführt wurde? Jude und Christ hatten in gleicher Weise dazu beigetragen, das Jahrhundert dorthin zu führen, wo es stand (*JZ*, p. 261).

Outdated Christian as well as Jewish morals have therefore proven to be inadequate when it comes to allowing people to have a liberal approach to sexuality. Instead, their repressive ways have led to the state of general depravity that turns out to be overwhelming for Agathon.

Towards the end of the novel Agathon and Jeanette both feel drawn towards the figure of the King, who, according to Jeanette, was 'für die Freude geboren' (*JZ*, p. 269). Given the time in which the novel is set, the King's mysterious death by drowning and the reference to his alleged insanity, it becomes clear that the novel refers to the Bavarian King Ludwig II (1845–1886). While Jeanette unsuccessfully attempts to become the King's mistress, Agathon decides to lead the people in an attempt to free the King, who has been arrested and incapacitated, a fate Agathon himself shares with the historical figure. The motivation behind this decision seems to be the King's function as a symbol for the detrimental consequences of the Church's oppressive power. The brief, sympathetic depiction of the King is that of a victim as he utters the following words:

> Was ist Majestät heute, daß sie sich beugen muß vor einem Krämer, der in einer guten Stunde unter Beihilfe seiner Schwäger und Tanten Minister wurde und zufrieden das christlich Hausbrot ißt? Eine schöne Majestät, die sich der Kirche opfern soll und keine Hand rühren darf ohne den Pfaffen (*JZ*, p. 267).

The negative influence of religion is thus shown to stretch far beyond people's daily lives, as it does not allow this King to reign, even though popular with the people. Agathon successfully motivates the peasants to try and free the King, yet before they can start marching they find out that he has drowned. Given Wassermann's later concern with homosexual outsider figures, King Ludwig II must be considered the first figure in that line, especially since he is described as a monarch 'der doch seit Jahren sich von allen Frauen ferngehalten. Er verachtete und geringschätzte die Frauen und war hart und brutal gegen sie' (*JZ*, p. 265). Moreover, as can be deduced from Heinz Häfner's biography, the king's homosexuality was already talked about during his lifetime, especially the sexual abuse of his soldiers, and hence Wassermann would no doubt have been familiar with this detail.[32]

The short-lived nature of Agathon's vision finds further emphasis in *Renate Fuchs*, in which, just before the end of his life, Agathon renounces his former beliefs:

32 Heinz Häfner, *Ein König wird beseitigt: Ludwig II. von Bayern* (Munich: Beck, 2008), pp. 50–76.

> Ich entäußerte mich alles Glaubens und sah in der entgötterten Welt starke Menschen sich zur Freude wenden. [...] Die Moral der Religionen und der Gesellschaft hatte mich erbittert und zum Kämpfer gemacht. Durch Andersthun, durch Worte glaubte ich wirken zu können. Heute glaub ich es nicht mehr (*RF*, pp. 472–73).

The idea of achieving happiness through the renunciation of religion is therefore denied and yet the search for happiness continues in *Renate Fuchs*, in which the topic of religion is moved to the margins. Even though Agathon's vision proves a failure, it nevertheless offers intriguing insights into the ways in which Wassermann perceived society at that point in his life.

Gudstikker – the Devil in Disguise?

As with the depiction of Jews and Christians in general, Wassermann demonstrates with the portrayal of the writer Gudstikker that making a distinction between Jewish and non-Jewish artists has become a futile and irrelevant pursuit since they are all affected by the same 'Literatentum'. Wassermann puts his point across by making the non-Jewish artist Gudstikker conform to all the stereotypes about non-creative Jewish artists as formulated by the anti-Semite Bojesen. Moreover, the character of Gudstikker is also a reflection on the role of the commercial artist, or 'Literat', in this troubled society. This reflection at times turns into moments of self-reflection on Wassermann's part, making them all the more intriguing.

Gudstikker represents the increasingly commercialized institutions of culture and thus the kind of artist whom Wassermann later describes as the 'Literat'.[33] Though Wassermann only introduces his concept of the 'Literat' in 1909, the figure of the inferior commercial man of letters is clearly anticipated in the character of Gudstikker. This figure stands in opposition to the true creative artist as he combines two trends which were common at the time: his books are mere 'products' and not inspired by true genius; or, as Wassermann puts it, they are simply produced instead of being born from contact with the divine.[34] Moreover, Gudstikker writes unworldly, merely aesthetic poetry which follows the doctrine of 'l'art pour l'art'. In 'Die Kunst der Erzählung' (1904) Wassermann rejects this watchword from the 1890s: 'Gewiß muß es [das Kunstwerk] um seiner selbst willen hervorgebracht werden. Aber es darf, wie das lebendige Geschöpf, nicht um seiner selbst willen existieren'.[35] In

33 Jakob Wassermann, 'Der Literat oder Mythos und Persönlichkeit', in *Lebensdienst*, pp. 502–50.

34 Wassermann, 'Literat', p. 503.

35 Wassermann, 'Die Kunst der Erzählung', in *Lebensdienst*, pp. 550–85 (p. 575).

his essay 'Der Literat oder Mythos und Persönlichkeit' (1909) Wassermann introduces the concept of the 'Literat' who has no true inspiration and thus turns literature into an article of mass production: 'Der Literat ist der vom Mythos losgelöste produktive Mensch'.[36] According to Wassermann, great literature should be based on timeless myths like those of Faust or Don Quixote. Moreover, Gudstikker considers his art to be a means to an end, or, as he puts it: 'Ich mache in Kunst' (*JZ*, p. 110). To Gudstikker writing is a job like any other and is not based on any genuine inspiration but merely on the desire to earn money.

In the novel, as well as in the essay, Wassermann is highly aware that most people are quick to associate the concept of the 'Literat' with the Jewish artist. Lindemann-Luiken tells us: 'Der "Jude" erweist sich für die völkische Literaturpolemik durch seine angeblich intellektuelle Arbeitsweise als Literat im Gegensatz zum intuitiv arbeitenden "arischen" Dichter und von daher gilt "jüdische Literatur" als artistisch-formal'.[37] Moreover, some critics even perceive this kind of art as a threat to genuine, profound German art and culture. As a rejection of this attitude, Wassermann seems to have created the character of Gudstikker in such a way that Bojesen's lengthy complaint about Jewish artists could as easily be read as a description of this Gentile 'Literat'. It is not therefore, as Lindemann-Luiken rightly observes, a moment of anti-Semitism by Wassermann himself:

> Sie [Jewish artists] sind Künstler, echte Künstler, daran ist nicht zu zweifeln. Aber sie richten uns zugrunde. [...] Sie haben keine Tiefe. Nur in die Breite gehen sie, und wenn sie tief scheinen, ist es eine Lüge. [...] Sie nehmen uns die Wahrheit und die Aufrichtigkeit in der Kunst [...]. Sie ersetzen es unbewußt mit dem Schein von Wahrheit, dem Schein von Aufrichtigkeit; sie bringen uns eine neue Art von Sentimentalität, die sich als Naivität gibt und mit grüblerischer Wehmut nach den Gründen der Dinge schreit (*JZ*, pp. 123–24).

Throughout the two novels, Gudstikker's art is also described as phony in the sense that it is written with virtuosity but is shallow, untrue and unable to leave a lasting impression. This kind of art is commercial and not meant to last. This description of Gudstikker culminates in a scene in which Agathon cannot help but think of the artist as the most Jewish person he has ever met: 'Es war die Lüge selbst, die ihm in ihrer ganzen brutalen Unbekümmertheit entgegentrat. [...] Agathon fand kein anderes Wort dafür als das Wort jüdisch, in seinem häßlichsten Sinn. Gudstikker schien ihm die jüdischste Natur, die er je getroffen' (*JZ*, p. 257). In this scene, in which a Jewish character

36 Wassermann, 'Der Literat', p. 544.

37 Lindemann-Luiken, *Auswirkungen*, p. 62.

accuses a non-Jewish character of being Jewish, it becomes apparent that for Wassermann the term 'Jewish' has turned, in this context, into a negative characteristic that has little to do with an actual religious affiliation. The artist whom many people think of as Jewish is simply, in his view, a type of modern artist. To distinguish between the Jewish and the non-Jewish artist is, therefore, a futile pursuit.[38]

In his essay on the 'Literat', Wassermann adds complexity to this point when he admits that there are indeed many Jews among these 'Literaten', a fact which he attributes to the contemporary exclusion of Jews from state employment. As a consequence many of them went into law, medicine and the arts. However, Wassermann is not entirely dismissive of these artists but rather argues that, even though their originality is artificial, they are capable of producing noteworthy works. Most importantly, though, in his view, no modern artist can help sharing some character traits with the 'Literat', something which raises this figure to a universal level, detached from any question of religious affiliation.

In accordance with this argument, the depiction of Gudstikker is not entirely negative. For instance, Agathon is shown to be aware of 'einen hohen Zug [...] durch den Gudstikker fähig war, das wirklich Große zu verstehen und sich ihm hinzugeben' (*JZ*, p. 195). The 'Literat' therefore remains an ambiguous and questionable figure, a necessary side-effect of modern life and a ubiquitous phenomenon but not an exclusively Jewish figure. Plöger is therefore right in asserting that Wassermann rejects the idea that inferior modern art is necessarily made by Jewish artists. However, her view that as a Jewish artist Wassermann was keen to distance himself from the figure of the 'Literat' at all costs does not do justice to the complexity of the matter.[39] Similarly, Erwin Poeschel is mistaken when he claims that Wassermann had identified the 'Literat' as a 'geheimer innerer Feind' whom he needed to make 'unschädlich'.[40] Joeris's claim that Wassermann here confirms Jewish stereotypes is as erroneous as her claim that his critique of the 'Literat' was aimed at Thomas Mann.[41] The latter is particularly problematic since Wassermann, despite a strong sense of rivalry, never doubted Mann's skill as an artist, a stance which can be inferred from a letter to Marta Karlweis in

38 Lindenmann-Luiken's claim that Wassermann does not react to the image of the Jew as a 'krankhaft sexuellen Triebwesen' is refuted by the fact that Gudstikker, with his very active sex life, could indeed be read as an indirect reaction to that prejudice (Lindemann-Luiken, *Auswirkungen*, p. 85).

39 Plöger, *Ästhet*, pp. 305–07.

40 Erwin Poeschel, 'Jakob Wassermann', in *Juden in der deutschen Literatur*, ed. by Gustav Krojanker (Berlin: Welt, 1922), pp. 76–101 (p. 83).

41 Joeris, *Aspekte*, pp. 65–67.

which he writes: 'und war dann über drei Stunden bei Thomas Mann. Er ist ja über jeder Kritik und jedem Lob'.[42]

Being a Jewish writer himself, Wassermann felt the need to make his own person part of the debate revolving around the 'Literat'. There are a few hints in the two novels that the figure of Gudstikker can also be understood as partly modelled on Wassermann himself. In *Zirndorf* Gudstikker leaves for Berlin because one of his plays is being performed, an ambition he shares with the young Wassermann, who, soon after the publication of *Zirndorf* in October 1900, travelled to Berlin, where his play *Hockenjos* was performed at the Sezessionsbühne alongside Hofmannsthal's *Der Tor und der Tod*.[43] In *Renate Fuchs* Gudstikker is writing a book about Renate in order to address the 'Frauenfrage', just as Wassermann does with his own novel. Moreover, in a letter to Gudstikker, Renate writes: 'Ich kann nur ihre Schrift schwer lesen. Sie ist so klein' (*RF*, p. 204) This minor detail becomes important in the context of Wassermann's own correspondence since some of his correspondents complained about his notoriously small handwriting, among them Martha Karlweis and Ferrucio Busoni.[44]

If Gudstikker is therefore to be understood as a reflection on Wassermann's own role as an artist in society, it reveals his concern with the possible limitations of that role. When confronted with the submissive behaviour of Käthe Estrich towards her fiancé Gudstikker, Agathon has an important insight: 'Er hat ihr den Glauben geraubt. Was hat er ihr dafür gegeben? Seine eigene Person' (*JZ*, p. 165). Nonetheless, as the two novels show, this type of artist is not a person in whom one should believe. Ruminating on her numerous encounters with famous poets in Berlin, Jeanette comes to a sobering conclusion: 'Aber wie schrecklich bin ich immer enttäuscht worden!' (*JZ*, p. 152). Most of the art in circulation, it seems, cannot offer any substantial or long-term relief to people. The kind of art that Gudstikker produces reaches many people, yet it is to no avail. It never leaves a lasting impression and even his book on the 'Frauenfrage' proves to be of no consequence to Renate. Even though aiming to become a commercial artist himself, Wassermann remains suspicious of the possible benefits.

This is because the notion of finding genuine happiness through art is not denied in the novel. In fact, it looks as if the only character to find happiness

42 Wassermann to Marta Karlweis, 18 February 1916 (DLA, call number: 73.205/).

43 Rodewald, *Ein Weg*, p. 45.

44 On 28 February 1916 Wassermann writes in a letter to Martha Karlweis: 'Liebste, so schreib ich also größer' (DLA, call number 73.205 / 7). On 8 April 1921 Wassermann writes to Ferruccio Busoni: 'Merken Sie, dass ich mich fortwährend bemühe, gross zu schreiben?' (DLA, call number 96.48.3 /16).

and contentment through art in the two novels is the minor character of Edward Nieberding's sister Cornely. Following an obsessive phase of believing herself to be a Christian, Cornely finally discovers writing poetry as a source of true happiness and liberation: 'Die Ruhe, die sie erfüllte, war so frauenhaft und ausgeglichen, daß sie sich ganz neubelebt fühlte. [...] Diese Empfindung des Losgelöstseins und der Leichtigkeit hatte sie wünschen lassen, nackt zu sein' (*JZ*, p. 254). Plöger is, therefore, mistaken in her claim that in the novel only Jeanette and Sema Hellmuth produce genuine art, even more so as neither of the two achieves happiness that way.[45]

An Emancipated Woman – Just a Dream?

The two figures in whom Wassermann is particularly interested throughout the two novels are the woman and the Jew. Even though he frequently denies any basis for making a distinction between the Christian and the Jew he is nevertheless aware of the mechanisms of exclusion affecting the latter. Seeing the woman and the Jew as parallel outsider figures in Wassermann's fiction offers a new way of looking at the two novels and the connections between them. In his book *Freud, Race and Gender* Sander L. Gilman offers an explanation of how the two can both be considered Others – albeit in different ways – in relation to the Gentile man. Gilman argues that within the categories of race and gender that prevailed in the nineteenth century, the stereotypes of the woman and the Jew were considered parallel categories to that of the Christian male. However, woman was not the opposite of man but his complement, needed for reproduction, and therefore the protected and inclusionary Other. By the end of the nineteenth century this conventional relationship had become strained and threatened by the figures of the prostitute and the intellectual woman, who were both considered the 'bad' Other, who stands in opposition to the good Other, that is, the figure of the obedient wife and mother. With the bad Other challenging male superiority as well as traditional family values, these women were perceived as a threat.

Historically, the Jew had also been a necessary inclusionary Other: 'Jews were the historical elements against which they [Christians] could define themselves.'[46] Nonetheless, when, in the course of secularization, religious categories gave way to racial ones and the Jew became the opposite, not of the Christian but of the Aryan, he was no longer needed and became the exclusionary Other. Thus, even though the Jew and the woman were not

45 Plöger, *Ästhet*, p. 303.

46 Sander L. Gilman, *Freud, Race and Gender* (Princeton: Princeton University Press, 1993), p. 9.

equivalent, the categories underwent similar changes and were both 'different from and less than the male'.[47] The idea of the woman and the Jew as suppressed Others in relation to the Gentile man explains why Wassermann was anxious to explore the contemporary situation of women in *Renate Fuchs*. Moreover, the status of the emancipated or 'fallen' woman as the bad Other, threatening conventional gender relations, seemed even closer to that of the Jew.

The concept of linking the woman and the Jew because of their similar status as outsiders can also be found in Hans Mayer's book *Außenseiter*. Mayer also adds the homosexual to the category of the existential outsider: an individual who is made an outsider by his or her birth, sex or any other mental or physical abnormality ('Eigenart'). Mayer goes on to argue that the bourgeois Enlightenment of the nineteenth and twentieth centuries failed in the face of these three outsiders. All that has been achieved is a form of tolerance which accepts the outsider without actually integrating him or her. For centuries these three outsiders have had to conform to the rules of a heterosexual, male-dominated and Gentile society: it was not acceptable for them to live their Otherness. Even though the category of the homosexual is more relevant for Wassermann's later fiction, Mayer's approach nevertheless allows it to be placed in a wider theoretical framework.[48]

Jeanette

Just like her cousin Agathon, Jeanette Löwengard breaks with the world of her father in search of a more pleasurable existence. As a woman, Jeanette is confronted with a problematic, though – as *Renate Fuchs* will show – not exclusively Jewish tradition: that is, marriage as merely a way of doing business. Despite her family's high level of assimilation, she is turned into a marriageable object (one could almost say a tradeable good). As Jeanette puts it: '[B]ei uns werden alle Mädchen verschachert wie Häuser und Grundstücke' (*JZ*, p. 95).[49] In his novel *Jüdinnen* Max Brod refers to this dilemma as 'das allgemeine traurige Schicksal der Mädchen, der jüdischen namentlich, die für keinen anderen Zweck als die Ehe erzogen werden'.[50] In the version of *Zirndorf*

47 Gilman, *Freud*, p. 9.

48 Mayer, *Außenseiter* (Frankfurt a.M.: Suhrkamp, 1975).

49 It is noteworthy that Wassermann uses such a strong term as 'schachern' here since it carries extremely negative connotations, not just because of the way it is used by Karl Marx in *Zur Judenfrage* (1844). Marx writes: 'Die Emanzipation vom Schacher und vom Geld, also vom praktischen, realen Judentum war die Selbstemanzipation unserer Zeit' (Karl Marx, 'Zur Judenfrage', in *Frühe Schriften I*, ed. by Hans Joachim Lieber and Peter Furth (Stuttgart: Cotta, 1962), pp. 451–88 (p. 481).

50 Max Brod, *Jüdinnen* (Leipzig and Vienna: Wolff, 1915), p. 174.

published in 1897 the controversy surrounding this practice is highlighted even further by the depiction of Jeanette's fiancé, the widower Salomon Hecht: 'Ein alter, grinsender, gebückt gehender Mensch mit brauner Perücke und gefärbtem Bart' (*JZ*, p. 97).[51] When Jeanette publicly refuses to marry this 'Greis', her longing for pleasure becomes immediately apparent: 'Was soll ich denn anfangen mit diesem Schwein in der Nacht, wenn ich von Männern träume, die nicht ein paar matte Nachtlichter im Kopf haben, sondern Augen, Augen, Augen?' (*JZ*, p. 100). Her decision to break with her family forever is, therefore, predominantly motivated by a longing for sexual freedom rather than emancipatory concerns.

Jeanette's means of escaping from a world where, as she puts it, 'die Lebensfreude bei der Prostitution anfängt' (*JZ*, p. 146) is dance.[52] The dance is important in her process of sexual liberation because it is an act of self-expression through the body. On stage Jeanette publicly exposes her body, an act which stands in strong opposition to the claim that women should dress modestly and cover themselves up. In Brod's *Jüdinnen* (1911) the character Irene Popper admires the famous female dancers of her time, yet when she tries to dance herself in front of the protagonist Hugo Rosenthal she trips and falls. Combined with her later 'traditional' marriage her inability to dance can be understood as a symbol for her failed attempt at emancipation or sexual liberation. Nevertheless, it remains questionable whether Jeanette herself achieves a form of emancipation or whether she simply remains an object of male sexual desire. In her job she dances for the entertainment of men, thus turning from an object of her father's business interests into a victim of male exploitation. Koester's claim that Jeanette is indeed a 'junge emanzipierte Jüdin' therefore remains dubitable.[53] At the end of the novel Jeanette returns from Paris an outsider figure who is dead to her father's household since her journey towards sexual liberation has proven a road of no return. As with Agathon, her final hopes lie with the Bavarian King as a potential bearer of joy.

Jeanette becomes the first important female figure in Agathon's life since she introduces him to her world of sensuality. In a society where joy in life equals prostitution, Jeanette is forced to lead a solitary, nocturnal existence with Agathon as the last member of her community she can hold on to.

51 In later versions of the novel this depiction is toned down as Hecht is described as 'ein elegant gekleideter, ziemlich fetter Mann' (*Die Juden von Zirndorf* (Berlin: Fischer, 1918), p. 105).

52 In later versions of the novel it reads: 'wo die Lebensfreude beim Verlust der bürgerlichen Ehre anfängt' (*Die Juden von Zirndorf*, p. 203). This shows that the young Wassermann was a fierce social critic who later, possibly with regard to his middle-class readership, toned down these criticisms.

53 Koester, *Wassermann*, p. 18.

Similarly to Gudstikker, she exposes him to the depravities of a 'vermorschte Gesellschaft' (*JZ*, p. 239) and at the end of it takes his virginity. This brings the story of Agathon's sexual awakening to a close, a process which he experiences as unpleasant due to its being a taboo in the society in which he grew up. However, it is important to point out that, according to David Biale, 'the Jewish tradition cannot be characterised as either simply affirming or simply repressing the erotic'.[54] The reader is thus confronted by Wassermann's subjective notion of society, which at the same time also reflects a conflict in Wassermann's own writing. Siegmund Bing emphasizes that Wassermann's entire work is characterized by what he refers to as 'Körperscheu', meaning that the author usually shies away from depicting sexual matters.[55] Agathon's troubled response to his own sexuality therefore mirrors a conflict present in Wassermann's entire work: the longing for sexual freedom combined with an inability to depict it.

Monika

The minor character Monika Olifat deserves a brief discussion, but not only because she becomes Agathon's first wife. Monika is not just a Jewish woman, but is also an Eastern European Jew, a fact which adds a heightened significance to her character. As mentioned above, *Zirndorf* can be considered a Jewish family novel, a genre which often bears testimony to the resentment felt by many Jews towards their counterparts from Eastern Europe, the so-called 'Ostjuden'. The latter frequently make an appearance in these novels in the form of 'unacculturated relatives who often turn up from Poland or Galicia and cause embarrassment by embodying the Gentile image of the hateful Jew from which the assimilationists are desperate to distance themselves'.[56] Jews from Eastern Europe were, therefore, often seen as outsiders within the Jewish community.

Even though *Die Juden von Zirndorf* offers traditional, if not stereotypical, depictions of contemporary Jewish culture, it also allows exceptions otherwise rarely to be found in Jewish family novels. Monika Olifat, who has emigrated from Poland with her mother and sister, is described as educated, fluent in standard German as well as Polish and good-looking; even her name is unusual. She is not portrayed as different from or inferior to other members of the Jewish community, which means that she is not an internal outsider, yet at the same time she is not shown to be exceptional for an Eastern European

54 Biale, *Eros*, p. 5.

55 Bing, *Wassermann*, p. 132.

56 Robertson, *'Jewish Question'*, p. 274.

Jew. Kraft's claim that Wassermann openly despised Jews from Eastern Europe is therefore in need of revision.[57]

Monika has an illegitimate child with Gudstikker, something which leaves her ostracized by her community in addition to already being an outsider figure within Gentile society. By marrying her, Agathon not only enables her to return to her own community (as depicted at the end of *Zirndorf*) but also bridges the gap between Eastern European and Western Jews. Even though it is mentioned in *Renate Fuchs* that Monika dies soon after the wedding (*RF*, p. 473), Agathon spends the rest of his life in Eastern Europe, in Moravia, a region with many Jewish communities where the son he has with Renate will also grow up. This suggests that the figure of Agathon also embodies the vision of a Jewish culture no longer separated by an East-West division. In fact, his marriage to Monika at the end of *Zirndorf* can be understood as the symbolic marriage of Eastern and Western Jewish culture. Wassermann thus offers one of the few exceptions to conventional representations of Jews, insofar as this work is free from stereotypical and derogatory depictions of ginger-haired and backward Jews from Eastern Europe. This notion of Agathon as a mediator between different worlds is a recurring theme and will be crucial to the understanding of the final scenes of *Renate Fuchs.*

Renate Fuchs

In *Renate Fuchs* the perspective is widened as the novel moves from the parochial setting of Franconia to that of the cosmopolitan Munich. After dealing with his immediate surroundings in *Zirndorf*, Wassermann is now able to explore the urban world and the world of women, that is, the 'other' Other. Following Gilman's as well as Mayer's, approach Renate can be seen as representing the other Other in relation to the Gentile man. As we have seen, at the time the woman and the Jew both experienced discrimination and were allowed only partial participation in a society dominated by Gentile men. Thus, despite the differences between them, they are both outsiders longing for emancipation from their outsider status.

Renate Fuchs is the story of a young and beautiful woman from a privileged background who breaks off her engagement to a duke by eloping with another man called Anselm Wanderer. Renate and Anselm live together for a while as an unmarried couple, yet after the loss of Wanderer's fortune Renate leaves for Vienna, where she starts selling her body as a high-class cocotte or prostitute. Unable to bear this situation, Renate tries to earn a living through manual

57 Kraft, *Wassermann*, p. 104.

labour, a situation which turns out to be equally unbearable. After many trials and tribulations Renate eventually meets the dying Agathon Geyer. In one night of love they conceive a child which Renate is to bring up on her own, away from society somewhere in the countryside in Moravia. Her quest for emancipation thus ends with motherhood.

Renate Fuchs marked the beginning of Wassermann's thriving career as a novelist, which led, as Karl Leydecker puts it, to 'an extremely lucrative relationship for Wassermann and Fischer'.[58] In *Die Bilanz der Moderne* (1904) Samuel Lublinski attributes the popularity of the novel, which for a long time remained Wassermann's most successful one, even after the publication of *Caspar Hauser*, to Wassermann's strong awareness of those issues in need of public discussion: in this case women's struggle for emancipation.[59] In 1903 Georg Brandes wrote: 'Er [der Roman] war vergangenes Frühjahr von allen Büchern das meist besprochene und meist gelesene'.[60] Thus, even though not all critics agree that the novel was actually a successful depiction of the issue of emancipation, it has struck a nerve and aroused extensive interest and discussion.[61]

Before looking at the novel's eponymous protagonist, the minor character Gisa Schumann needs a brief discussion at this point. With Gisa, Wassermann chooses a Jewish woman to become the ultimate sexual object, the victim of other people's longing for pleasure. Wassermann here designates the Jewish woman as the ultimate outsider whose situation is far worse than that of the male Jew or the Gentile woman. Gilman tellingly refers to the situation of being Jewish and female as a 'double-double bind'.[62] Gisa stands at the centre of the novel's opening scene: she runs away, naked, from Renate's fiancé Rudolf. She has been tricked and essentially sold by her parents to Rudolf, who could not resist her beauty. Conversely, her nudity underlines the fact that she is a defenceless object.

Just after the wedding to a man she does not love, Gisa has a violent fit of madness. Throughout the novel, she hardly ever speaks: 'Gisa Schumann sprach nicht, auch schien man nicht zu erwarten, daß sie rede' (*RF*, p. 2. Madness is therefore not shown to be subversive. Instead, Marta Canimero-Santangelo's theory applies: namely, that the figure of the madwoman 'provides

58 Leydecker, 'Case', p. 86.

59 Samuel Lublinski, *Die Bilanz der Moderne* (Berlin: Crombach, 1904), pp. 245–46. The relevant reference is quoted in Neubauer, *Schriftsteller*, p. 31.

60 Georg Brandes, *Gestalten und Gedanken: Essays* (Munich: Langen, 1903), pp. 25–30 (p. 25).

61 For a more detailed discussion of the novel's reception, see Plöger, *Ästhet*, pp. 346–49.

62 Gilman, *Freud*, p. 21.

a symbolic resolution whose only outcome must be greater powerlessness'.[63] Moreover, Wassermann evokes the image of the sensual Jewish woman, the *belle juive*. In the nineteenth and early twentieth centuries the Jewish woman is frequently depicted as a highly sensual *femme fatale*.[64] Due to her status as a double outsider, the Jewish woman is, therefore, in Wassermann's view, at a far greater risk of becoming subject to male exploitation. Her longing for emancipation can, it seems, as in the case of Agathon's sister Miriam, only be satisfied if she is willing to relinquish all sexual pleasure in order to focus on her education instead. Female madness as the only way out of a hopeless situation will remain a constant theme throughout Wassermann's entire oeuvre.

The character of Renate Fuchs is Wassermann's main contribution to the so-called 'Frauenfrage'. As a character, Renate is probably best understood if seen as a victim of the various mechanisms of exclusion affecting her life. After all, she spends almost all her life in complete social isolation. In depicting her Wassermann seems less interested in concrete emancipatory concerns than in conveying the psychological situation as well as the daily life of a naive young woman who chooses what looks like a free life of pleasure over a lucrative marriage to a middle-aged man. Herbert Tiefenbacher, in one of the few existing critical discussions of *Renate Fuchs*, describes this process as follows: 'Sehnsucht nach Ich-Findung [...] verbunden mit der Ahnung, zu Höherem berufen zu sein, sind die Kräfte, die die Heldin zu dem für die Gesellschaft so außergewöhnlichen Handlungsschritt bewegen'.[65] Moreover, through Renate's eyes Wassermann seeks to explore the lives of a number of women ranging from a baroness to a prostitute.

At the beginning of the novel the connection between the situation of the woman and the Jew is made apparent through Renate's strong attachment to the Jewish writer Süssenguth. The latter has to be seen as a major influence on Renate's decision to elope with Anselm Wanderer. Süssenguth, a self-declared 'Retter der Frauen und Mädchen' (*RF*, p. 17), is an acute observer of the troubled situations many women experience. His status as a distanced observer standing outside society is highlighted by the fact that he lives 'im letzten Haus der Stadt, mitten in der Wiesen-Einsamkeit' (*RF*, p. 24). Even though he is far below her social status Renate feels irresistibly drawn towards this man, who eventually talks her out of a marriage that is based solely on

63 Marta Caminero-Santangelo, *The Madwoman can't speak, or, Why Insanity is not subversive* (Ithaca & London: Cornell University Press, 1998), p. 3.

64 Mayer, *Außenseiter*, p. 318; and Ritchie Robertson, 'Historicizing Weininger: The Nineteenth-Century German Image of the feminized Jew', in *Modernity, Culture, and 'the Jew'*, ed. by Bryan Cheyette and Laura Marcus (Cambridge: Polity Press, 1998), pp. 23–39 (pp. 28–29).

65 Herbert Tiefenbacher, *Textstrukturen des Entwicklungs - und Bildungsromans* (Königstein: Forum Academicum, 1982), p. 105.

rational, material interests and that would leave her emotionally isolated: 'Jedes wird seiner Vereinsamung müde werden, frieren, innerlich absterben, elend und verlassen sein' (*RF*, p. 33). Similarly to Jeanette, Renate would thus simply be married off. Moreover, Süssenguth opens her eyes to the existing discrepancy in sexual experience between men and woman when they enter a marriage: 'Er [Süssenguth] meint, daß alle die körperlichen Tugenden, die die Männer von uns verlangen, nichts als Lug und Trug sind. Er meint, daher kommt es, daß so viele, viele Frauen zu Grunde gehen' (*RF*, p. 18). Renate's life-changing decision to break off her engagement, to look for happiness and to explore the lives of the 'Frauen unten' (*RF*, p. 71), is thus based at least partly on her contact with the other outsider.

For a brief period after her escape, Renate finds the 'beglückende Lebensfülle' that she had been seeking. Renate and Wanderer live as an unmarried couple, with Renate frequently rejecting Wanderer's attempts to marry her or, as he puts it: 'ihren Bund gesellschaftlich zu sanktionieren' (*RF*, p. 117). The price for this lifestyle is high since her father disowns her and she is forced to live in complete social isolation in a house close to the woods. At the same time Wanderer is still able to enjoy, at least to a certain extent, a social life outside their relationship. Once Wanderer has lost his entire fortune and their relationship falls apart, it soon becomes clear that Renate's previous life and education have left her too inexperienced to support herself:

> Aber was hatte sie gelernt? Ein altersgraues Vorurteil hatte sie daran gehindert, ihre Sinne zu sammeln für eine Thätigkeit, ihre Gedanken zu gewöhnen an ein übersichtlichtes Maß von Geschäften, ihre Hände zu üben in Stetigkeit und Ausdauer [...]. Mußte also ein Weib das Edelste ohne Zögern feilbieten, wenn sie sich im grauenhaften Kampf der Existenzen behaupten will? (*RF*, pp. 254–55).

As soon as other men realize that Renate has lived with a man without being married, she is considered an object of prey. As a result she finds herself almost automatically drawn towards a life of degradation. After several attempts at earning her own living – as a governess, a factory worker and as an accompanist to a female choir – she arrives at the conclusion that women's working conditions do not allow them to lead an independent existence, let alone to find true happiness. Selling her body becomes the only way to make a living outside wedlock. Tellingly, Renate is also referred to as a 'Heimatlose' (*JZ*, p. 292) by Gudstikker, a status which brings her into close proximity with many Jews who were equally denied their claim to a 'Heimat' – albeit for different reasons – by the greater part of Gentile society.

The majority of women in the novel are prevented from experiencing sexuality as a source of happiness or pleasure. Instead, it becomes a space in which they are subject to humiliation and powerlessness, since they are either, like Renate, confronted by domestic violence or stuck in a loveless marriage or relationship. These women are contrasted to a whole array of female students whom Renate meets during her time in Switzerland. The depiction of these women is predominantly negative and clichéd, as the portrayal of Gertrud Werkmeister shows: 'Ihr Gang war vernachlässigt (absichtlich watschelnd), wie alles an ihr vernachlässigt war. Eine dürftige Kleidung schlotterte an ihrem Körper, und die kurzgeschnittenen Haare gaben dem Gesicht trotz seiner Blässe etwas Pausbäckiges' (*RF*, p. 379). The common denominator to most of these almost caricatured figures is that they are 'durchaus geschlechtslos' (*RF*, p. 381). The possibility of intellectual emancipation in combination with sexual fulfilment is seemingly denied. The narrator's reaction to the intellectual woman is, therefore, surprisingly unsympathetic as they are on the whole ridiculed and denied all feminine qualities. In a similar vein, Renate is only allowed to experience a form of physical, that is, sexual, freedom while her mental faculties are shown to be limited.

This allows the novel to be placed in the context of writers such as Elsa Bernstein and Lou Andreas-Salomé, even if these do not necessarily caricature their 'new women' in the same way as Wassermann. The figure of the intelligent, yet therefore rather masculine, woman can also be found in the character of Sabine Graef in Elsa Bernstein's play *Dämmerung* (1893): the possibility of being happy as an unmarried and educated woman is seemingly denied. In fact, Sabine dreams about marrying Ritter, after which she will eventually be 'ganz glücklich dumm'.[66] Similarly, in Lou Andreas-Salomé's two short stories *Fenitschka* and *Eine Ausschweifung* (1898), the female protagonists remain strangely incapable of living up to their emancipated claims.[67] During Wassermann's time in Munich (1894–98) he and Andreas-Salomé frequently spent time together, a fact which allows us to suspect that he was familiar with her work.[68] Wassermann is, therefore, no exception when he eventually denies his protagonist an emancipated lifestyle.[69] It makes it, however, doubtful whether the novel, despite its awareness of the complicated situation of women, actually supports their liberation and independence.

In its latter stages the novel moves from a realist presentation of women's situation to a more symbolic, even allegorical bond between two outsiders,

66 Elsa Bernstein, *Dämmerung: Schauspiel in fünf Akten*, ed. by Susanne Kord (New York: The Modern Language Association of America, 2003), p. 121.

67 Lou Andreas-Salomé, *Fenitschka. Eine Ausschweifung: Zwei Erzählungen*, ed. by Ernst Pfeiffer (Frankfurt a.M. & Berlin: Ullstein, 1983).

68 Lou Andreas-Salomé, *Lebensrückblick*, ed. by Ernst Pfeiffer (Frankfurt a. M: Insel, 1974), p. 110.

69 This view is supported by Plöger's findings. See Plöger, *Ästhet*, pp. 360–61.

namely Agathon and Renate. This union stands in strong opposition to Mayer's claim that solidarity between the outsiders cannot exist.[70] Instead, Lindemann-Luiken is right in claiming that Renate is the 'nicht-jüdische Pendant zu Agathon'.[71] The two are united and designated outsiders by another curious fact: their proximity to animals. Agathon is frequently compared to animals while Renate's companion throughout the entire novel is a dog named Angelus with whom she can communicate. The idea of linking the outsider with animals, thus underlining their Otherness, reappears and features most strongly in *Caspar Hauser* (1908). Renate realizes that the inner voice she has been following actually belongs to Agathon. In their one night of love she becomes pregnant with their son, the first member of a 'neues Geschlecht'.

The Jew and the Gentile woman thus unite in order to make the Gentile man superfluous from their point of view. It is the attempt to found a society in which they could both participate fully without being classed as inferior which clearly adds more significance to the ending than Koester allows in his interpretation, in which he refers to 'ein[en] kaum nachvollziehbare[n], unglaubwürdige[n] Ausklang'.[72] However, this union would only prove to be a noteworthy alternative if the relationship between them were based on equality and respect, meaning that women would no longer depend on men because of their weaker legal status, lack of education and confinement to the domestic world. Nevertheless, this remains one of the drawbacks to the thought-provoking solution, which simply excludes the oppressor: it signifies an escape from a world in which all Renate's attempts at emancipation have failed. Even though the idea of a union between the two outsiders remains appealing, it therefore also proves unsatisfactory in other aspects: is a life removed from society the only way in which a woman can experience freedom? Where does the union of the two outsiders leave the Jewish woman? Is madness her destiny?

As a result of Wassermann's engagement with the question of belonging or not belonging to a community, the reader is made aware of the parallel dilemmas surrounding the discrimination of women and Jews. Wassermann's conclusions are in many ways remarkable. In the course of his two novels he makes it clear that for both of them the 'Gleichheit der Ausgangschance'[73] – for Mayer one of the key prerequisites for the outsider's integration – is still out of reach and both outsiders are denied their 'Heimat'. In the case of the Jew, Wassermann demonstrates that, concerning people's daily lives in particular,

70 Mayer, *Außenseiter*, p. 464.
71 Lindemann-Luiken, *Auswirkungen*, p. 201.
72 Koester, *Wassermann*, p. 24.
73 Mayer, *Außenseiter*, p. 387.

there is no longer a difference between non-Jews and Jews which could in any way make discrimination against the latter seem justifiable. His awareness of the plight of women is, with the exception of his depiction of the intellectual woman, highly sympathetic. Moreover, even though the end of *Renate Fuchs* might appear conservative and antiquated to a modern eye, it remains altogether unusual for a novel written at that time to allow a woman to combine the otherwise contrasting types of 'whore' and 'mother'. Moreover, it is important to acknowledge that the parallels drawn between the woman and the Jew are not negative in themselves, meaning that the Jew is not depicted as effeminate as, for instance, Otto Weininger was to do only a few years later.[74] In terms of the overall picture of society here, the insight into the general lack of pleasure offers a simple, yet telling, understanding of how Wassermann perceived the world around him at the turn of the century.

74 Otto Weininger, *Geschlecht und Charakter: Eine prinzipielle Untersuchung* (Berlin: Kiepenheuer, 1932), pp. 39–441; and Robertson, 'Historicizing Weininger'.

CHAPTER 2

Talk to Me – on the Life of the Child in *Caspar Hauser* (1906)

'Die Zeit wird kommen, in der das Kind als heilig angesehen werden wird.'[1]

Introduction

The novel *Caspar Hauser oder Die Trägheit des Herzens* (1908) is one of Wassermann's best known works to this day and has received a fair amount of critical attention. It was one of Kafka's favourite books[2] whilst Erich Kästner still felt the need to mock the 'Trägheit des Herzens' in his novel *Fabian* in 1931.[3] Thomas Mann considered it to be Wassermann's 'erstes Meisterwerk'.[4] *Caspar* tells the story of the historical figure of Kaspar Hauser from his sudden appearance in Nuremberg in May 1828 to his death in Ansbach in December 1833. With the story of the mysterious foundling, Wassermann chose a subject that not only inspired subsequent artists[5] but also remains a hotly debated topic to this day, with books still being written on the subject. Wassermann thus uses the material of a widely familiar story as the basis for his novel – with the exception of *Alexander in Babylon* (1905) and *Donna Johanna von Castilien* (1906),[6] this is a unique instance in his oeuvre.[7] Yet while Joana of Castile and Alexander the Great are figures from different and more distant historical

1 Ellen Key, *Das Jahrhundert des Kindes*, trans. by Francis Maro (Weinheim & Basel: Beltz, 1992), p. 36.

2 Max Brod, *Über Franz Kafka* (Frankfurt a.M.: Fischer, 1974), p. 276.

3 Erich Kästner, *Fabian: Die Geschichte eines Moralisten* (Munich: DTV, 2011), pp. 10, 35, 40.

4 First printed in Karlweis, *Wassermann*, p. 334. See also Thomas Mann, *Große kommentierte Frankfurter Ausgabe*, xv: *Essays II (1914–1926)*, ed. by Hermann Kurzke and others (Frankfurt a.M.: Fischer, 2002), pp. 354–55.

5 For the most famous examples, see Georg Trakl, *Kaspar Hauser Lied* (1913); Klaus Mann, 'Kaspar-Hauser-Legenden', in *Vor dem Leben* (1925); Peter Handke, *Kaspar* (1967); and Werner Herzog's movie *Jeder für sich und Gott gegen alle* (1974). See also Kálmán Kovács, *Kaspar-Hauser-Geschichten: Stationen der Rezeption* (Frankfurt a. M.: Peter Lang, 2000).

6 Jakob Wassermann, 'Donna Johanna von Castilien', in *Die Schwestern* (Berlin: Fischer, 1906), pp. 9–69.

7 Tellingly, Wassermann considered *Die Schwestern* practice for his *Caspar Hauser.*

periods, the figure of Kaspar Hauser is closer in time to Wassermann's own life, thus serving an altogether different purpose. 'Das Kind von Europa', as Kaspar was frequently called, became Wassermann's chance to present the outsider par excellence, namely the child. In Wassermann's view children are generally misunderstood, forced to live by the rules of the adult world yet unable to have their say in it. He is particularly intrigued by the language barrier that separates adults and children and makes it difficult for the latter to articulate their needs and wishes, leaving them excluded from the world of their parents. Critics have shown how the figure of Caspar in the novel can be understood as a Jewish or a homosexual figure,[8] yet while the figure certainly lends itself to these interpretations, it is even more intriguing to complete this notion of Caspar as the ultimate outsider by showing how he is ostracized as a child without a childhood and no chance of ever growing up. Wassermann's general concern with the figure of the child here reaches an early climax as he dedicates an entire novel to the mechanisms of exclusion that do not allow children to participate fully in a society of adults. The creation of his Caspar therefore becomes Wassermann's discovery of childhood as a space of oppression and exclusion.

Wassermann's use of the original sources of the historical Kaspar Hauser case will be analysed in the first part of this chapter. Given the author's growing interest in the question of character, it is most important to see how he uses or changes the historical material in order to create his characters while sticking to the original cast. Analysis will show how this confined creative space nevertheless allowed Wassermann to come up with his own version of character and to offer not only a critique of Biedermeier society but also of the Wilhelmine Germany with which he was confronted. The history of the novel's genesis will reveal how it has to be understood as the fusion of contemporary and historical material in the sense that it was initially intended to have a modern setting. The final result is a work of cultural criticism in thin historical disguise.

When looking at Caspar as a child, it will be necessary to take into account the fact that during the process of writing Wassermann was inspired by his first son, Albert, then a toddler, whose linguistic development in particular is reflected in the figure of the foundling. Tellingly, Caspar's literal and symbolical inability to communicate stands at the centre of his exclusion from the adult world as he seems to be forever misunderstood. Moreover, those who do

8 Stimilli, 'Findlinge', 478–500; and Roman Graf, '"Alles ist Verdächtig": Zum Thema der "Homosexualität" in den Bearbeitungen der Kaspar-Hauser-Legende von Jakob Wassermann, Klaus Mann und Werner Herzog', in *Der Imaginierte Findling*, ed. by Ulrich Struve (Heidelberg: Winter, 1995), pp. 103–23.

understand him are also branded outsiders, namely the homosexual character Lord Stanhope and the intellectual woman Klara von Kannawurf. As in his early novels, Wassermann highlights a network of loyalties between those who cannot find access to a society dominated by the ideals of the heterosexual Gentile man.

Fact or Fiction?

The question of fact or fiction in this context is not aimed at establishing the level of Wassermann's historical accuracy. Such a purpose would already be defeated by the opaqueness of the subject matter as well as Wassermann's own rejection of the question's relevance: 'Bei der Konzeption des Romans und der Vision der Caspar-Hauser-Gestalt mußte mir die historische Grundlage schließlich ebenso gleichgültig werden, wie die kriminalistischen und genealogischen Forschungsergebnisse'.[9] Wassermann's spelling of his protagonist's first name with a 'C' instead of the 'K' can therefore be read as a constant reminder of the author's fictional intentions. After all, his novel was not to be understood as another contribution to the ongoing debate about Kaspar Hauser's origins. Similarly, even though convinced of Hauser's princely identity, Wassermann refrains in the novel from using the full name of his alleged mother – Stéphanie de Beauharnais, Grand Duchess of Baden. Given this strong emphasis on the novel's fictional nature, it will be even more revealing to look at the ways in which Wassermann made use of the original sources.

To begin with, however, it is necessary to take the novel's genesis into consideration in order to understand its underlying structure. The intention to write a novel about the foundling dates back to the seventeenth year of Wassermann's life.[10] Similarly to *Zirndorf*, this novel is another expression of the author's concern with the 'Heimat' of his childhood and youth, yet in the case of *Caspar* Wassermann was for a long time unsure about the time-frame in which to set his novel. On 30 March 1904 Wassermann notes in his diary that he has started to occupy himself with a fictional account of the life of Kaspar Hauser yet he soon lost interest in the material.[11] Instead, he focused on a novel set in contemporary Ansbach which was going to be entitled *Die Trägheit des Herzens*. In this version the figure of the foundling was to be

9 Jakob Wassermann, 'Meine persönlichen Erfahrungen mit dem Caspar-Hauser-Roman', in *Lebensdienst*, pp. 123– 49 (p. 143).

10 Wassermann, 'Meine persönlichen Erfahrungen', p. 129.

11 Wassermann kept a diary between 6 March 1903 and 16 July 1904 for his eldest son Albert. So far it has only been reprinted in Karlweis, *Wassermann*, pp. 115–63 (p. 155).

reduced to a symbolic figure with a clear focus on contemporary events. It was not until 3 December 1905 that he wrote in his diary: 'Die ganze Tragödie stand gewaltig da und der Titel war mit leuchtenden Lettern an die Wand gemalt: Caspar Hauser oder die Trägheit des Herzens'.[12] Apart from revealing Wassermann's vanity in comparing himself to the biblical character of Daniel,[13] this means that the final product is a fusion of two rather different projects: one novel dealing with the historical figure of Kaspar Hauser and another concerned with life in the Ansbach of the early 1900s. The final novel is set exclusively in the cities of Nuremberg and Ansbach between 1828 and 1833 ,and yet analysis will show that it can be related to Wassermann's own time, to which he later referred as an 'Epoche der Auflösung'.[14]

This description of the early twentieth century is significant because it points us to another reason for Wassermann's choosing the Biedermeier period as his main focus. We have the impression that he was simply overwhelmed by the task of describing his contemporary world and therefore chose to change the period as a means of facilitating the writing process. Evidence for this can be found in his diary: 'Das Resultat ist bei einem unleugbar großen Talent wie dem meinen [...], daß es seiner großen, vielfältig bewegten Zeit, einer ungeheuren Epoche, nahezu ohnmächtig gegenüber steht'.[15] By taking a step backwards in time, Wassermann makes use of the Biedermeier setting in order to create, as Schmitz-Emans puts it, a 'panoramatisches Bild der zeitgenössischen Gesellschaft',[16] thus formulating a cultural critique of his own time.

In order to see whether and how Wassermann has or has not modified the historical characters it is necessary to look at some of the original sources. In a letter to the writer and publisher Alfred Walter von Heymel, Wassermann mentions the sources on which he mostly relied for his novel: 'Meine Quellen sind hauptsächliche die Daumerschen und Feuerbachschen Bücher und das schauderhafte Aktensammelsurium des Julius Meyer gewesen'.[17] This means that Wassermann used Georg Friedrich Daumer's three sympathetic publications on Hauser: *Mitteilungen über Kaspar Hauser* (1832), *Enthüllungen über Kaspar Hauser* (1859) and *Kaspar Hauser: Sein Wesen, seine Unschuld*

12 Karlweis, *Wassermann*, p. 188.

13 In the *Book of Daniel*, Daniel is famed for his great wisdom and is the only one who can interpret the writing on the wall at Belshazzar's feast.

14 Wassermann, *Hofmannsthal der Freund* (Berlin: Fischer, 1930), p. 61.

15 Karlweis, *Wassermann*, p. 201.

16 Monika Schmitz-Emans, *Fragen nach Kaspar Hauser: Entwürfe des Menschen, der Sprache und der Darstellung* (Würzburg: Königshausen & Neumann, 2007), p. 82.

17 Jakob Wassermann in a letter to Alfred Walter von Heymel, 23 May 1908 (DLA, call number: 62.1894)

(1873). Moreover, he is referring to Anselm von Feuerbach's *Kaspar Hauser, Beispiel eines Verbrechens am Seelenleben des Menschen* (1832) and Julius Meyer's damning *Authentische Mittheilungen über Kaspar Hauser* (1872). Since the story of Kaspar Hauser is very complex, Wassermann had to simplify it by leaving out certain characters and events in the life of the foundling. Similarly, this analysis will only be concerned with some of the novel's main characters, namely Daumer, Quandt, Hickel, Lord Stanhope and Feuerbach.

Daumer – the Failure of the Intellectual

The figure of Daumer serves as one of Wassermann's first examples of the failure of the intellectual in the face of the modernity crisis. Georg Friedrich Daumer (1800–75), Hauser's first foster father, was a poet and a philosopher of religion whose publications frequently caused controversy. Combined with his poor health, these controversies led to him resigning from his post as a teacher at the Egidiengymnasium in Nuremberg. The real Daumer was, therefore, a disputatious character, who dared to speak his own mind and occupied a prominent place in the dispute that broke out just after the foundling's death. Throughout his life Daumer strongly contested the idea that Hauser had been a mere impostor. His book *Kaspar Hauser: Sein Wesen, seine Unschuld* (1873) has been called the 'bedeutendste [Schrift] über Kaspar Hauser im 19. Jahrhundert'.[18] For Daumer, Hauser was the proof 'daß der Mensch edel geschaffen ist und daß die Bestialität nicht die Grundlage seiner Natur bildet'.[19] To him Hauser was a miracle that ought not to be meticulously questioned but accepted with simple belief, albeit not in a religious sense but with reference to the 'Anerkennung des Außerordentlichen, auch wenn es der allgemeinen Begriffswelt widerspricht'.[20] His view of the foundling was, therefore, diametrically opposed to the materialistic approach of his opponents in whose understanding there was no such thing as a soul, let alone a miracle.

The view of Daumer as a romantic dreamer and a dubious scientist was further encouraged by the numerous experiments he carried out with Hauser in connection with mesmerism, spiritualism and homeopathy.[21] Despite the great caution Daumer claims to have exercised, these experiments had alarming physical consequences as he reports that Hauser 'am ganzen Leib

18 Peter Tradowsky, 'Einleitung', in Georg Friedrich Daumer, *Kaspar Hauser: Sein Wesen, seine Unschuld*, ed. by Peter Tradowsky (Dornach: Gerring, 1984), pp. 3–11 (p. 5).

19 Daumer, *Wesen*, p. 28.

20 Daumer, *Wesen*, p. 35.

21 On the topic of mesmerism, see also Jürgen Barkhoff, *Magnetische Fiktionen: Literarisierung des Mesmerismus in der Romantik* (Stuttgart: Metzler, 1995).

gelb wurde [...], die Augen tränten [...], Nasenbluten, Erbrechen, schnelle Abmagerung'.[22] Wassermann, who otherwise entertained a favourable view of him, is rather critical of Daumer in this regard: 'Er [Daumer] sah nicht den Menschen, er sah nur seine Idee vom Menschen'.[23] This critique of Daumer as lost in the world of the mind becomes even more apparent in Wassermann's rendering of the fictional Daumer.

Nonetheless, even though Hauser soon lost his extraordinary skills (he was, for instance, able to read in the dark or to detect metals without seeing them) as well as his absolute love for truth through the corruption of a 'täuschungsvolle Welt',[24] Daumer never ceased to think highly of him. Even more importantly, he always remained in contact with Hauser, who visited him in Nuremberg in the autumn of 1833 just a few months before his death. The real Daumer gave up fostering Hauser because of his poor health and, following the first attack on the foundling, the lack of security that his house offered. Despite his view that Hauser was a miracle, he was also able to see that Hauser would inevitably become a more ordinary person one day and therefore deliberately helped the latter to free himself from some of his special skills which had become a burden to Hauser. These details are important when it comes to distinguishing the real from the fictional Daumer in order to understand how Wassermann modified his sources to come up with the figure of the discerning yet impractical intellectual.

In Wassermann's version, Daumer is equally drawn to Caspar because of the latter's romantic nature as well as his special gifts. Daumer despises most people for being rational 'Philister' and is accordingly convinced that his experiments with Caspar will provide 'gültige Beweise [...] für die Existenz der Seele, die von allen Götzendienern der Zeit mit elender Leidenschaft geleugnet wird'.[25] Caspar thus becomes his weapon in his struggle against the rationalistic mindset of his time. Daumer's great sense of compassion for Caspar is thus inextricably linked with his own scientific as well as philosophical purposes. 'Er muss mir leben' (*CH*, p. 43) are the words that Daumer utters just after Caspar has fallen seriously ill for the first time. Although Daumer is genuinely worried about Caspar, the 'mir' nevertheless denotes his egoistic pursuit. The experiments that Daumer carries out in the novel are exactly the same as those

22 Georg Friedrich Daumer, *Mitteilungen über Kaspar Hauser*, ed. by Peter Tradowsky (Dornach: Geering, 1983), p. 18.

23 Wassermann, 'Erfahrungen', p. 138.

24 Daumer, *Wesen*, p. 165.

25 Jakob Wassermann, *Caspar Hauser oder Die Trägheit des Herzens* (Munich: DTV, 1983), p. 21. This edition does not differ from the first edition. For the original edition see Jakob Wassermann, *Caspar Hauser oder Die Trägheit des Herzens* (Stuttgart & Leipzig: Deutsche Verlags-Anstalt, 1908).

described by the real Daumer. However, in the novel these experiments come across as far worse because they have been turned into a performance that people enjoy as an entertainment, with Caspar as a 'dressiertes Äffchen' (*CH*, p. 54) and Daumer delighted with all the attention. Meanwhile nobody notices that Caspar is 'blaß und mit kühlem Schweiß bedeckt' (*CH*, p. 53), with his state of mind being equally ignored. The narrator therefore describes the theories that Daumer follows so passionately as 'Theorien, die mit der Seele des Menschen hantieren wie ein Alchimist mit dem Inhalt einer Retorte' (*CH*, p. 53).

Apart from treating Caspar like an object when it comes to his experiments, the fictional Daumer is also guilty of abandoning Caspar once he has turned into a mere ordinary person. Daumer thus lets his personal disappointment with the foundling prevent him from helping Caspar, even though he knows the latter will suffer at the hands of other people:

> Aber ist dies etwa ein Grund, den Geschehnissen wie einem Feind, der das Schwert erhoben hat, in die Arme zu fallen und den Schlag abzuwenden? Nein, es ist kein Grund. [...] Darin haben die Idealisten und Seelenforscher nichts voraus vor Dieben und Wucherern (*CH*, p. 133).

This serves as an illustration of what Wassermann considers to be the 'Trägheit des Herzens'. It also tallies with what Eda Sagarra describes as the Germans' reputation for 'impractical idealism', especially before 1848. This passive character prompted the writer Ludwig Börne to refer to the Germans as 'a nation of flunkeys'.[26]

Wassermann understood the story of Hauser to be not just the case of a pitiable individual but also a political issue with a far wider significance. In his version a whole section of society is suppressed alongside the foundling. Wassermann does not allow his Daumer to be as eccentric and outspoken as the historical character; instead, he shows him to be hemmed in and oppressed by the provincial society around him. He is unable to give public voice to the critique of society that Caspar inspires in him. As a result of his lack of personal freedom in the face of authorities, who dismiss the concept of 'Freigeisterei', Daumer has developed what could be called 'Untertanengeist', a mindset also described by Heinrich Mann in his novel *Der Untertan* (1918). Although Daumer often feels offended and humiliated by Feuerbach's harsh behaviour or Frau Behold's possessive attitude towards Caspar, he is meek and obedient in their presence. Daumer is only able to voice his complaints in the safety of his own home.

Wassermann despised this submissiveness towards the authorities yet considered that it was still present at the beginning of the twentieth

26 Eda Sagarra, *Tradition and Revolution: German Literature and Society 1830–1890* (London: Weidenfeld and Nicolson, 1971), p. 64.

century. He refers to it as the 'dem Deutschen anerzogenen Glauben an die Unantastbarkeit gekrönter Häupter. [...] man konnte im Notfall darüber tuscheln [...]; in der Öffentlichkeit hieß es kuschen und schweigen. Das war bis zum Jahr 1918 nicht anders'.[27] In this context Caspar's tragic end can be understood as an illustration of the acute danger lying beneath this mindset, for it makes people susceptible towards manipulation as well as cold towards vulnerable outsiders such as Caspar. Jutta Schlich therefore rightly concludes that it is Wassermann's way of showing his 'Publikum [...] wohin Nichtstun führt – ein indirekter [...] nachhaltig wirkender Appell an dessen tatkräftige Entschlossenheit im Vorfeld des ersten Weltkrieges'.[28] Wassermann has thus modified the figure of the historical Daumer in order to show how the figure of the Romantic intellectual was unable successfully to overcome the strict social hierarchy of his time or to oppose the strict Biedermeier mindset, even more so as he is himself affected by it. The failure of Daumer's Romanticism as well as his other theories is an early example of Wassermann's overall dismissal of ideologies or any other theoretical approach as a means to overcome the general malaise which in his view affected society.

Quandt – the Revolt Underneath the Surface

Quandt is the only character whose fictional name differs from that of the historical model and yet this character has been changed the least. He is based on the figure of the teacher Johann Georg Meyer, who became Hauser's foster father when the latter moved to Ansbach in December 1831. Hauser lived with the Meyer family until his death in 1833. This was followed by the publication of Meyer's *Notizen über Kaspar Hauser*, in which the foundling is described as an impostor who accidentally killed himself. Meyer, therefore, never considered Hauser a miracle nor did he ever believe that he was dealing with a prince. Nonetheless, despite this great congruence the figure of Quandt is interesting because of the ways in which his character has been created as well as his double-identity: he is the combination of a doctor character from Wassermann's modern Ansbach story and the one based on the historical teacher Meyer: '[U]rplötzlich war mein Arzt und Ehemann zum Lehrer Quandt geworden'.[29] Moreover, just as the character is based on two rather

27 Wassermann, 'Erfahrungen', p. 136.

28 Susanne Havekost and Axinja Heß, 'Caspar Hauser oder Die Trägheit des Herzens', in "*Warum fliegen da so schwarze Würmer herum?*": *Das Kaspar-Hauser-Syndrom in Literatur und Film, Forschung und Lehre*, ed. by Jutta Schlich (Würzburg: Königshausen and Neumann, 1999), pp 49–70 (p. 57).

29 Wassermann, 'Erfahrungen', p. 131.

different sources, the figure in the novel is equally split into two, meaning that this character embodies the past as well as the potential future.

In the novel, Quandt is on the outside the archetypal representative of a German citizen during the Biedermeier period. He repudiates the idea of social and political change, proves himself to be a loyal subject accepting of the strict social hierarchy and is also the proud patriarch of an orderly and conventional household. Quandt is frequently described as wearing a nightcap, slippers and a 'Schlafrock' (*CH*, p. 313, p. 456). In the nineteenth century the latter was a symbol for the conservative preference for a peaceful domesticity. People who wore a 'Schlafrock' at home in order to spare their clothes were equally considered to be sleepy in a political sense since they were sparing themselves instead of making personal sacrifices to bring about change. A well-known example of this 'Schlafrock' symbol is Heinrich Heine's poem number LVIII from *Die Heimkehr*:

> Zu fragmentarisch ist Welt und Leben!
> Ich will mich zum deutschen Professor begeben.
> Der weiß das Leben zusammen zu setzen,
> Und er macht ein verständlich System daraus;
> Mit seinen Nachtmützen und Schlafrockfetzen
> Stopft er die Lücken des Weltenbaus.[30]

As a 'provinzlicher Schultyrann'[31] the teacher Quandt is also a main source for the propagation of those strict and pious principles governing Biedermeier life. In his obsession with uncreative book learning and his unfeeling treatment of Caspar, Quandt becomes a relevant figure for the critique of the educational system at the beginning of the twentieth century. Quandt serves as a perfect illustration of Ellen Key's critique of the pedagogical system as formulated in *Das Jahrhundert des Kindes.* Wassermann met Key during a stay in Rome[32] and was familiar with some of her work.[33] Quandt not only believes in the benefits of caning his pupils, and even threatens to beat Caspar at one point, but he is also the archetypal pedagogue who acts according to doctrine and is always suspicious of the child:

> Man lehrt die neue Seele, nicht zu stehlen, nicht zu lügen, auf ihre Kleider aufzupassen, ihre Lektionen zu lernen, mit ihren Groschen hauszuhalten, Befehlen zu gehorchen, älteren Personen nicht zu widersprechen, Gebete zu sagen und sich hie und da zu balgen, um tüchtig zu werden.[34]

30 Heinrich Heine, 'Die Heimkehr', in *Buch der Lieder*, ed. by Pierre Grappin (Hamburg: Hoffmann & Campe,1975), pp. 204–334 (p. 270).
31 Wassermann, 'Erfahrungen', p. 133.
32 Müller-Kampel, *Collage*, p. 51.
33 Plöger, *Ästhet*, p. 140.
34 Key, *Jahrhundert*, pp. 81–82.

In this interpretation the child is an object that requires shaping according to very strict rules and ideas, something which Key considered detrimental to the child's development. Rudolf Koester observes how Wassermann himself would have been subject to this kind of education, thus adding to the notion that it has indeed undergone very little change between Hauser's time and Wassermann's.[35]

The following passage from Hermann Hesse's novel *Unterm Rad* (1906) can serve as one example for Wassermann's simultaneous engagement with with a popular literary topos:

> Seine [the teacher's] Pflicht und sein ihm vom Staat überantworteter Beruf ist es, in dem jungen Knaben die rohen Kräfte und Begierden der Natur zu bändigen und auszurotten und an ihre Stelle stille, mäßige und staatlich anerkannte Ideale zu pflanzen. [...] Der Mensch, wie ihn die Natur erschafft, ist etwas [...] Gefährliches.[36]

This is a direct continuation of Wassermann's critique of the educational system in his earlier novels and confirms Theisz's view that *Caspar* is 'eine Kritik der Erziehung der Zeit'.[37] Moreover, as Schmitz-Emans points out, stories revolving around the relationship between teachers and students were a popular means at the time for the 'literarische Auseinandersetzung mit Machtstrukturen und gesellschaftlichen Ordnungen'.[38] At the same time this teacher-pupil dynamic, which stretches into all areas of Caspar's private life, helps to confine him permanently to the space of childhood. In his review, Stefan Zweig therefore refers to the novel as a 'pädagogisches Gleichnis'.[39]

However, there is still that other side of Quandt. As the public person ‚Quandt is a citizen, taxpayer and patriot, in other words a 'Heros der Tugend' (*CH*, p. 280) who prides himself on never having told a lie. Then there is the 'Quandt an sich' who rejoices every time a misfortune occurs: 'Der Quandt an sich hatte etwas von einem Revolutionär und war immer auf dem Posten, um der Weltregierung auf die Finger zu schauen' and 'er belauerte die liebe Gotteswelt' (*CH*, p. 281). This 'heimlich aufrührerische[r] Quandt' is full of envy, highly critical of the authorities and frustrated with his situation as an underpaid teacher. This contrast often makes Quandt an exceptionally

35 Koester, *Wassermann*, p. 7.

36 Hermann Hesse, *Unterm Rad*, in *Sämtliche Werke* (Frankfurt a.M.: Suhrkamp, 2001), II, ed. by Volker Michels, pp. 137–280 (pp. 172–73).

37 R. D. Theisz, 'Kaspar Hauser im zwanzigsten Jahrhundert: Der Außenseiter und die Gesellschaft', *German Quarterly*, 49 (1976), 168– 80 (p. 171).

38 Schmitz-Emans, *Fragen*, p. 82.

39 Stefan Zweig, 'Jakob Wassermann', *Die Neue Rundschau*, 23 (August 2012), 1131–40 (pp. 1141–42). Quoted in Neubauer, *Wassermann*, p. 40.

funny character as he is, according to Thomas Mann, 'mit einer so klug-ergötzlichen Heiterkeit behandelt'.[40] As Quandt is the only character of whom the narrator gives such an explicit account, we may assume that he is supposed to represent a type, namely the narrow-minded bourgeois. By turning Quandt into a type, Wassermann is able to show that an authoritarian regime, whether during the Biedermeier or the Wilhelmine era, produces obedient yet frustrated subjects. Moreover, as can be seen with Quandt, these subjects were even likely to develop an initially unconscious sense of revolt, despite a strong sense of loyalty.

Quandt therefore also functions as a symbol of change. Schmitz-Emans has rightly pointed out that the novel 'eine Zeit im Umbruch, des Wertewandels und Werteverfalls [spiegelt]'.[41] The inevitability of change is not only mirrored in Quandt's other personality but also in his encounter with Ludwig Feuerbach at the end of the novel. During their conversation Quandt is highly critical of the first railway, which is about to start operating between Nuremberg and Fürth in 1835 (*CH*, p. 449), yet the reader finds himself in a position of superior knowledge, sure that Quandt's scepticism will be of no use. By mentioning this encounter with Feuerbach, Wassermann reminds the reader that the intellectual forces opposing the Biedermeier mindset were already at work. Feuerbach was one of the intellectual leaders of the *Vormärz* movement which led to the revolutions of 1848/49.[42] However, Feuerbach was also important for the later Materialist philosophy of which the novel is highly critical. The reference to Feuerbach therefore seems to suggest that the changes were inevitable, yet not necessarily positive in the long run. Given Wassermann's aversion towards the idea of an actual revolution, he was faced with a similar dilemma at the beginning of the twentieth century.

Hickel – Dreams of Power

The even darker aspects of life in Biedermeier Germany are represented by the figure of Polizeileutnant Hickel. The biographical situation of this figure is

40 Thomas Mann, 'Jakob Wassermanns "Caspar Hauser oder Die Trägheit des Herzens"', in *Gesammelte Werke* (Frankfurt a.M.: Fischer, 1960), ed. by Peter de Mendelssohn, II, pp. 553–55 (p. 554).

41 Schmitz-Emans, *Fragen*, p. 83.

42 *Vormärz* refers to a period of German history that preceded the revolution in March 1848. Also known as the Age of Metternich or the Biedermeier age, this period is characterized by police states in Austria and Prussia which led to revolutionary uprisings and calls for liberalism. *Vormärz* combines oppositional and revolutionary works by writers such as Karl Gutzkow, Heinrich Laube, Theodor Mundt and Georg Büchner.

rather complex. The historical Hickel was never hostile towards Hauser and the foundling seems to have been close to him and his wife, yet after Hickel's death Dr Julius Meyer, son of the teacher Meyer, published a collection of Hickel's letters according to which Hickel considered Hauser to be an impostor. In 1956 Hermann Pies proved that the so-called 'Hickelschen Briefe' were forgeries.[43] Even though Daumer had already hinted at the possibility of the letters being a fraud, it cannot be established whether or not Wassermann was aware of it. In any case, the letters clearly served him as an inspiration for 'his' Hickel.

In Wassermann's version Hickel becomes the representative of a nineteenth-century police state which closely monitors and oppresses its subjects, above all through intimidation and rigid censorship. By refraining from actually depicting the rulers of a country, governed in unfathomable ways with dark intrigues as part of the system, Wassermann emphasizes the powerlessness and insecurity of its subjects. Hickel is a violent character who throughout the novel is associated with the night, which he uses to spy on other people. He is fuelled by disgust and indifference for the people around him: 'Mochten sie einander die Köpfe abhacken, [...] mochten sie morden, stehlen, einbrechen, schänden und betrügen [...], ihm war schließlich alles Schwindel' (*CH*, p. 318). At the same time Wassermann does not fail to reveal Hickel as a banal figure who is emotionally inept and tries in vain to overcome his lower-class background by exercising power over people of a higher class. The figure of Hickel can thus be understood as a hint that Wassermann perceived his own time as repressive and illiberal.

Stanhope – the Stranger Makes an Appearance

The depiction of Philip Henry Stanhope (1781–1855), the Fourth Earl of Stanhope, led to a controversy in the course of which Wassermann was forced by the Lord's family to sign a document stating that 'der Stanhope des Buches und der Stanhope der Wirklichkeit nichts mit einander zu tun hätten'.[44] Stanhope was an intellectual and politician who studied in Germany, travelled extensively in Europe and was known to be eccentric and estranged from his wife and his two children. He was an enthusiastic admirer of Hauser, whom he met for the first time in May 1831, when Stanhope came specially to visit him in Ansbach. He spoilt Hauser with luxurious presents and in December 1831 officially became his foster father. However, some sources suggest that the love he bore for Hauser was not that of a father but of a lover. Daumer quotes an

43 Hermann Pies, *Die Wahrheit über Kaspar Hausers Auftauchen und erste Nürnberger Zeit* (Saarbrücken: Minerva, 1956), p. 313.

44 Wassermann, 'Erfahrungen', p. 146.

eye-witness reporting 'wie sich der Graf von H. küssen und streicheln ließ'.[45] Even though there are no more definitive historical proofs for Stanhope's homosexual inclinations, this would tally well with Stanhope's behaviour after Hauser's death. In 1835 he published a collection of letters under the title *Materialien zur Geschichte Kaspar Hausers* in which he portrays Hauser as an impostor who eventually killed himself. Stanhope bribed and re-interviewed former witnesses and thus came up with a new version of Hauser's story in which he considered himself betrayed by the foundling. This could indeed be the behaviour of a disappointed lover, now ashamed of his former affections, though other people saw the behaviour of a spy working for Hauser's murderers in this extreme change of attitude.

The novel picks up the ambiguity surrounding the character of Stanhope, making him one of its most intriguing figures, not only because of his apparent homosexuality (which will be discussed in the second part of this chapter) but also because Stanhope becomes Wassermann's first likeable villain. This is a figure that will return most prominently in the character of Warschauer-Waremme in *Der Fall Maurizius* (1928), with whom Stanhope also shares the tendency towards homosexuality as well as the need to act as part of their everyday lives. In the novel Stanhope is gradually revealed as a diabolic figure who is being paid to kill Caspar. At the same time, the reader is also offered an insight into this character, whose life as an impoverished noble forces him to play a role with which he can no longer identify. He finds himself haunted by the person he used to be: '[D]er Doppelgänger stand an seiner Seite, dieser Schattenleib des Gelebten, Begangenen, Versäumten' (*CH*, p. 227). Nevertheless, even though he is a 'Meister in der Kunst, seine wahren Absichten zu verschleiern' (*CH*, p. 170), Stanhope gradually loses control over his character as he can no longer distinguish between his performances and his genuine feelings. This becomes most apparent when he shares his employers' secrets with Caspar and Feuerbach and actually considers escaping with the foundling. Towards the end of his life the extreme discrepancy between the private and the public Stanhope can be considered the first signs of madness in an actor who is not allowed to give up his role. Even though the narrator leaves us in the dark as to the motives of Stanhope's eventual suicide, it can be seen as partly motivated by his growing mental instability.

This suicide is a considerable deviation from reality (the real Stanhope died naturally in England in 1855) and caused the above-mentioned controversy. At the same time it helps to turn this complex outsider figure into a tragic and more humane character. Otto Hartwich's description of Stanhope thus appears adequate: '[Stanhope] ist ein Lucifer, eine moralisch gesunkene, göttliche

45 Daumer, *Wesen*, p. 288.

Größe, die bei aller Gemeinheit ihren heiligen Ursprung nie ganz vergessen kann'.[46] The complex structure of Stanhope's personality and the depiction of his character testify to Wassermann's growing interest in the question of character and his incipient doubts as to whether such a thing actually exists. Stanhope therefore has to be acknowledged as in many ways his most modern character before the publication of *Christian Wahnschaffe* (1919).

Feuerbach – the Revolution from Within

Wassermann's Feuerbach is based on Paul Johann Anselm von Feuerbach (1775–1833), one of the greatest German legal scholars of his time, who became famous for his reform of the Bavarian penal code, which included the abolition of torture. His son Ludwig, in his preface to *Paul Johann Anselm Ritter von Feuerbachs Leben und Wirken* (1852), describes him as 'eine durchaus dramatische Persönlichkeit, mit allen Tugenden, aber auch Fehlern einer solchen behaftet'.[47] This description helps to shape the image of a man who officially lived with his mistress and liked to sign his letters 'Vesuvius', a rather appropriate self-description. In a letter to Kriminaldirektor Hitzig, Feuerbach remarks: 'Seit Jahren ist er [Hauser] der erste und wichtigste Gegenstand meines Beobachtens, Forschens und Sorgens, meiner höchsten Teilnahme als Mensch, Gelehrter und Staatsbeamter'.[48] The great interest he took in the foundling was largely motivated by his firm belief that the latter was a prince; however, Feuerbach's untimely death from a stroke prevented him from continuing his struggle for Hauser's rights.

Feuerbach's *Beispiel eines Verbrechens am Seelenleben eines Menschen* is a very affectionate and lenient depiction of the foundling as the victim of a 'partiellen Seelenmordes'.[49] As a result of Feuerbach's own psychological studies, this work gives vital insights into Hauser's psyche. While Feuerbach's opponents dismissed it as mere fiction, Wassermann makes extensive use of it for his depiction of Caspar. Wassermann greatly admired Feuerbach and referred to him as a 'Reformator aus Leidenschaft und Menschenliebe'.[50] In the

46 Otto Hartwich, 'Feinde der Natürlichkeit. Wassermann: *Caspar Hauser oder Die Trägheit des Herzens*', in *Kulturwerte aus der modernen Literatur* (Bremen: Leuwer, 1911), pp. 247–73 (pp. 263–64), as quoted in Neubauer, *Wassermann*, p. 43.

47 Ludwig Feuerbach, 'Vorwort', in *Paul Johann Anselm Ritter von Feuerbachs Leben und Wirken*, ed. by Ludwig Feuerbach (Berlin: Akademie-Verlag, 1976), pp. 1–19 (p. 10).

48 Quoted in Johann Friedrich Karl Merker, *Kaspar Hauser: Nicht unwahrscheinlich ein Betrüger* (Berlin: August Rücker, 1830), p. 13. The date of the letter is 15 May 1830.

49 Anselm von Feuerbach, *Kaspar Hauser oder Beispiel eines Verbrechens am Seelenleben eines Menschen* (Stuttgart: Klett, 1984), p. 32.

50 Wassermann, 'Der Kriminalist Feuerbach', in *Lebensdienst*, pp. 30–37 (p. 31).

novel Wassermann also provides the reader with a summary of Feuerbach's other work on Hauser, the *Memoire* (*CH*, pp. 123–26), only published in 1853, which stays true to Feuerbach's language but without revealing the actual names of the people involved. In that way Wassermann avoids direct borrowings from Feuerbach's text.

In the novel Wassermann portrays Feuerbach as a tragic figure of resistance who struggles to remain a loyal subject in the face of a corrupt and inefficient legal and court system that is indifferent towards human rights and suffering. It is, therefore, not a demagogue or a young revolutionary who rebels but a *Staatsrat* who is part of the ruling class, thus operating from within the system. Even more than Quandt, Feuerbach symbolizes the angry passions beneath the surface that first led to smaller revolutions which caused the accession to the French throne of Louis Philippe in 1830 and eventually the revolutions of 1848. Feuerbach is the most political figure in the novel as he also seems to embody the debate over Hauser's origins that soon turned into a political issue, with nationalist forces seeking to destroy the myth of his princely descent. Feuerbach's strong will to see crimes punished even if they are 'mit einem Purpurmantel bedeckt' (*CH*, p. 219) ends in failure, which in the novel is emphasized further by the inescapable hints that Feuerbach has been poisoned. Murdered for political reasons, he becomes an even more heroic figure while the true, brutal nature of the regime is fully exposed. In the world that Wassermann depicts here, justice is simply unavailable.

At the same time Wassermann is keen to show how the frustration with this system has even corrupted a figure like Feuerbach. Abused by his rulers for many years, Feuerbach's strong will to seek justice for Caspar carries connotations of revenge and a desire for self-vindication. He openly admits that the achievement of his aims would be worth Caspar's death. For the fictional Feuerbach the case is, therefore, not so much about Caspar as a person than ultimately about the question as to whether his lifelong struggles have been a futile pursuit: '[O]b denn alles Geopferte und Gewirkte umsonst gewesen [...]; ich muß wissen, ob ich in Wind geredet und auf Sand geschrieben habe' (*CH*, pp. 225–26). To him Caspar becomes living proof, a weapon that is supposed to help him in his struggle to make the crown a symbol of humanity. Feuerbach is driven by 'die bis zur Selbstverleugnung getriebene Erfüllung der Idee' (*CH*, p. 348), which makes him exploit Caspar for an egoistic goal. With Feuerbach, Wassermann makes the figure of the politically motivated fighter an altogether questionable one.

Wassermann thus modifies his sources in order to carve out the picture of a society affected by an oppressive regime which in the course of history might have changed its name – from Biedermeier to Wilhelmine – but not its nature. In his version all areas of people's lives are shaped by a lack of personal freedom that corrupts even the best of intentions. At the same time he seems confident that this state of oppression cannot last, yet he is apprehensive of the future. Throughout the novel Caspar functions as the focalizer in order to highlight how people's hearts and minds have been corrupted. For the rest of the chapter the role of Caspar as a child as well as his relationships with the other two outsiders, Stanhope and Klara von Kannawurf, will stand at the centre of the analysis.

Caspar – the Child Does Not Speak

Caspar's status as an eternal child is confirmed throughout the novel by his childlike appearance, yet most of all by his inability to communicate with the people around him. Jan Cölln has rightly concluded that Wassermann was deeply concerned with the question of why communication fails.[51] Caspar's story is that of exclusion through language for even after he has learnt to use it he is still not able to communicate with others. He is prevented from integrating fully because he is forever at a loss to understand the actions and emotions of the people in charge of him, a failure which in turn leads to their rejection of this most innocent figure. Tellingly, Caspar's strong attachment to the other outsiders in the novel, namely Stanhope and Klara, can be seen as the result of their ability to understand him due to their similar status in society. This time, therefore, Wassermann portrays the homosexual, the child and the intellectual woman as outsiders, with none of them surviving to the end of the novel.

As we can learn from Wassermann's diary, he has integrated into the novel the process of language learning that he witnessed with his first son Albert. Some of the things uttered by Caspar at the beginning of his familiarization with the German language are, therefore, direct quotations from an infant trying to grapple with verbal techniques. One example is Caspar's way of conveying that he is afraid of the dark: 'In der Nacht sitzt das Finstere auf der Lampe und brüllt' (*CH*, p. 63).[52] Wassermann has, therefore, literally allowed the language of the child into his novel and, in an intriguing experiment, confronts it with the language of the adult. As this entails a childlike perception of things it often results in endearing as well as amusing scenes: for instance, when Caspar thinks that an apple rolling along the pavement must be exhausted; or when he is unable to understand why Stanhope kneels

51 Jan Cölln, 'Von der Gewalt und Ohnmacht der Worte: Eine literarische Psychologie gestörter Kommunikation im Werk Jakob Wassermanns', in *Deutscher – Jude – Literat*, pp. 29–45 (p. 29).

52 Karlweis, *Wassermann*, p. 179.

down to pray: 'Caspar, peinlich berührt, schaute sich unwillkürlich um, ob niemand Zeuge dieser demütigen Handlung sei. [...] Warum krüppelt er sich so zusammen, dachte er verstimmt, Gott kann doch nicht im Boden drinnen sein' (*CH*, p. 278). However, this other way of looking at the world soon becomes a problem as it turns Caspar into a figure of initially unconscious resistance.

Once Caspar has overcome the obvious lack of vocabulary with which he started, the people around him immediately expect him to be able to speak their language. This not only includes the verbal skills to allow him to communicate, but refers just as much to social conventions. Throughout the novel Caspar fails to comply with the rules of politeness and when confronted with the news of the suicide of his former foster mother, Frau Behold, he has nothing nice to say about her: 'Sie war ein schlechtes Weib, Herr Lehrer' (*CH*, p. 326). As a consequence, much of the language by which he is surrounded in the adult world is simply meaningless to him. On the occasion of one of the numerous parties he is being forced to attend his feelings towards that language are described:

> [E]s schien ihm gefährlich zu sprechen, es war, als ob alle Worte zwiefach vorhanden wären, einmal offenbar, das andre Mal verhüllt, und so wie die Worte, hatten auch die Menschen etwas Zwiefaches, und unwillkürlich suchten seine Blicke in ein und derselben Person die zweite, die lauernd hinterherging und verführerisch mit den Fingern winkte. Es war ihm unverständlich, was sie von ihm wollten, ihre Kleidung, ihre Gebärden, ihr Nicken, ihr Lächeln, ihr Beisammensein, alles war ihm unverständlich, und auch er selbst, er selbst fing an, sich unverständlich zu werden (*CH*, p. 102).

As a child, Caspar is unable to participate in the language games and conventions of the adult world. Caspar is, therefore, excluded from society not just because he is, as Graf argues, a 'feminisierter Mann' lacking the power of the phallus,[53] but because he is unable to become an adult. This, however, does not provoke a reaction of compassion in people but instead makes them suspicious of the foundling.

The above-mentioned negative reaction is epitomized in the figure of Quandt, who is determined to discover Caspar's 'secret', meaning that he wants to prove that the story of the foundling's incarceration is simply a lie. Moreover, Quandt is keen to prove that Caspar is generally a dishonest person, while many of these so-called untruths are based on the latter's inability to understand his foster father (for example, *CH*, p. 425). The more lenient view of these so-called lies, proposed by the priest Fuhrmann, is confirmed by Key's view, according to which children are often unaware of their lies and not driven by evil intentions.[54]

53 Graf, 'Verdächtig', p. 106.
54 Key, *Jahrhundert*, p. 102.

Quandt, however, does not refrain from accusing Caspar of being a liar even after he has been fatally wounded, an act which reveals the outright brutality of the teacher's views. The lie therefore becomes a symbol of the educator's cold-hearted refusal to engage with the child on a level that does the latter justice.

Even though Caspar fails to communicate with most of the adult world – significantly he acts a silent part in a play performed at Frau von Imhoff's – there are nevertheless moments in which he acts as a figure of resistance. This resistance finds its strongest expression in the diary that Caspar successfully hides from Quandt and subsequently destroys before anyone can read it. When once again pressed by Hickel and Quandt to produce the diary, Caspar cries out: 'Ja, bin ich denn ein Eigentum von einem andern? Bin ich denn wie ein Tier?' (*CH*, p. 344). These two questions confirm the proximity of Caspar's status to that of animals, creatures which in this society are eaten, kept as pets or even violently mistreated, as shown in the scene of the carter and the horse or the blackbird killed by Frau Behold. Moreover, Kálmán Kovács draws an interesting parallel: 'Caspars Gemeinsamkeit mit den Tieren [zeugt] von dem Urstandscharakter der Existenz des Protagonisten.'[55] At the same time, however, Caspar's utterance denotes not only an awareness of his problematic status but also a growing will to show resistance to a humiliating form of control and mistrust. When Caspar grabs his diary from Hickel's hands the latter feels 'als werde er zermalmt oder zertreten' (*CH*, p. 345) and cannot prevent the foundling from incinerating it. Caspar consideres the diary (and thus his own text documenting his progress) to be his only true possession, which makes it a powerful reminder of text as a space of privacy, personal development and eventually resistance.

Despite outward signs of puberty, Caspar never leaves the realm of childhood behind. This is confirmed when, just before his death, Caspar still talks to the wooden horse, his companion during his weeks in the prison tower in Nuremberg. Moreover, his notion of what it actually means to be a prince is childlike and far removed from the realities of ruling a country. Tellingly, throughout the novel Caspar is not interested in the various theories about his origins – he is described as 'unneugierig' about them (*CH*, p. 361): all he cares about is his mother. Caspar frequently expresses a longing to meet his parents and in particular his mother. He shows himself to be highly conscious of lacking a place in life because he does not have a family.

If we briefly return to Ellen Key, who places an equal significance on the role a mother plays in the life of a child, a new understanding of Caspar's being a prince becomes available. Key writes:

55 Kálmán Kovács, 'Ein Fall für zwei: Anthropologische Konzepte in Wassermanns *Caspar Hauser oder Die Trägheit des Herzens* und in Peter Handkes *Kaspar*', in *Die Zeit und die Schrift*, ed. by K. F. Auckenthaler (Szeged: JATE, 1993), pp. 261–77 (p. 263).

> Bevor nicht Vater und Mutter ihre Stirne vor der Hoheit des Kindes in den Staub beugen; bevor sie nicht einsehen, daß das Wort Kind nur ein anderer Ausdruck für den Begriff Majestät ist [...] – werden sie auch nicht begreifen, daß sie ebensowenig die Macht oder das Recht haben, diesem neuen Wesen Gesetze vorzuschreiben [...]; wenn der Vater in seinem Kinde den Königssohn sieht, dem er in Demut mit seinen eigenen besten Kräften dienen soll – dann kommt das Kind zu seinem Rechte![56]

The novel's insistence on the special role Caspar ought to occupy in society could therefore also be understood as a plea to improve the situation of the child in general. The rights of which he has been deprived would therefore be not his claim to an actual throne but rather his claim to be treated with dignity and respect. The outrage expressed in the face of Caspar's constant mistreatment at the hands of adults can therefore be read as an indictment of the treatment children receive in this society. Goldmann is, therefore, right to refer to the novel as depicting the 'ewige Tragödie menschlicher Kindheit'.[57] This view finds support in the depiction of Frau Behold's daughter, who is obviously neglected by her parents and can therefore be seen as another victim of the adult world. Moreover, Key considers the situation of the child to be increasingly defined by 'Heimatlosigkeit', a notion that, as we have seen in the previous chapter, is essential to Wassermann's understanding of the outsider.[58] If the child were indeed treated with reverence, the face of society would be altered in a way Wassermann seemingly approved of. Given Wassermann's overall concern with the figure of the child, beginning with the early novella *Hier ruht das kleine Öchslein* (1896) or Agathon's return to the world of the child at the end of *Zirndorf*, it seems plausible that he would have considered them to be kings and queens in their own right.[59]

Caspar and Klara

Klara von Kannawurf is able to develop an important relationship with Caspar because despite being an adult she has retained many childlike qualities and, like the foundling, is an orphan. She is not only described as having a 'kindliche Gestalt' (*CH*, p. 377), 'große Kinderaugen' (*CH*, p. 389) and the facial expression of an 'aufmerksamen Kindes' (*CH*, p. 379) but is also the only character in the novel who is willing to accept Caspar as a child.

56 Key, *Jahrhundert*, p. 120.

57 Goldmann, *Wassermann*, 88.

58 Key, *Jahrhundert*, pp. 137–44.

59 Koester also observes this continous interest in the 'Kinderseele'. See Koester, *Wassermann*, p. 14.

Moreover, during her stay in Ansbach she is frequently seen walking the streets surrounded by a 'lärmenden Schwarm von Knaben und Mädchen' (*CH*, p. 401). Her willingness to allow Caspar his status as a child finds its strongest expression in their communication. They see each other every day or write letters and yet their conversations never touch on anything that is remotely profound. The content of their letters is 'unverfänglich' and the same applies to their conversations if they talk at all, for they often spend hours without saying a word (*CH*, p. 387). In his relationship with Klara, Caspar is therefore not expected to comply with the rules and conventions of the adult world. Moreover, when Caspar hears about Klara's life story and the death of her brother, he is for the first time able to feel the pain of another human being: '[W]ie durch den Wink eines unsichtbaren Geistes öffnete sich zum erstenmal sein Herz den Leiden eines andern Ichs, einer fremden Existenz' (*CH*, p. 298). Throughout the novel Klara remains the only character whose words and actions are always understandable to him.

Klara's understanding of Caspar's situation even reaches far enough for her to understand that he will never be mature enough to have a sexual relationship with her. As Klara finds herself falling in love with Caspar she decides to leave: 'Ihn anzutasten! Seinen Schlummer stören! O verbrecherische Lippen, denen ein Kuß nichts bedeutet! Hätt' ich's getan, ich müßte seine Mörderin heißen, was kann ich Besseres tun als fliehen?' (*CH*, pp. 412–13). Even though Caspar occasionally seems to reciprocate Klara's sexual feelings, she is right in assuming he would be at a loss to actually understand them. This view is confirmed when, in their only moment of intimacy after having performed together in the play, Caspar tries to touch her yet calls her 'Schwester' (*CH*, p. 410), thus revealing his state of emotional confusion.

Without parents, Klara is also without a place in life and can therefore be seen as a parallel outsider figure to Caspar. Moreover, her strong attachment to him makes her suspicious in the eyes of the world: 'Wahrscheinlich ist sie eine Demagogin, hieß es' (*CH*, p. 401). This watchword of the Biedermeier period clearly denotes Klara as standing on the margins of society. In this context a demagogue would be a young, hot-headed person who believed in the ideals of the French Revolution and would later support the ascension of Louis Philippe to the French throne. Moreover, in the context of the novel, the supporters of the prince-theory are equated with demagogues, something which foreshadows the historical dispute that broke out soon after Hauser's death. Klara is indeed depicted as a political activist who has dedicated her life to improving the situation of the poor. She has studied politics, law and national economy in a small, unspecified university town, spends most of her time travelling on her own, is childless and lives apart from her husband. She therefore forms a strong contrast to the Biedermeier ideal of womanliness, which was, according to Sagarra, 'a motherly figure yet full of girlish innocence'.[60]

Klara's level of education, her independent character and her depiction as a potential lover rather than a wife make her resemble prominent figures such as Rahel Varnhagen, Bettina von Arnim and Charlotte Stieglitz. Bettina von Arnim was well educated and a writer who actively tried to help the poor and underprivileged members of society. Charlotte Stieglitz was also a writer; and Rahel Varnhagen was famous for her salon in Berlin, which was frequented by such people as Alexander and Wilhelm von Humboldt and Heinrich Heine. Rahel Varnhagen is of particular importance in this context, not only because she knew Hauser's alleged mother Stéphanie de Beauharnais, whom she described in a letter as a 'metaphysische[n] Kopf',[61] but also because Daumer compared Rahel Varnhagen to Hauser, as they were both disadvantaged yet gifted with extraordinary talents: 'Sie war eine Art von Kaspar Hauser'.[62] Rahel Varnhagen was weak in the sense that as a Jew and a woman she struggled with social boundaries and exclusion; these are comparable to Caspar's situation yet in the novel have also been transferred to Klara.

The notion of Klara as a successful fighter for human rights is gradually deconstructed throughout the novel as she fails to save Caspar. Her failure, it seems, is based on the romantic and childlike nature of her ideals as well as on the fact that as a woman she will never be taken seriously enough to oppose successfully the regime represented by Hickel. The only plan to save Caspar that Klara ever devises is for the two of them to run away together, which sounds more like the adventure of two children than a feasible option in face of the severity of Caspar's situation. Caspar consequently refuses the idea of the two of them escaping to her house in the Swiss mountains, symbols of a liberty that can never be achieved. Moreover, his life there would simply be another form of social isolation, something which Klara fails to see when trying to convince Caspar: 'Das Haus liegt vollständig einsam zwischen hohen Bergen im Tal und an einem See' (*CH*, p. 379). This plan of running away to Switzerland because it is the country especially associated with popular democracy, is therefore dismissed as too abstract to solve Caspar's situation. As with Daumer, Klara's romanticism is of no use when it comes to fighting an authoritarian regime.

Moreover, Klara's situation is complicated further by the fact that she is a woman. This problematic situation is depicted in her relationship with Hickel.

60 Sagarra, *Tradition*, p. 19.

61 Rahel Varnhagen von Ense, *Ein Buch des Andenkens für ihre Freunde* (Berlin: Dunker und Humblot, 1834), III p. 329. Quoted in Daumer, *Wesen*, p. 458. The letter is dated 18 March 1828.

62 Daumer, *Wesen*, p. 458.

Instead of suspecting Klara because of her political activities and her close relationship to Caspar, Hickel merely finds her attractive, so much so that he spends time underneath her window at night. To Klara's great disappointment, the sexual attraction Hickel feels towards her becomes her only chance to save Caspar. In a rather chilling scene, Hickel asks her to give in to his sexual desire and offers a favour in return: 'Madame, von Ihrem Mund hängt zur Stunde manches ab [...]. Hier steh' ich und bettle. Verleugnen Sie nicht ihr Gesicht, das einen Engel glauben läßt!' (*CH*, pp. 413–14). Klara simply storms past Hickel and leaves Ansbach the next morning as this scene clearly confirms her defeat as a political activist and a woman. This can be understood as a continuation of Wassermann's portrayal of the situation of women at the turn of the century in *Renate Fuchs*. The intellectual woman now receives a more favourable depiction but still fails, while at the same time being reduced to her sexual functions. As with Stanhope, Klara is not to survive the end of the novel. Even though she is physically alive, we are told that: 'Sie war wahnsinnig geworden. Noch am selben Tag wurde sie in eine Anstalt gebracht. Mit der Zeit verging die Raserei, aber ihr Geist blieb umnachtet' (*CH*, p. 458). Klara is therefore to be seen as standing in one line with Caspar and Stanhope, while at the same time she is another woman whose weakness finds a strong expression in her insanity.

Caspar and Stanhope

Stanhope is a character of great interest because he must be seen as the first in a number of outcasts with a clear homosexual tendency who make an appearance in Wassermann's works. Graf has shown how Stanhope can be understood as a homosexual character, yet goes too far in assuming that Stanhope's and Caspar's deaths are solely based on their being rejected as homosexuals.[63] It is more rewarding to see the link between those two characters not in a potentially homosexual relationship but in their status as outsiders. Similarly, when looking at Stanhope it is more intriguing to look at the ways in which his homosexuality affects his status in society instead of searching for hints of an actual relationship with Caspar.

From the beginning Stanhope is clearly constructed as an exotic figure and can be seen as a version of the eccentric English lord that was popular in nineteenth-century German literature: for example, in Goethe's *Die Wahlverwandtschaften* (1809) and Nestroy's *Die beiden Nachtwandler* (1836). In this function he allows a different and more sophisticated perspective on life in Germany around 1830. Stanhope's observations strongly resemble those

63 Graf, 'Verdächtig', p. 110.

of foreign visitors to Germany during the Biedermeier period as described by Sagarra: 'The consensus of opinion among foreign visitors was that the Germans were pedantically self-sufficient, contented and well-mannered'.[64] By also turning him into a sexual outsider, Wassermann arrives at an even more damning picture of a society that is forever suspicious of the Other. Moreover, in the portrayal of Stanhope, Wassermann makes it clear that parallels between the figure of the Jew and the homosexual as outsiders do exist. Stanhope compares himself to Ahasver and seemingly shares the pain of this 'auf immer Verstoßenen'. The narrator describes him thus: 'Vater und Mutter tot, ehemalige Freunde gegen den edlen Sproß des Hauses verschworen, und er, ein Mann von fünfzig Jahren, ohne Heim und Weib und Kind, Ahasver!' (*CH*, p. 180). The character of Stanhope can therefore be understood as a continuation of Wassermann's concern with society's outsiders as well as a broadening of this theme since he now fully adds the homosexual to that group.

Nevertheless, the relationship between Caspar and Stanhope cannot be considered mutually homosexual. The most remarkable thing about Stanhope is that he not only calls Caspar 'Liebling' and caresses him but is happy to do so in public: '[E]r gebärdete sich wie ein Verliebter, der seine Empfindungen ohne Scheu preisgibt' (*CH*, p. 175). When Caspar and Stanhope walk around arm in arm, 'achteten sie der Blicke nicht, die sie verfolgten' (*CH*, p. 177). However, rumours begin to spread, with people asking for Caspar's protection again the 'Machenschaften des englischen Grafen' (*CH*, p. 181). Caspar, however, is far from suspecting the lord's true intentions and is happy about the latter's attentions. Caspar soon grows attached to his new protector and to a certain extent adopts his lifestyle, making him a similarly suspicious figure in the eyes of the world.

As with Stanhope, who offends the bourgeois citizens with his decadence, Caspar is criticized for his vanity. Frau Quandt complains: 'Immer müsse er herausgeputzt sein wie eine Docke, und schon in aller Herrgottsfrüh fange er an, seine Kleider zu bürsten' (*CH*, p. 317). Caspar is, therefore, emulating the behaviour of a man who rejects the idea of becoming a Catholic monk because having to grow a beard would be too disgusting for him. Caspar also begins to dream of travelling to Italy, yet his ideas about it are those of a child, while Stanhope might well have Italy in mind as the country that, as James W. Jones tells us, was considered a place of homosexual freedom.[65] Caspar's strong attachment to Stanhope can, therefore, partly be explained because

64 Sagarra, *Tradition*, p. 5.

65 James W. Jones, *"We of the Third Sex": Literary Representations of Homosexuality in Wilhelmine Germany*, German Life and Civilization, 7 (New York etc.: Peter Lang, 1990), p. 282.

the latter satisfies many of the foundling's childlike desires since he showers him with presents and tells him exciting stories about foreign lands. Their relationship is comparable to that between Waremme-Warschauer and Etzel Andergast in *Maurizius* in that there the homosexual attraction is also one-sided and undermines conventional power relations. In both cases it is the love for a young man that not only makes the 'evil' character confess but also paralyzes their bad intentions.

Moreover, as another outsider, Stanhope is full of understanding for Caspar's refusal to comply with many of society's rules and regulations. Even though Stanhope immediately becomes the talk of the town in Ansbach, with people being all too keen to invite him to their parties, his private views about them could not be more damning. In a letter to his employer, Stanhope writes: 'Das [...] Volk ist kaum der Rede wert. Die guten Deutschen sind servil bis zum Erbrechen. [...] Nichts hindert mich, hier eine Art Caligula zu spielen' (*CH*, pp. 261–62). Albeit for different reasons, Stanhope is also bored as well as disgusted by a society in which he, too, is forced to play his role. It is, therefore, largely due to Stanhope's influence that Caspar is 'dem Kreis friedlicher Bürgerlichkeit entwachsen' (*CH*, p. 242).

The other aspect of Caspar's life from which Stanhope is happy to free him is the regular schedule that has been imposed on the foundling. Since he is staying with von Tucher as well as with Quandt, Caspar's life is subject to the strictest schedule that leaves nothing to chance. Stanhope regularly estranges Caspar from this routine and could not care less when listening to Quandt's complaints about Caspar's scholarly shortcomings, 'wobei die Langeweile seine Nasenflügel auseinander dehnte' (*CH*, p. 287). Finally, when Stanhope and Caspar fall out over the diary which the latter refuses to share with the lord, his motives for wanting to see it could not be more different from those of Hickel and Quandt:

> Er hatte gehofft, aus den Aufzeichnungen des Jünglings manches über sich selbst zu hören. Dies lockte. Er wußte, daß er dort auf einem hohen Postament stand und daß er vergöttert worden war [...]. Dies lockte. An das Verräterisches des Büchleins dachte er nicht (*CH*, p. 291).

Nonetheless, even after their relationship has cooled down considerably, Caspar and Stanhope still spend time together regularly because for both of them this relationship has become a mutual space of freedom. Stanhope also feels liberated in Caspar's presence: 'Der Lord fand sich durch diese Form eines Verkehrs lebhaft angezogen, ja, im wahrsten Sinn ergriffen. Durfte er sich doch einmal wieder unbefangen fühlen' (*CH*, p. 284). The love between the two outsiders that Wassermann depicts here is, therefore, an expression of their longing for a space where they can enjoy freedom away from society's rules and regulations.

With the figure of Caspar, Wassermann's concern with the outsider as a faultless character who mirrors society's failings comes to an end. In his subsequent works his understanding of this figure becomes increasingly complex, alongside his more critical way of looking at the possibilities of human character. In that sense *Caspar* has to be seen as a prime example of the kind of work which Wassermann produced before World War I and which became impossible after four years of hitherto-unknown human suffering. As will become apparent in the next chapters, the works that Wassermann produced during the Weimar Republic differ greatly from his previous ones as they become more and more pessimistic, dark and at times even opaque. In *Christian Wahnschaffe*, the subject of the next chapter, the link between Wassermann's depiction of character and of society will come under close scrutiny. It will become clear that the state of innocence embodied in the figure of Caspar is now forever out of reach as the Great War proves to be the most significant caesura in Wassermann's life as a writer.

CHAPTER 3

If You Could See Me – A Modern Version of Sainthood in *Christian Wahnschaffe* (1919)

Introduction

In pre-war Germany, a decadent young man leaves his family, his wealth and eventually his name behind in order to become a modern saint. This is, in a nutshell, a summary of Wassermann's 1919 novel *Christian Wahnschaffe*. Although it was an immediate commercial success, the novel has to this day attracted surprisingly little critical attention. *Wahnschaffe* signifies in many ways a turning point in Wassermann's writing as he, for the first time, explores new ways of handling issues of style, characterization and form. The novel marks the beginning of Wassermann's career as a writer in the newly-founded Weimar Republic as it proves to be a radical departure from his previous works. It is an ambitious project that attempts to offer a panorama not only of pre-war Germany but also of Europe, and thus deals with a world that had ceased to exist by 1918. However, unlike his previous works such as *Zirndorf* and *Caspar*, Wassermann has now left behind the small world of provincial Germany, the petty bourgeoisie and the question of 'Heimat'. With it he puts aside the aim of creating psychologically rounded characters or naturalistically 'real' people in favour of a more radical and therefore modern approach to the question of character. Indeed, the novel could be referred to as Wassermann's truly modern work: it is a conscious reflection of a 'modern condition' and thus of the fact that the world around him is no longer the same. In it we see Wassermann take in his altered surroundings and apply his findings to his narrative technique, with the result that he partly abandons more traditional forms of narration. Changing modes of perception and life in the Berlin metropolis stand at the centre of a journey undertaken by the eponymous protagonist which will lead to the end of the self. This makes him stand out amongst Wassermann's characters, for Christian Wahnschaffe is the only one of them literally to overcome his self instead of just taking on a new identity. Inspired by the story of St Francis of Assisi,[1] this subject enables Wassermann to combine his by now intensified concern with the question of character with the subject of perception in the modern world. Moreover, this new take on an old saint allows Wassermann to be placed in the context of various movements that, following the 'Entkirchlichung' at the end of the nineteenth century, were looking for meaning by aesthetic, social and artistic means.[2] Wassermann's new narrative technique results in the disappearance or dissolving of character (Christian gradually vanishes throughout the novel) and at the same time defines an altered perception as a form of modern sainthood. Written between 1915 and 1918 and thus under the influence of the Great War, Wassermann's novel tells a striking tale of overcoming one's self as the only way to remain human in a modern world.

In order to make the concept of sainthood as perception understandable and to link it to Wassermann's new narrative techniques, our analysis requires three steps. The novel's form will be the focus of the first section. After showing how it can be related to the newly emerging cinema, the novel's form will be analysed further in the context of accounts of modern life by three major thinkers of the early twentieth century: Georg Simmel, Sigmund Freud and Walter Benjamin. Through the linking of some of their thoughts about modern life with each other as well as the novel, the latter's form will become understandable as a direct response to the ways in which modern life has altered our perception, that is, how we see and process the world around us. This will also serve as the foundation for an understanding of how Wassermann's concept of sainthood has its roots in a concern with the question of human perception. Another technique used in the novel to highlight the importance of an altered perception will be discussed in the second section, namely the appearance of three allegorical figures representing, respectively, art, religion and political ideology. By experimenting with these allegorical figures, Wassermann finds a new way of revealing ostensible forms of sainthood to be unhelpful in the face of modern life. Neither art, religion nor political ideology is of much help when it comes to improving people's daily lives since not one of them allows the human being in crisis to be seen. Moreover, this use of allegorical figures instead of 'realistic' characters becomes another way for

1 St Francis of Assisi (1181/1182 – 3 October 1226) was an Italian Catholic friar and preacher who became one of the most important religious figures in the history of the Catholic church. He is the patron saint of Italy as well as of animals and nature. The son of a wealthy silk merchant, St Francis left all his riches behind and lived according to humble precepts. The order he founded had a large following during his lifetime and still exists.

2 Jütten, *Diskurse*, p. 84. Jütten also points out the following:'Die verschiedenen kulturellen, religiösen, okulten und lebensreformerischen Sinnstiftungsangebote sind der Versuch, eine angemessene Haltung zur Moderne zu finden' (*Diskurse*, p. 87).

Wassermann to reflect on the ways in which people perceive each other in a world in which the individual has become invisible. The third section will analyse how these 'false' saints are contrasted to Christian's development, one which eventually leads to the end of his self. Given the overall structure of the novel, it is most appropriate to trace this evolution via the protagonist's encounters and relationships with other characters. In this way his gradual development, namely the disappearance in stages of aspects of his character, will become visible. At the same time it will also become clear that in Wassermann's version sainthood is part of the everyday and not something remote or abstract. Sainthood here is about the ways in which we, on a daily basis, share a world with each other.

Perception in a Modern Age

On 11 January 1919 Thomas Mann writes in his diary:

> Abends Fortsetzung des Wassermann [*Wahnschaffe*]. Kostbar. Das Kino läuft, flirrt, zeigt alles und das Erdenklichste [...]. Alles in einem geläufigen, wohlgesetzten, konservativen, mundwässerig-schwatzhaften Erzählstil, der selbst sprachliches Kino ist. Nichts kann komischer sein.[3]

A few days later Mann adds that the novel contains 'tausend flirrende Bilder'.[4] The repeated use of the word 'flirren' (to flicker) underlines its importance in this context since it immediately conveys the sense that these images change so rapidly that it is impossible to contemplate them at length or in great detail. More generally, Mann's emphasis on the cinematic nature of the novel offers a good starting point for a new understanding of it: *Wahnschaffe* can be understood as a response to the ways in which modern life has changed our perception and thus estranged us from, as Detlev Peukert puts it, 'die traditionelle Ästhetik des Sehens'.[5] Our altered surroundings have, therefore, changed not just the way we see the world, but also our aesthetic needs.

It is the form of the novel that makes the connection to the cinema comprehensible. Its chapters each consist of up to thirty short, numbered passages, which could be referred to as episodes or narrative units. At the same time Mann's use of the word 'Bilder' implies the use of images, something which highlights the episodes' scenic nature and gives them a visual quality. These

3 Thomas Mann, *Tagebücher 1918–1921*, ed. by Peter de Mendelssohn (Frankfurt a. M.: Fischer, 1979), p. 133.

4 Mann, *Tagebücher 1918–1921*, p. 142.

5 Detlev J. K. Peukert, *Die Weimarer Republik: Krisenjahre der klassischen Moderne* (Frankfurt a. M.: Suhrkamp, 1987), p. 80.

episodes, often no longer than one page, tell the stories of numerous characters in numerous places. Indeed, many of the characters travel frequently all over Europe and even to South America. They make full use of modern means of transport, something which no longer allows them to be associated with one particular place or language, as most of them are shown to be fluent in various European languages. They are restless characters, modern life not allowing them to slow down. Some of the storylines are only loosely connected and the images often change abruptly with no transition from the previous one. This abruptness itself mimes the shock effect which, as we shall soon see, has often been ascribed to modern urban life. This effect is intensified even further by the flamboyant and at times dramatic nature of these episodes: with very colourful language, characteristic of Wassermann, they tend to focus on one particular feature of a person or a place, without giving much context. The reader is therefore often left with what is best described as a 'Momentaufnahme', which means that s/he is confronted with isolated moments. Altogether this makes for the quick and thus modern pace of the novel. Critics such as Koester, who claim that Wassermann adhered to 'aus dem neunzehnten Jahrhundert überkommenen Formgesetzen epischer Komposition', will therefore be proven wrong.[6] Moreover, *Wahnschaffe* has frequently been criticized for introducing too many characters and thus creating unnecessary confusion,[7] yet, as this chapter will show, it is precisely the novel's kaleidoscopic nature which makes it so relevant in the context of modern, urban life.

That there are certain similarities between the form of a movie and that of a novel was also observed by Kurt Pinthus in his introduction to the *Kinobuch* (1913). Contrary to the drama, he argues, the novel and the film both open the doors to a realm of endless possibilities: limits of time and space no longer apply as we can follow a protagonist from one corner of the earth to another in no time. It is this new freedom of movement, as Pinthus emphasizes, that separates the novel and the movie from the drama, in which 'die Personen auf der Bühne festgehalten sind'.[8] With its quick pace the novel strongly echoes these new possibilities as we follow its characters on their endless journeys

6 Koester, *Wassermann*, p. 83.

7 Klaus Karlstetter writes: 'Dabei steht Wassermann immer in der Gefahr, die einzelnen Elemente nicht zur großen Einheit zusammenschmelzen zu können, sondern dysfunktional werden zu lassen' (Klaus Karlstetter, *Das Bild des Jugendlichen in der deutschsprachigen Erzählliteratur der Zeit zwischen dem Ersten Weltkrieg (1918) und der Diktatur (1933)* (Stockholm: Almquist & Wiksell, 1980), p. 53). Similarly, Jürgen Jacobs denies that the novel succeeds in presenting an 'überzeugendes Totalbild' (Jürgen Jacobs, *Wilhelm Meister und seine Brüder: Untersuchungen zum deutschen Bildungsroman* (Munich: Fink, 1972), p. 211).

8 Kurt Pinthus, 'Das Kinostück (1913)', in *Das Kinobuch*, ed. by Kurt Pinthus (Frankfurt a. M.: Fischer, 1983), pp. 19–29 (p. 21).

across the globe. Pinthus remained critical of the attempt to turn novels into movies, as the silent films with which he would have been familiar could function merely as the illustration of a novel. Nevertheless, his analysis of the relationship between movie and novel is vital in the context of this chapter as he arrives at the following conclusion: 'Das Kinopublikum ist im wesentlichen ein Romanlesepublikum'.[9]

The novel appealed strongly to contemporary taste, yet among the critics only Erwin Poeschel and Moritz Heimann, Wassermann's friend and editor, seem to have understood the meaning of the novel's form. Heimann writes:

> Je energischer der Roman seinem Thema zustrebt, um so breiter wird das Bett der Erzählung; und wenn wir zurückblicken, erscheint uns die frühere Sprunghaftigkeit als ein zwar noch immer bedenkliches, aber doch als ein Mittel, auch durch die äußere Form, die innere Zerrissenheit und seelische Zufälligkeit, das Unfruchtbare und Zerflatternde der Luxuswelt fühlen zu lassen. Es ist einer der schönsten Siege eines Dichters, wenn er uns zwingt, auszulegen und Sinn und Symbol dort zu entdecken, wo wir geneigt waren, Willkür oder Laune und Schwäche anzuklagen. Daß wir bei diesem Buche Wassermanns den umeinander wirbelnden hundert Figuren, den Kühnheiten, ja Dreistigkeiten der Erfindung nachträglich Bedeutung für das Ganze zuschreiben, ist ein solcher Sieg; und er ist in der Folgerichtigkeit der Entwicklung Christians, als der geistigen Einheit des Romans, begründet.[10]

Heimann thus points out the episodic character of the novel and shows how the form brings out the fragmented and arbitrary nature of the social world the work depicts. Moreover, Heimann makes it clear that this is the essential setting for Christian's spiritual development. Poeschel rightly remarks that through its form, the novel becomes 'ein vollkommener Abglanz des Lebens. Die Oberfläche bekommt etwas Flimmerndes, Bewegtes, die vorgetäuschte Wahllosigkeit des wirklichen Lebens'.[11] Even if only Heimann and Poeschel analysed the form of the novel in that way, it nevertheless struck a chord. The novel was not only popular in the German-speaking world: translated by Ludwig Lewisohn as *The World's Illusion* in 1921, it was the first of Wassermann's works to become an international success and the translation of other works followed soon after. Moreover, the novel was made into a movie by the Danish director Urban Gad in 1921.[12]

9 Pinthus, 'Das Kinostück', p. 21.

10 Moritz Heimann, 'Das jüngste Gericht im Roman', *Die Neue Rundschau*, 30 (1919), 367–73 (p. 372).

11 Poeschel, *Wassermann*, p. 99.

12 For further details regarding the novel's reception, see also Müller-Kampel, *Collage*, pp. 156–59.

Simmel and the City

In his essay 'Die Großstädte und das Geistesleben' (1903) Georg Simmel argues that what separates life in a modern city from life in a rural area is, among other things, the '*Steigerung des Nervenlebens*, die aus dem raschen und ununterbrochenen Wechsel äußerer und innerer Eindrücke hervorgeht'.[13] Life in a big city challenges our nervous system much more than in a rural area because the stimuli that a city offers are constantly changing, while those in a rural area tend to remain the same. In *Der Mann ohne Eigenschaften,* Robert Musil also comments on this phenomenon:

> Könnte man die Sprünge der Aufmerksamkeit messen, die Leistungen der Augenmuskeln, die Pendelbewegungen der Seele und all die Anstrengungen, die ein Mensch vollbringen muß, um sich im Fluß einer Straße aufrecht zu halten, es käme vermutlich – so hatte er [Ulrich] gedacht und spielend das Unmögliche zu berechnen versucht – eine Größe heraus, mit der verglichen die Kraft, die Atlas braucht, um die Welt zu stemmen, gering ist, und man könnte ermessen, welche ungeheure Leistung heute schon ein Mensch vollbringt, der gar nichts tut.[14]

The modern individual, the city-dweller, is thus confronted by a constant wave of new sensations; and the only form of protection against this sensory overload is to react to it with the intellect rather than the emotions (Simmel uses the word 'Gemüt' in this context). The city has, therefore, produced what Simmel refers to as the 'Verstandesmensch[en]'. However, these intellectual properties come at a high cost: life in the city is impersonal; inner lives are impoverished and affectionate relationships with other people are increasingly out of reach. Instead, relations in the city are instrumental and practical, with money as the only value that matters: in the city everything has its price, including human beings. Nevertheless, as Simmel argues, we can never be truly indifferent towards one another. Our human nature inevitably compels us to react somehow when confronted with another human being. However, our nervous system cannot afford to react with empathy towards every person we encounter. As a consequence, the only reaction we have left is antipathy. It is a form of protection as well as the 'elementare Sozialisierungsform' of the city.[15] In *Wahnschaffe* the minor character of Dr Voltolini seems like an illustration of Simmel's theory when he says to the protagonist:

13 Georg Simmel, 'Die Großstädte und das Geistesleben', in *Das Abenteuer und andere Essays*, ed. by Christian Schärf (Frankfurt a.M.: Fischer, 2010), pp. 9–26 (pp. 9–10).

14 Robert Musil, *Der Mann ohne Eigenschaften*, in Robert Musil, *Gesammelte Werke*, 9 vols, ed. by Adolf Frisé (Reinbek bei Hamburg: Rowohlt, 1978), I, p. 12.

15 Simmel, 'Großstädte', p. 17.

> [I]n dieser großen Stadt [Berlin] ist es möglich, sich eine Einsamkeit zu schaffen, in die kein unberufener Blick zu dringen vermag. Lange Zeit konnte ich meinen Beruf nur ausüben, wenn ich vergaß, daß es Menschen waren, mit denen ich zu tun hatte; es waren Mechanismen für mich [...]. Begreifen Sie diese Fühllosigkeit und Verachtung? (*CW*, pp. 310–11).[16]

Voltolini has thus used his intellect as a means of protection against the sensory overload of a metropolis like Berlin. Christian's approach, however, will aim for the opposite: on his way to sainthood he develops a perception that is not predominantly based on the intellect but instead on the 'Gemüt'.

At the same time, because it is so crowded, the physical proximity of life in the city offers anonymity, mental distance and therefore personal freedom. The city-dweller has successfully left behind the small social circles or groups, still to be found in rural areas, that exercise control over their members: 'Je kleiner ein solcher Kreis ist, der unser Milieu bildet, je beschränkter die grenzenlösenden Beziehungen zu anderen, desto ängstlicher wacht er über die Leistungen, die Lebensführung, die Gesinnungen des Individuums'.[17] The bigger a group is, therefore, the more personal freedom it will grant its members even though this freedom is not necessarily perceived as pleasant. After all, one can be nowhere as lonely as in the crowd in a modern city.

In fact, the crowd becomes the space for one of the key struggles of the city-dweller, namely to assert his or her individuality. Simmel here talks about the 'Widerstand des Subjekts, in einem gesellschaftlich-technischen Mechanismus nivelliert und verbraucht zu werden'.[18] Moreover, city-dwellers are not only part of the same crowd but are united further by the same aim: money. Money, however, and thus the 'Verstandesmensch' who is desperate to possess it, is indifferent towards all matters of individuality. Money reduces objects and people to their mere financial value without paying attention to any individual characteristics. Simmel therefore refers to money as the 'fürchterlichste[n] Nivellierer'.[19] Affective relationships ('Gemütsbeziehungen'), however, are based on people's individual character and personality, a link which makes us keen to preserve our individuality. This leads to the eccentric characters one is likely to encounter in a big city: '[...] deren Sinn gar nicht mehr in den Inhalten solchen Benehmens, sondern nur in seiner Form des Andersseins, des Sich-Heraushebens und dadurch Bemerklichwerdens liegt'.[20] Moreover, encounters in the city tend to be brief and rare. The individual is, therefore, forced to give

16 The edition of the novel published in 1932 is changed and abridged considerably; Jakob Wassermann, *Christian Wahnschaffe* (Berlin: Fischer, 1932).

17 Simmel, 'Großstädte', p. 18.

18 Simmel, 'Großstädte', p. 9.

19 Simmel, 'Großstädte', p. 15.

20 Simmel, 'Großstädte', p. 22.

a performance that is as memorable and characteristic as possible. At the same time, money has led to the devaluation not only of objects and other human beings, but also of ourselves. To be noticed by others is, therefore, often the last chance to save some self-esteem ('Selbstschätzung'): eccentricity is the only way we can be heard by ourselves as well as others. In his novel *Die Stadt des Hirns*, Otto Flake is also concerned with this phenomenon and diagnoses a loss of human individuality as a result. He arrives at the sobering conclusion 'daß es in Wirklichkeit überhaupt keine für sich existierenden "Individuen" gibt', for individuality is nothing but 'die arme Lüge'.[21]

The exaggerated self-representation required by modern life allows Wassermann's novel to be related to Simmel's essay even if there is no proof that he was familiar with the latter's work. In *Wahnschaffe* the reader has only brief encounters with its characters, during which they all come across as remarkable in some way. They may deliberately present themselves as such, or they may have been shaped by peculiar circumstances. As Simmel rightly remarks, modernity has led to a seeming domination of form over content: our perception is already so challenged by the exterior of people and things that it can hardly afford to pay attention to their interior. In the modern world it is therefore the exterior that matters most. The novel itself, as well as each of its episodes, can be understood as an expression of this shift in meaning.

To begin with, the opening line of each passage has the crucial function of drawing in the reader. This helps to create the impression of a particular, ephemeral moment rather than a continuing narration: 'Auf den Samtsofas des Restaurants lagen Tote und Verwundete' (*CW*, II, p. 36) is a typical example of this technique. These suspense-creating opening lines are usually followed by exuberant descriptions of characters and events which, however, give very little space to people's inner lives. Opulence and misery are presented in their most extreme forms since sharp contrasts are used to create strong images: Christian's mother wears the most expensive necklace to be found in Europe, with pearls the size of a child's fist, while the children of the imprisoned worker Kroll lie naked on the floor of an overcrowded room, their skin covered in rashes. The dancer Eva Sorel wears a shawl so expensive that the annual salary of a general in the Russian army would equal a mere fraction of its value. The unspeakable riches of the Russian as well as the German upper classes are contrasted to the endless suffering of the Russian people as well as life in the poor parts of Berlin. Wassermann seemingly perceives the world around him as torn apart by contrasts that cannot be bridged. Koester's negative criticism that the novel merely achieves a 'reißerische Wirkung' through its 'stilistische

21 Otto Flake, *Die Stadt des Hirns* (Berlin: Fischer, 1919), p. 293.

Erhöhungen' therefore misses the point.[22] In a similar vein, Blankenagel is unable to see anything but 'strained artifice' in this technique.[23]

Most of the characters stand out, whether because of their beauty or their ugliness, their wit or their evil nature, their great talents or their lifestyle: by whichever means, most of them have found a way to be remarkable. Moreover, the characters interact in conspicuous ways as the novel contains intrigues, love affairs, a mysterious diamond, fortune-telling, murder and other dramatic deaths: for instance, when the animal tamer Adda is killed by her own lions. However, as Simmel analyses it, this hunt for individuality leaves little room for genuine and meaningful relationships. People react to each other with antipathy because their nervous system can no longer afford positive emotions. Amadeus Voss therefore appositely refers in the novel to the 'einsamen Menschen mit ihren Augen ohne Gnade' (*CW*, I, p. 228).

Freud – the Shock Cannot be Remembered

Freud takes up the idea again of the need for protection against the sensory overload resulting from modern life in his essay 'Jenseits des Lustprinzips' (1921). The context of this essay is sensory overload of a more drastic kind, as it deals with the traumas suffered by shell-shocked soldiers during World War I. Freud argues: 'Die meiste Unlust, die wir verspüren, ist ja Wahrnehmungsunlust, entweder Wahrnehmung des Dränges unbefriedigter Triebe oder äußere Wahrnehmung'.[24] Simmel's city-dweller reacts to the world around him with the intellect ('Verstand'); by coming back to this theory Freud refines it and differentiates Simmel's concept of the intellect further. Freud's theory is largely based on the idea of a correlation between consciousness and memory. Instead of using Simmel's term 'Verstand', Freud arrives at a definition of human consciousness in connection with the senses as the individual's 'Reizschutz'. According to Freud, it is human consciousness that separates the inner from the outer world as well as the individual himself from the world. Stimuli ('Erregungsvorgänge') first come into contact with a person's psyche via his or her consciousness, yet unlike other systems within the human psyche, they leave no traces behind. Since consciousness remains unaltered by these stimuli, they are also unlikely to become part of a person's memory: '[Erinnerungsreste] sind oft am stärksten und haltbarsten, wenn der

22 Koester, *Wassermann*, pp. 57–58.

23 Blankenagel, *Writings*, p. 174.

24 Sigmund Freud, 'Jenseits des Lustprinzips', in Sigmund Freud, *Studienausgabe*, 11 vols, ed. by Alexander Mitscherlich and others (Frankfurt a.M.: Fischer, 1975), III, *Psychologie des Unbewußten*, pp. 215–73.

sie zurücklassende Vorgang niemals zum Bewußtsein gekommen ist. [...] *das Bewußtsein entstehe an Stelle der Erinnerungsspur*'.[25] Consciously experienced stimuli are therefore doomed to disappear soon after they have reached consciousness. This also implies that most sensations never actually reach the inner person but remain on the threshold. By using the senses as antennae, consciousness is thus enabled to function as a kind of breakwater. These antennae take samples of the outside world and pass them on to different mental systems only in a diluted form. Freud therefore considers 'Reizschutz' to be almost more important than 'Reizaufnahme', since the breakdown of this protective system would inevitably lead to trauma. In the context of *Wahnschaffe* and, in particular, the protagonist's personal development, it is also noteworthy that, according to Freud, 'Reizschutz' can only protect us from outside stimuli and is of no use when it comes to protecting the individual from his or her inner life or inner stimuli.

Benjamin – the Desire to be Shocked

Freud's concept of 'Reizschutz' and stimuli that will not be remembered reappears in Benjamin's essay 'Über einige Motive bei Baudelaire' (1939). If we take Benjamin's analysis of modern perception into consideration, it will be easier to understand Christian's gradual move towards sainthood as a move towards a new kind of perception. Benjamin starts his description of our altered perception by claiming that the conditions for the reception of poetry have worsened, a claim which seems to be confirmed in the novel when Christian is at a loss to understand why his friend Crammon reads poetry (*CW*, I, p. 27). At the heart of this altered perception stands, according to Benjamin, the constantly decreasing relevance of 'Erfahrung' and the rise of what he refers to as 'Erlebnis'. He defines 'Erfahrung' thus: 'In der Tat ist die Erfahrung eine Sache der Tradition im kollektiven wie im privaten Leben. Sie bildet sich weniger aus einzelnen in der Erinnerung streng fixierten Gegebenheiten denn aus gehäuften, oft nicht bewußten Daten, die im Gedächtnis zusammenfließen'.[26] In other words, 'Erfahrung' is a collective as well as an individual experience. It is not remembered as a particular moment in time, but rather can be understood as sediment on which our life is based. Since the modern city-dweller is, however, isolated, s/he can only have an 'Erlebnis'.

25 Freud, 'Jenseits des Lustprinzips', pp. 234–35.

26 Walter Benjamin, 'Über einige Motive bei Baudelaire', in *Illuminationen*, ed. by Siegfried Unseld (Frankfurt a. M.: Suhrkamp, 1977), pp. 185–230 (p. 186).

It is the unconsciously remembered data that are crucial in this context, for they lead Benjamin to make the distinction between the *mémoire volontaire* and the *mémoire involontaire* based on Marcel Proust's novel *A la recherche du temps perdu* (1913–27). The *mémoire volontaire* is part of our intelligence and can be used at any given moment, yet 'von ihr gilt, daß die Informationen, welche sie über das Verflossene erteilt, nichts von ihm aufbehalten'.[27] As Christian puts it in the novel: 'Ich habe kein Gedächtnis für das, was ich erlebt habe' (*CW*, II, p. 185). The more meaningful memory is thus part of the *mémoire involontaire*, which, as in the case of Proust's famous madeleine, can only be triggered by an object. In fact, it is linked to one particular object. Whether or not one will ever be able to find the relevant object in order to gain access to a particular memory, and thus to a picture of oneself, remains a matter of chance. Only things that have not been consciously 'erlebt' can therefore become part of the *mémoire involontaire.* This peculiar state of our memory is, however, not a natural one but a result of our modern way of life as the inner person has become private and isolated. One reason for this isolation is the fact that the 'äußeren Anliegen' (information, sensations) can no longer become part of a person's 'Erfahrung', but instead have turned into a mere 'Erlebnis'.

At this point, Benjamin connects his theory to Freud's previously mentioned ideas about the 'Reizschutz':

> Im Jahre 1921 erschien der Essai 'Jenseits des Lustprinzips', der eine Korrelation zwischen dem Gedächtnis (im Sinne der mémoire involontaire) und dem Bewußtsein aufstellt. [...] Die Überlegungen, die sich im folgenden an sie anschließen, werden nicht die Aufgabe haben, sie zu beweisen. Sie werden sich begnügen müssen, die Fruchtbarkeit derselben für Sachverhalte zu überprüfen, die weit von denen abliegen, die Freud bei seiner Konzeption gegenwärtig gewesen sind.[28]

Benjamin thus applies Freud's theory, based on the experience of shell-shocked soldiers, to modern life in general. Every impression delivers a slight shock to our system, therefore what Freud's soldiers went through is only an extreme version of something we experience on a daily basis. Nonetheless, our reaction to these constant shocks is of a two-sided nature. Our initial reaction is to refuse to assimilate those shocks as we want to expel them out of ourselves instead of making them part of our 'Erfahrung'. The more our consciousness has to function as a 'Reizschutz' against the shock-like ('chockförmige')[29] nature of an impression, the less likely that it will become part of our 'Erfahrung'. Benjamin

27 Benjamin, 'Motive bei Baudelaire', p. 188.

28 Benjamin, 'Motive bei Baudelaire', p. 190.

29 Benjamin, 'Motive bei Baudelaire', p. 208.

therefore describes the result of the 'Chockabwehr' as follows: 'dem Vorfall auf Kosten der Integrität seines Inhalts eine exakte Zeitstelle im Bewußtsein anzuweisen'.[30] Modern life, with its constant shocks, as can be experienced when using public transport in a big city, has therefore forced people to accept an altered perception.

However, at the same time Benjamin describes a new 'Reizbedürfnis' which can be understood as a significant by-product of this new perception. Contrary to what one might expect, namely that these shocks are merely unpleasant, the city-dweller also develops a need for such stimulation and seeks an equivalent in aesthetic experience. This new desire to be shocked is best satisfied by the movie: 'Im Film kommt die chockförmige Wahrnehmung als formales Prinzip zur Geltung'.[31] In this context, *Wahnschaffe* can therefore be thought of as an attempt to create a form of art that would correspond to its readers' 'chockförmige Wahrnehmung' of the world around them. The novel is an endeavour to satisfy the perceptual needs of a readership used to a new rhythm of life and a sensory overload. Comparable to the scenery of an urban landscape, the novel is designed to over-stimulate its reader's nervous system: rather than counterbalancing the shock modern life has caused, it reinforces it.

Apart from trying to satisfy its reader's 'Reizbedürfnis', the novel is also highly critical of the consequences of this altered, modern perception. Initially, Christian's life is shown to be made up of 'Erlebnisse' in the Benjaminian sense, as he is happy to embrace many aspects of modern life: Christian travels all over Europe, indulges in luxury, has an adventurous love life and, with no real purpose in life, constantly seeks new sources of entertainment to satisfy his ever increasing 'Reizbedürfnis'. To him the world is purchasable, ephemeral and essentially meaningless. He is unwilling, as well as unable, to engage seriously with himself or other people. His transformation from a decadent young man to a modern saint therefore begins with a change in his perception: initially, however, not of people, but of objects.

Objects are also central to Benjamin's argument, not only because of their potential to trigger our *mémoire involontaire*, but also because he attributes an aura to objects. Benjamin writes:

> Wenn man die Vorstellungen, die, in der mémoire involontaire beheimatet sind, sich um einen Gegenstand der Anschauung zu gruppieren streben, dessen Aura nennt, so entspricht die Aura am Gegenstand einer Anschauung eben der Erfahrung, die sich an einem Gegenstand des Gebrauchs als Übung absetzt.[32]

30 Benjamin, 'Motive bei Baudelaire', p. 193.
31 Benjamin, 'Motive bei Baudelaire', p. 208.
32 Benjamin, 'Motive bei Baudelaire', p. 221.

What characterizes the experience of the aura is the fact that it enables objects to return a human gaze, that is, to play a significant role in our lives and thus make a reciprocal relationship with them possible. Moreover, such an experience cannot become part of the *mémoire volontaire*. Modern life has largely led to the destruction of the aura, which means that we are no longer capable of looking at objects in this way. In other words, of observing an object steadily, for a long time and with concentration: our eyes have forgotten how to gaze. This, according to Benjamin, is the price we pay to experience the sensation of modernity: 'die Zertrümmerung der Aura im Chockerlebnis'.[33]

Christian has the first experience of what could be referred to as the aura in the squalid flat of a poor worker's wife and her five children:

> Sein Blick fiel auf einen Waschkrug mit abgebrochenem Henkel; [...] einen einzelnen Stiefel mit einer dicken Kotkruste [...]. Dann fesselte eine Strick seine Beachtung, [...] dann die kleine Petroleumlampe [...]. Nur Dinge, an denen sich sein Auge festsaugte. Aber die Dinge gingen in ihn über, und er verwandelte sich in sie. [...] Er wurde in einem Schmelzfeuer umgeformt, Gestalt wechselte mit Gestalt, [...] und obwohl er auch die Menschen [spürte], [...] war es sein innigstes Bemühen, sie noch von sich abzuhalten, eine kleine Weile noch, ehe sie mit ihrer Qual, ihrer Verzweiflung, ihrer Besessenheit, ihrer Grausamkeit über ihn stürzten: wilde Hunde über ein Stück Fleisch (*CW*, I, pp. 161–62).

The essential first step in his transformation is, therefore, a change in the way he perceives objects. Before Christian can open his eyes to the human wretchedness around him, he has first to familiarize himself with the material misery. Christian even develops a reciprocal relationship with these objects: not only does he 'turn into' them, but they also reappear, seemingly against his will, as a *mémoire involontaire*. In Wassermann's version, the object therefore becomes more than just a trigger for a particular memory but part of the memory itself. In this context, the character of Christian offers parallels to Hofmannsthal's Lord Chandos (*Ein Brief* (1902) and Rilke's Malte (*Die Aufzeichnungen des Malte Laurids Brigge* (1910)), who find significance in precisely the most commonplace objects. This fascination with the banal objects of the everyday enables us to place *Wahnschaffe* in the context of a widespread interest in perception also to be found in other fiction from the beginning of the twentieth century.[34] Another parallel could be seen in the Dada movement that began in 1916 in Zürich and also, among other things, demonstrated a considerable interest in objects of the everyday

33 Benjamin, 'Motive bei Baudelaire', p. 229.

34 See also Naomi Segal, *The Banal Object: Theme and Thematics in Proust, Rilke, Hofmannsthal, and Sartre* (London: Institute of Germanic Studies, 1981).

'vom Gebrauchsgegenstand bis zum Gebrauchstext'.[35] When Christian later remembers these broken objects, they will prove to have a major influence on the path his life is going to take, as if through his engagement with these objects his eyes had been opened to the world outside his bubble of decadence and pleasure. Christian's altered character is, therefore, predominantly defined by his altered perception: objects are given back their aura and his eyes are eventually enabled to gaze again.[36]

How Not to Do It – the Blind Saints

Apart from a new form the novel also confronts its reader with a fresh approach to the question of character. Up to this point Wassermann was keen on creating psychologically rounded characters whereas now, amongst other things, he becomes interested in exploring the use of allegorical types instead. This new approach not only corresponds to the end of his concern with a realistic depiction of the petty bourgeoisie's provincial world but also tallies with the ways in which modernity has changed our perception: Wassermann's fresh approach is also an attempt to mirror the ways in which we perceive the people around us on a daily basis. The most poignant aspect of this is the fact that the reader may well have forgotten about some of the novel's characters by the time s/he has finished it. A popular point of criticism, this overdose of characters could equally be seen as one of the novel's most modern features, which is why Poeschel's claim that it is merely an expression of Wassermann's 'Unersättlichkeit nach Menschen' is inaccurate.[37] It demonstrates that we are no longer able to remember all the people we encounter. Moreover, as we have learned from Simmel, eccentricity is the only way to be seen in a modern society. Tellingly, the eccentric characters are those we are most likely to remember at the end of the novel.

Another aspect of the new way in which we perceive people, apart from forgetting about them altogether, is that it is no longer possible to get to know their private *persona*. At best we might be able to catch a glimpse of it, for it is

35 Peukert, *Die Weimarer Republik*, p. 167.

36 In his interpretation Karlstetter is aware of the importance of perception for Christian's spiritual development, yet he does not link it to the development of perception in the modern world (Karlstetter, *Bild des Jugendlichen*, p. 76). Hermann Greissinger writes that Christian's decision to leave his world behind leads to a 'Wahrnehmungserweiterung' but, like Karlstetter, he does not link this to other, more general developments in perception (Hermann Greissinger, *"In die vierte Existenz vielleicht": Konzeptionen von 'Leben' und 'Nicht-Leben' im Werk von Jakob Wassermann und in den Erzähltexten der frühen Moderne* (Bern, Frankfurt a.M., New York: Lang, 1986), p. 86).

37 Poeschel, *Wassermann*, p. 86.

otherwise completely isolated. This means that to our eyes people are mainly made up of 'äußere Anliegen' and it has become increasingly difficult to see the individual human being behind them. The novel echoes this effect as it does not allow most of its figures to turn into fully developed characters. Instead, Wassermann uses them as allegories, in particular Eva Sorel (art), Iwan Becker (political ideology) and Amadeus Voss (religion). These three figures are most suitable to highlight Wassermann's new technique of characterization and will therefore be discussed below. Moreover, there is a strong link between the depiction of character and its content, meaning that all three represent failed attempts at finding salvation which stand in stark contrast to Christian's eventual sainthood and his desire to place the individual human being above everything. Jütten refers to the 'religionskritische Haltung der Moderne'[38] and shows how this has led to a search for new spiritual options.[39] In this context, the abundance of potential new saints can be seen as a reflection of a situation in which people experienced a spiritual void they were desperate to fill. The failure of these three attempts can again be linked back to the question of perception, thus completing the picture that Wassermann draws of society immediately before the Great War.

Eva Sorel – the Power of Art

The figure of the dancer Eva Sorel offers a good starting point as the way she is presented clearly links back to the connection made previously between the novel and the cinema: more than any other character in the novel Eva is presented like a silent movie star. Her appearance and her dance, that is, her movements, stand at the centre while her personality retreats into the background. This character is made up mainly of visible features which do not allow significant psychological depth. Whenever Eva is present the reader knows what she is wearing and how she moves. However, since Eva is a rather quiet character with no inner monologues, we rarely find out anything about her inner life. Even the conversations she has are described as beautiful but meaningless, while her dress and her movements, her dance, are exceptional, eccentric and memorable. They are frequently referred to as new, unheard-of or mesmerising. The character of Eva therefore lends itself perfectly to the creation of those 'images' that are so vital for the form of the novel.

In fact, Eva's rapidly changing and extravagant outfits, which greatly influence the fashion of her day, are yet another indicator of the new

38 Jütten, *Diskurse*, p. 110.

39 For a further discussion of those options, see Jütten, *Diskurse*, p. 86.

'Reizbedürfnis' resulting from the ways in which modernity has changed our perception. Simmel observes this phenomenon in his essay 'Die Mode' (1905): 'Daß in der gegenwärtigen Kultur die Mode ungeheuer Überhand nimmt [...] ist nur die Verdichtung eines zeitpsychologischen Zuges. Unsere innere Rhythmik fordert immer kürzere Perioden im Wechsel von Eindrücken'.[40] Our desire to be shocked and to experience sensory overload therefore also extends to the world of fashion and it is one of the functions of Eva's character to fulfil this desire. All these properties of her character also lend themselves to allegorical use, as Eva becomes a significant symbol of her time as well as an allegory for the role of art in it. Eva advances within ten months from a dancer in a backstreet theatre in Paris to an international star and, immediately surrounded by a group of adoring followers, she becomes an idol and symbol of hope for many people:

> [I]hre Kunst galt als hohe Blüte der Epoche. Es lagen ihr alle zu Füßen, deren geistig-unruhigem Verlangen sie eine Gestalt dargeboten hatte. Die Vorläufer der gehetzten Menschheit schöpften Atem und blickten zu ihr empor. Die Anbeter der Form und die Verkünder eines neuen Rhythmus warben um ein Lächeln ihres Mundes (*CW*, I, p. 59)

Eva thus represents the new era with its new, faster pace. At the same time people see her art as a source of comfort, to the extent that, as suggested by the choice of words, she is worshipped in a semi-religious way. However, as Wassermann already hints in *Zirndorf* and *Renate Fuchs*, the artist, in that case the 'Literat' Gudstikker, is not a figure to be believed in, let alone worshipped. The character of Eva thus has to be seen as a continuation of Wassermann's concern with the role of the artist in society. Moreover, as a dancer Eva also becomes a later and more successful version of Jeanette Löwengard. Eva is not only successful as an artist but both her emancipation and her sexual liberation are credible.

Eva's function as an allegory begins when she is made aware of the sheer, endless agony of the Russian people under authoritarian rule. As a consequence she decides to redeem the world through her art: 'Die Verdammnis will ich tanzen. Die Verdammnis in der Hölle und die Erlösung' (*CW*, I, p. 61). She thus attributes a (religious as well as political) purpose to a form of art that has hitherto been an ephemeral source of entertainment. Through her art, Eva wants to bring people the salvation they are so desperately seeking. Contrary to the comfort commonly found in art she wants to take it to the level of international politics. Initially some people are thrilled by her taking that step: 'Es gab verzückte Propheten, die behaupteten, sie tanze das neue

40 Simmel, 'Die Mode', in *Das Abenteuer*, pp. 58–92 (p. 69).

Jahrhundert, den Untergang der alten Ideen, die kommende Revolution' (*CW*, I, p. 61). However, there is already a hint in the artwork that becomes a great inspirational source for Eva that art would betray its purpose under these circumstances: namely, the thirty-third canto of the *Inferno* from Dante's *Divine Comedy*. Significantly, the canto deals with traitors who find themselves in the ice of Cocytus. It is there that:

> we have the last state of the corruption of love; that every devouring passion, sexual or otherwise, that sets itself against the order of God and the City, bears in itself the seeds of treachery and a devouring passion of destruction.[41]

This is a first hint at Eva's inevitable fall and the megalomania that leads to her destruction. The passage quoted in the novel (beginning with 'Lo pianto stesso li pianger non lascia' (*CW*, I, p. 61)) describes traitors' inability even to weep because their tears are frozen, which foreshadows not just Eva's downfall but also her increasing inability to see and thus to love and show empathy.

When art comes into contact with worldly powers, its fall becomes inevitable and Eva is branded a traitor. In this context the figure of the dancer becomes a particularly fruitful representative of art because as a dancer Eva and her work are inseparable: the dancer is the art work itself. In order to influence his decisions, Eva becomes the mistress of the Russian Großfürst Maidanoff, who has allegedly spilt enough blood to drown the whole of Moscow. The allegorical nature of these two figures is further underlined by the lack of any historical foundation for the figure of Maidanoff.[42] Moreover, Maidanoff can hardly be referred to as a character at all since he is represented as a dark force that is rarely physically present. Maidanoff has only a few lines of speech throughout the novel, a silence which adds to the sense that in this society people are ruled by an anonymous force rather than actual, tangible people. In the figure of Maidanoff, Wassermann depicts the most sinister aspect of modern society, namely the brutality of a regime that has seemingly lost all human qualities.

It does not take long before art becomes corrupted by the game of international politics as well as defeated by Eva's own desires. The Russian Iwan Becker observes: 'Sie empfängt die Minister und fremden Gesandten wie eine gekrönte Herrscherin' (*CW*, II, pp. 67–68). Art is thus seated on the throne of worldly powers, allowing Eva to live a life of almost unspeakable luxury in Russia. Her initial aim is soon forgotten: '[I]ch will den Tiger [Maidanoff] an

41 Dante Alighieri, *The Divine Comedy. 1: Hell*, trans. by Dorothy L. Sayers (London: Penguin, 1949), p. 282.

42 See, for example, Orlando Figes, *A People's Tragedy: the Russian Revolution, 1891–1924* (London: Pimlico, 1997).

die Kette legen' (*CW*, II, p. 260). She had hoped to persuade Maidanoff to adopt more humane politics but instead no longer minds the sacrifice of human lives for the satisfaction of her own desires. Art has thus been betrayed, even destroyed (as indicated by Eva's eventual suicide) in her attempt to influence politics. As soon as Eva becomes the tyrant's lover, her art ceases to be a source of relief for her audience as she is never again able to perform her dance of 'Freiheit und Erlösung' (*CW*, I, p. 264). In other words, salvation through art is, therefore, only possible if the latter is free from any worldly purpose. This understanding of the role of art in society can be linked to *Zirndorf.* Here, only the minor character of Cornely Nieberding finds salvation through her art while the commercial artist Gudstikker instrumentalizes his work to the extent that it became meaningless. Similarly, in her function as an allegory, Eva becomes a potent reminder that art and power should stay apart to prevent art from becoming superficial as well as to avoid a situation in which the artist is worshipped like a god.

Iwan Becker – Revolution at Any Cost

The Russian revolutionary leader Iwan Michailowitsch Becker represents another failed attempt at bringing people salvation. Once again, Wassermann carefully avoids presenting an actual historical figure. Instead, he makes allegorical use of it in order to depict the failure of political ideology as well as the dangers lurking behind any kind of mass movement. There is an earlier, similar version of the figure of Becker, named Rachotinsky, in *Der goldene Spiegel*, a first indicator that Becker is more of a type than an individual character.[43] Moreover, Robert Service tells us that the politically persecuted Russian in exile was a familiar sight in early twentieth-century Europe, which makes Becker an easily identifiable and imaginable figure.[44] Otto Flake's concern with the figure of the Russian revolutionary in 'Der Tausch', as well as with the artist Lutz, who joins the Communist movement in Russia, offers another literary parallel.[45]

However, even though Becker gives the usual account of horror and agony under the Tsarist regime, Wassermann neither seems interested in creating a heroic, martyr-like figure nor does he give in to the fear of revolution that had reached its height in Germany just after World War I. At that time Germany went through a number of revolutions or revolutionary outbreaks, notably the

43 Jakob Wassermann, 'Aurora', in *Der goldene Spiegel: Erzählungen in einem Rahmen* (Berlin: Fischer, 1911), pp. 291–323.

44 Robert Service, *Trotsky: a Biography* (Basingstoke & Oxford: Pan Books, 2010), pp. 87–114.

45 See Flake, *Stadt*. 'Der Tausch' is one of the stories within the novel (pp. 150–90).

Munich *Räterepublik* of 1918, the Spartakus uprising and the Kapp putsch, which caused widespread alarm.[46] By making Becker have a radical change of heart, abandon the revolutionary cause and join a pro-Tsarist movement, Wassermann instead aims at a more general rejection of any kind of political extremism taken up by a mass movement. This depiction tallies with the author's critique of the figure of the intellectual in his earlier novels. Becker's decision to abandon the revolutionary cause shows him to be blind to the suffering of the people for whom he is ostensibly fighting. Following the insight that ever since the beginning of the revolutionary movement in Russia (1905) more blood has been shed than before, Becker decides to turn his back on the political left. Tellingly, this insight does not prevent Becker from spilling even more blood as he first leads a workers' movement in support of the Tsar and later becomes the head of a group of violent ex-soldiers who terrorize entire regions on the coast. In fact, it is one of these groups that storms Eva's castle, prompting her to commit suicide. The false saints are therefore shown to be without mercy for each other, with 'false' meaning they are perceived as a contrast to Christian and the promises and ideologies they stand for offer no consolation to people and their everyday trials and tribulations. During all this time, Becker wears the dress of an Orthodox priest and the men revere him as a saint: '[E]r galt ihnen als der Heilige des Volkes und der Prophet des neuen Reiches' (*CW*, II, p. 414). Becker thus runs the gamut from a revolutionary leader to an Orthodox 'saint' with the result that all his endeavours have led to the loss of further lives. Becker is obviously unable to see the human being behind his various political causes.

By placing Becker in the context of his opponent Maidanoff, Wassermann illustrates how tyranny and revolutionary endeavour potentially lead to the same outcome. Even though unable to predict what the future will hold, Wassermann clearly feels the need to issue a warning against any kind of extremism, be it revolutionary or authoritarian. In order to put his point across, he refrains from using fully developed characters or actual historical figures but instead relies on their symbolic significance. In this way he arrives at an overarching critique of the consequences of ideology being put to the test. Moreover, Becker's attempt at bringing people salvation and relief through mass movements, including the use of violence, stands in stark contrast to Christian's approach, which aims at saint-like behaviour in an everyday context. As Koester puts it: Christian's aim is 'seine Nächstenliebe

46 See, for example, Harry Graf Kessler, *Tagebücher 1918–1937*, ed. by Wolfgang Pfeiffer-Belli (Frankfurt a.M: Insel, 1996), pp. 6–87; and Thomas Mann, *Tagebücher 1918–1921*, pp. 3–119.

praktisch zu leben'.[47] Blankenagel's criticism that Christian lacks any interest in 'organized philanthropy' therefore clearly misses the point.[48]

Amadeus Voss – Religion in Need of Salvation

With the character of Amadeus Voss, Wassermann dismisses religious dogmatism as a means of finding salvation. It might seem that religion offers the most obvious way to achieve salvation, and yet the novel confronts us with a form of religious dogmatism that is itself in need of salvation. Voss is the representative of this dogmatism and even though he is a less obvious allegorical figure, it soon becomes apparent that his symbolic value by far exceeds his importance as a character. In this context Karlstetter is seriously mistaken when he identifies Voss as a 'Zivilisationsliterat', trying to place him in the context of Thomas Mann's critique of that persona.[49] An eccentric figure like Voss is clearly a very different kind of person from the liberal, Francophile, secular type that Mann had in mind and later embodied in Settembrini:

> Der Typus dieses deutschen Anhängers der literarischen Zivilisation ist, wie sich versteht, unser *radikaler Literat*, er, den ich den 'Zivilisationsliteraten' zu nennen mich gewöhnt habe, – und es versteht sich deshalb, weil der radikale Literat, der Vertreter des literarisierten und politisierten, kurz, des demokratischen Geistes, ein Sohn der Revolution, in ihrer Sphäre, ihrem Lande geistig beheimatet ist.[50]

Wassermann himself associated this term with Heinrich Heine, a very plausible antecedent of the 'Zivilisationsliterat', which shows that he understood the term as Mann did.[51]

Although the reader is provided with some information regarding Voss's background and personal development, his religious fanaticism predominates. He is shown to be a tormented character who received his education at a Catholic seminary and is unable to free himself from an extreme form of religiosity. The extent of his fanaticism becomes apparent when he does not refrain from using physical abuse as a means of educating his pupils during a brief interval as a private tutor ('Hofmeister'). He reports his treatment of the two boys as follows:

47 Koester, *Wassermann*, p. 57.

48 Blankenagel, *Writings*, p. 277.

49 Karlstetter, *Bild des Jugendlichen*, p. 71.

50 Thomas Mann, *Betrachtungen eines Unpolitischen* (Frankfurt a.M.: Fischer, 1983), p. 76.

51 Wassermann, 'Mein Weg', p. 74. See also Anne-Liese Sell, *Das metaphysisch-realistische Weltbild Jakob Wassermanns* (Bern: Paul Haupt, 1932), p. 21. For a more detailed discussion of Wassermann's relationship to Heine, see Markus May, 'Die Wunde Heine', in *Deutscher – Jude – Literat*, pp. 91–109.

> Sie mußten beten, einmal in der Woche fasten, auf harten Lagerstellen schlafen und des Morgens um fünf Uhr aufstehen. Ich brach ihren Trotz auf alle Weise, ihre dumpfe Trägheit, ihre Lüsternheit, ihre Ränke. [...] Ich züchtigte sie. Ich schlug sie bei der geringsten Widersetzlichkeit mit der Peitsche. Ich lehrte sie den Schmerz. Nackt mußten sie vor mir liegen, mit den blutigen Striemen auf der Haut, da sprach ich ihnen vom Martyrium der Heiligen (*CW*, I, pp. 207–08).

Even Voss's language is soaked in the vocabulary of Christian extremism, making it difficult to trace any personal aspect to it. This is emphasized further by his frequently quoting or reading from the Bible when he wants to make a point; this renders him less individual as his words are not his own. Voss's personality has, therefore, been taken over by dogma to the extent that hardly any individuality remains. Nevertheless, it is important to bear in mind, as Elisabeth Jütten observes, 'dass sich die Kritik des Romans gegen jegliches religiöse Dogma, das religiöse Intoleranz erzeugt, nicht jedoch gegen den Glauben als solchen wendet'.[52] The figure of Voss is, therefore, a continuation of Wassermann's criticism of religion in *Zirndorf*. Moreover, this rejection of dogmatism and, more generally, the superiority of one religion over another, is an important step towards the search for a more syncretic approach towards spirituality as presented in *Kerkhoven*.

Hatred stands at the centre of Voss's world view, making him, among other things, a radical anti-Semite. The idea of religion as a means to channel one's hatred is fundamentally opposed to Christian's approach, which is why Voss becomes the latter's opponent. Voss has been blinded by his dogmatism and consequently fails to see the human being, a failure which becomes most apparent in his open contempt for the prostitute Karen. Voss's blindness to life and love is underlined by several references to his face being 'augenlos' (see, for example, *CW*, I, p. 173). Greissinger rightly remarks that Voss rejects 'die wesentlichen Transformationen: [...] die von Wahrnehmung und Erkenntnis'.[53] In this version, religion therefore prevents the individual from altering his or her perception so as to be able to see the human being. Christian and Voss thus find themselves on opposite journeys: Christian towards light and the ability to see despite the blinding influences around him and Voss towards darkness and the inability to see beyond his hatred.

As an allegorical representation of religion, Voss also functions as a foil for Christian in order to demonstrate how the latter, as a modern saint, is without religion. In an ironic scene, when Voss mentions St Francis of Assisi

52 Jütten, *Diskurse*, p. 117.

53 Greissinger, *Vierte Existenz*, p. 117.

to Christian, the latter replies: 'Ich weiß von ihm nichts' (*CW*, II, p. 209). In the novel Christian's behaviour is thus, at least from his perspective, not inspired by any known religious movement. Moreover, while Voss constantly has to force himself to be religious, Christian's development comes across as natural. This becomes most apparent in their different approaches towards sexuality: as a follower of a fanatical Catholicism, Voss has learnt to suppress his sexuality even though this is against his nature. He therefore constantly expresses his hatred for sexuality as well as for women who arouse these forbidden desires in him. Christian's sexual abstinence, by contrast, seems to be a natural part of his transformation and is at no point depicted as a struggle against himself. Religiosity and even sainthood, it seems, have therefore to be the result of an inner, natural development that cannot be forced onto somebody, whether from the outside as Voss tries to do with his pupils, or from the inside as he tries to do with himself. A religious dogmatism, as represented by Voss, that is so fundamentally opposed to human nature can thus never be a source of salvation for the victims of modernity. Religious dogma is shown to stand between a religious figure and the people instead of facilitating contact between them. Wassermann insists that the human being should always come before any kind of dogma, be it religious or political, as with Becker. The inability to focus on the individual human being has led to the failure of all these three false saints. The depiction of them as 'semi-characters' helps to show how Wassermann's criticism is inextricably linked to the way he creates his characters.

Wassermann and his Saint

On 29 May 1916 Wassermann writes in a letter to his friend, the pianist and composer Ferruccio Busoni: 'Ich arbeite seit Monaten an einem grossen Roman mit religiöser Grund-Idee, einem modernen Franz v. Assisi-Stoff. Er hat mich ganz und gar verschluckt, und die Widerwärtigkeiten der Welt klopfen nur, schreckhaft genug, doch im tiefsten machtlos, an das Schneckengehäuse'.[54] These lines not only justify commentators in comparing Christian to St Francis.[55] They also highlight the significance the figure of Christian had for Wassermann in a period of great distress, namely the years of the Great War.

54 Wassermann to Ferruccio Busoni 29 May 1916 (DLA, call number: 96.48.3 /1–33, A: Wassermann, 1911–1924).

55 See, for example, Joeris, *Aspekte*, p. 123. For a more general discussion of the reception of the story of St Francis at the turn of the century and the influences of Buddhism on the novel, see Jütten, *Diskurse*, pp. 107–10 and pp. 124–31.

During that time he noted in his diary: 'Ich blicke in eine zerstörte Welt. Es ist, als ob die Menschheit sich selbst verloren, Gott verloren hätte'.[56]

In 1920, only one year after *Wahnschaffe*, Wassermann published the first volume of a collection of novellas entitled *Der Wendekreis*. 'Der unbekannte Gast', the first of these novellas, can be understood as a reflection on the comfort Wassermann found, not only as a writer, in the figure of Christian. In the novella we meet a middle-aged writer named Mörner, who is presented in a way that recalls Wassermann himself. Mörner finds himself in a personal and professional crisis, as he has lost faith in his own mission, namely his art, as well as in the people around him. He therefore refers to the 'Zerstörung der Geister und Seelen. [...] War jemals eine Menschheit so zu Boden getreten?'[57] Even though there are no direct references to the Great War in the novella, this quotation is very similar in tone to that from Wassermann's own diary. Moreover, according to Mörner, recent events have left society in a state too devastated for humanity to receive or that is able to inspire great works of art. One evening Mörner suddenly finds himself in the presence of a nameless visitor described in a way that suggests he is an aged version of Christian. This ghostlike visitor has come to cure Mörner of his negative, unproductive views, the result of his diseased perception: '[D]as Ganze ist eine Erkrankung des Auges; freilich nicht des physischen Auges; was darf nicht alles Auge heißen bei den Edleren: das Herz ist selber Auge'.[58] By recounting numerous instances of human suffering he has witnessed all over the world, the visitor demonstrates that the human soul is invincible. Even the most tragic events bear witness to its omnipresence and its beauty. He also reminds Mörner that it is his duty to continue writing, as his soul has not been directly affected by this recent wave of destruction: 'Ist das eigene Auge und die eigene Seele unzerstört, so ist die Welt unzerstört'.[59] When the visitor vanishes, Mörner has won new faith in the human soul and, to all appearances, can continue with his work. The use Wassermann makes of the word 'Auge' confirms that, for him, goodness is initially a matter of perception.

This comforting aspect of the figure of Christian and thus of *Wahnschaffe* sheds light on another potential reason for the work's great popularity and commercial success: it might have been a source of hope to those whom the War had left bereft and / or impoverished. The uplifting nature of the novel is

56 During the Great War, between 25 July 1914 and 25 December 1915, Wassermann kept another diary. See Karlweis, *Wassermann*, pp. 242–75 (p. 243).

57 Jakob Wassermann, 'Der Unbekannte Gast', in *Der Wendekreis: Erste Folge* (Berlin: Fischer, 1920), pp. 7–45 (p. 15).

58 Wassermann, 'Der Unbekannte Gast', p. 23.

59 Wassermann, 'Der Unbekannte Gast', p. 42.

confirmed by some of the contemporary reviews. Max Rychner, for instance, refers to Christian as 'ein Regenerationsheld in der Niederbruchszeit'.[60] Koester therefore rightly observes that Wassermann was, amongst other things, concerned with the 'seelischen Wiederaufbau im Nachkriegsdeutschland'.[61] At that time the idea of finding a source of hope and renewal in a spiritual yet non-religious way was, of course, not exclusive to Wassermann. Hermann Hesse, who also wrote a brief text about St Francis,[62] displays a similar attitude towards religion, the need for spiritual renewal and even altered perception in his novel *Demian: Die Geschichte von Emil Sinclairs Jugend* (1919). In the novel, Sinclair is looking for a 'Weltgefühl, das über allen Bekenntnissen stand'.[63] In the course of the novel he realizes that the world does not need new gods or a new religion but that only the altered behaviour of each individual will make the difference. His mentor Pistorius teaches him that the equivalent of a modern saint must want nothing but his own destiny:

> Wer wirklich gar nichts will als sein Schicksal, der hat nicht seinesgleichen mehr, der steht ganz allein und hat nur den kalten Weltenraum um sich. Wissen Sie, das ist Jesus im Garten Gethsemane. [...] Wer nur noch das Schicksal will, der hat weder Vorbilder noch Ideale mehr, nichts Liebes, nichts Tröstliches hat er! [...] Er darf auch nicht Revolutionär, nicht Beispiel, nicht Märtyrer sein wollen.[64]

The parallels to the path that Christian follows are rather striking. Sinclair tries to follow this path together with his other mentor and friend Max Demian. As with Christian, this new way of life is linked to altered perception: '[W]ir waren von der Mehrzahl der Menschen nicht durch Grenzen getrennt, sondern nur durch eine andere Art des Sehens'.[65] The novel ends with the beginning of the Great War and Sinclair, like so many others, senses potential for renewal in this collapse. However, this collapse will have rendered all previous ideas of religion and morality obsolete and only the new, individual path he has discovered will be a means of salvation.

Another novel that offers parallels to *Wahnschaffe* is Gerhart Hauptmann's *Der Narr in Christo Emanuel Quint*, most notably in its lenient depiction of

60 Max Rychner, 'Ein neuer Roman Jakob Wassermanns. "Christian Wahnschaffe"', *Neue Züricher Zeitung*, 6 July 1919, p. 1 (quoted in Neubauer, *Schriftsteller*, p. 56).

61 Koester, *Wassermann*, p. 61.

62 Hermann Hesse, 'Aus der Kindheit des Heiligen Franz von Assisi', in Hermann Hesse, *Legenden*, ed. by Volker Michels (Frankfurt a.M.: Suhrkamp, 1975), pp. 162–73.

63 Hermann Hesse, 'Demian: Die Geschichte von Emil Sinclairs Jugend', in *Sämtliche Werke*, 21 vols, III, *Die Romane*, ed. by Volker Michels (Frankfurt a. M.: Suhrkamp, 2001), pp. 233–366 (p. 311).

64 Hesse, 'Demian', p. 336.

65 Hesse, 'Demian', p. 348.

prostitutes and the fact that Emanuel's companion Ruth also becomes the victim of a sexual murder.[66] Apart from Hesse, Rilke was also fascinated by the idea of the 'new saint' and wrote about St Francis in the third section of his *Stundenbuch* (1905), entitled 'Von der Armut und vom Tode'. In his version Rilke is also concerned with the 'tiefe Angst der großen Städte' in which people live 'schlecht und schwer', thus offering a parallel to Christian's life in Berlin and the misery he witnesses.[67] Moreover, highly critical of modern life in the city, Rilke also comments on people's exaggerated self-representation and their inability just to be themselves: 'Es ist als ob ein Trug sie täglich äffte, / sie können garnicht mehr sie selber sein'.[68] In spite of Rilke's strong emphasis on nature as opposed to the city, his version offers marked parallels to Wassermann's treatmet of the 'new saint'. Another parallel can be seen in Adolf von Hatzfeld's story *Franziskus* (1918), an important work of German Expressionism in which the young protagonist questions the rules and structures imposed by religion, the family and the state.[69]

Against this background it is also important to mention that *Wahnschaffe* can also be seen in the context of late Expressionism's concern with the idea of the 'new man'. Wasserman's relationship with Expressionism is complex and cannot be explored at length here; instead, it will be mentioned as a starting point for further research. Wahnschaffe could, for instance, be compared to figures such as Ernst Toller's protagonist Friedrich in his play *Die Wandlung* (1920); or to the figure of Hans Iver in Ernst Barlach's play *Der arme Vetter* (1918). Similarly to Christian, Iver is confronted with a world in which most people are unable to see each other and think that 'die ganze Erlöserei [...] ein himmelschreiender Mumpitz [ist]'.[70] However, the Expressionist novel that cannot be ignored in this context is Otto Flake's *Stadt des Hirns*.[71] Published in 1919, the same year as *Wahnschaffe*, the novel bears some striking similarities to Wassermann's work. Flake's protagonist Lauda also decides to leave his life behind and sever all ties with his family; in the course of the novel he sometimes compares himself to Buddha, a figure to whom Wahnschaffe has also been contrasted.[72] As mentioned before, Flake's novel is also highly critical of the concept of a fixed character and reveals personality to be the

66 Gerhart Hauptmann, *Der Narr in Christo Emanuel Quint* (Berlin: Fischer, 1910).

67 Rainer Maria Rilke, *Das Stundenbuch* (Wiesbaden: Insel, 1955), pp 89–91.

68 Rilke, *Das Stundenbuch*, p. 107.

69 Adolf von Hatzfeld, *Franziskus* (Berlin: Paul Cassirer, 1919).

70 Ernst Barlach, *Der arme Vetter* (Stuttgart: Reclam, 1992), p. 39.

71 My thanks to the reader of my dissertation for the Bithell series for alerting me to this work and the potential for comparison.

72 Jütten, *Diskurse*, p. 106.

'lügnerischstes Wort'.[73] More importantly though, Lauda considers the eye to be the 'primäre[s] Organ vor aller Seele', thus also placing an emphasis on the importance of perception.[74] The figures of the prostitute and the dancer also feature in Flake's novel and his protagonist likewise attempts to live in self-imposed sexual abstinence, yet unlike Christian he fails. Nevertheless, at the end of the novel Lauda marries Claire, who reminds him that 'Demut' will make him worthy of being loved.[75] 'Demut' is also one of the main aims to which Christian aspires, so both protagonists end their quest for meaning on a similar note. The figure of Christian is therefore of significance to Wassermann beyond the actual novel as well as being part of a wider search for spiritual renewal following the devastation caused by the Great War.

Even though Christian is not presented as a religious saint, it is important to acknowledge that his character is inspired by the thirteenth-century saint Francis of Assisi. It is safe to say that Wassermann used *Saint François d'Assise: sa vie et son oeuvre* (1910), by the Danish writer Johannes Jørgensen, as a source for his novel, a copy of the book having been found in the author's private library.[76] Generally, it can be said that Wassermann relies heavily on Jørgensen's account, with some striking parallels between the novel and the biography. Moreover, in the early chapter 'Der Globus auf den Fingerspitzen einer Elfe' (*CW*, I, pp. 59–104), the poet Ermelang is said to recite a poem about St Francis, yet the novel offers only a summary of it. This is in large part a direct quotation from Jørgensen's book.[77] In this scene St Francis is asked by Brother Matteo why he, in particular, is so popular among the people and why they have started to follow him. St Francis replies:

> Warum mir alle nachfolgen? Das hat mir der Blick des allmächtigen Gottes ersehen, der allerorten auf Guten und Bösen weilt. Denn seine heiligen Augen sahen unter den Sündern keinen, der elender war denn ich, keinen, der untüchtiger war denn ich, keinen, der ein größerer Sünder war denn ich; und um das wundersame Werk zu vollbringen, das er sich vorgenommen, fand er kein Geschöpf auf Erden, das armseliger war denn ich. Darum hat er mich auserwählt, um die Welt zu beschämen mit ihrem Adel und ihrem Stolz (*CW*, I, p. 78).

73 Flake, *Stadt*, p. 62.
74 Flake, *Stadt*, p. 128.
75 Flake, *Stadt*, p. 567.
76 Johannes Jørgensen, *Saint François d'Assise : sa vie et son oeuvre*, trans. by Teodor de Wyzewa (Paris: Perrin, 1910). Wassermann's private library now belongs to the Stadtbibliothek, Nuremberg. The book was first published in Danish: Johannes Jørgensen, *Den hellige Frans af Assisi* (Copenhagen: Gyldendals, 1907).
77 Johannes Jørgensen, *Saint Francis of Assisi: A Biography*, trans. by T. O'Conor Sloane (New York etc.: Longmans, Green & Co., 1912), p. 74.

This emphatic reference to St Francis early in the novel is a major clue about how we are to read the work and what to expect from it. By becoming the lowest of the low Christian will demonstrate that salvation can only be achieved if one recognizes one's own insignificance and as a result overcomes one's self. The reference to God's holy eyes is another hint at the idea that in the novel the ability to see is depicted as a divine quality.

The Disappearance of Character

In Wassermann's 'Der Unbekannte Gast', the mysterious visitor is nameless, a final confirmation of the fact that for Wassermann the idea of sainthood is strongly connected to that of the disappearance of character. The nameless visitor has disappeared for the benefit of others and all that is left of him, really, are his good deeds in everyday life and his unusual perception. The notion of sainthood with which Wassermann presents us is thus predominantly based on an altered perception that results from the overcoming of the self. He tries to depict this in *Wahnschaffe* by using a new narrative technique: he gradually makes his protagonist disappear until he vanishes completely at the end of the novel. In *Wahnschaffe* the question of the outsider therefore retreats into the background since Christian's character can no longer be seen in relation to society. By his virtually ceasing to exist, it has indeed become impossible for society to exclude him. Given the complex structure of the novel, it is most reasonable to trace Christian's development from a rich, decadent young man to a modern version of St Francis through his relationships with some of the other characters. Each of these relationships leads to the loss of an aspect of his former character until Christian eventually disappears altogether. Moreover, it will also become apparent that Koester's interpretation of Christian's development is in need of qualification: '[D]ie Entwicklung der Hauptfigur verliert sich schließlich in legendenhaft-idealistischer Verschwommenheit'.[78]

Katharina Zöllner

Regarding his inner development, Christian's first important moment with another character is his encounter with Katharina Zöllner, the daughter of a sailor and generally a minor character. This meeting documents the beginning of the changes in Christian's perception while at the same time serving as a first hint at his later practice of sexual abstinence. In a town on the Rhine, just after leaving Paris and Eva Sorel, Crammon and Christian witness Katharina

78 Koester, *Wassermann*, p. 57.

being molested by numerous drunken men in a beer garden where she has come looking for her father. Neither of them attempts to help her, even though the situation is traumatic: 'Ihr Haar war aufgelöst, ihre blaue Bluse zerrissen, daß man die nackte Brust gewahrte, ihr Gesicht voll häßlicher Flecken. Sie suchte sich aufrecht zu halten, nach einigem Umsichtasten brach sie zusammen' (*CW*, I, p. 110). Though he is not yet ready to interfere, the event nevertheless leaves Christian doubting his lifestyle for the first time: 'Glaubst du [Crammon], daß ich richtig lebe, so wie ich lebe?' (*CW*, I, pp. 111–12). Apart from guilt, Christian is driven by a strange curiosity, keen to explore how 'diese Sorte Mensch' lives. Together with Crammon he visits Katharina at her parents' home, conquering for the first time the disgust that regularly affects him when confronted with poverty. Unable to offer any genuine support to the traumatized girl and her family, all Christian has to give is a diamond ring as he is literally struck speechless by what he sees. This inability to find one word that would not be 'überflüssig und gemein' (*CW*, I, p. 115) shows that the need for a different way of seeing the world is deeply connected to the need to find a way back to more supportive and meaningful human relationships.

At this point Christian is unable to interact with any of the family members, a failure which is, significantly, expressed in his inability to return their gaze. Nonetheless, this marks a pivotal moment in the development of his altered understanding, as becomes apparent when Christian's perception is compared with Crammon's. While the latter can see nothing but a squalid room inhabited by poor members of the lower classes, Christian can see beyond that:

> Was Crammon sah und was Christian sah, war nicht dasselbe. [...] Für Christian war es wie ein Traum vom Fallen. Auch er sah den Schiffer, das abgehärmte Weib, den schlafenden Burschen, den Säugling in der Wiege und das Mädchen, [...] aber er sah es wie man Bilder sieht, während man in einen Schacht heruntergleitet; Bilder, die beständig wiederkehrten und von anderen abgelöst wurden, die sich von oben her dazwischen schoben. So sah er Eva, die einem ihrer Affen eine Walnuß reichte [...] und jedes Ding, auf das sein Auge fiel, hatte Bezug auf ein anderes aus der andern Welt (*CW*, I, pp. 113–14).

Another technique used here by Wassermann to highlight the importance of altered perception becomes apparent. In these early stages, Christian can only sense his viewpoint is about to change as part of a gradual process stimulated by recurring images rather than as a sudden transformation. The reader and Christian therefore have a similar experience as they are both confronted by rapidly changing images that potentially inspire a different way of looking at the world. At the same time these images are a great challenge affecting reader and protagonist in a similar way. This passage precedes the one quoted above, in which Christian first perceives spiritual significance in mundane objects in the flat of the worker's wife. Now he starts to connect objects from the world of the poor to objects in his own world. Christian thus becomes increasingly aware of the discrepancy between the two worlds, here hinted at by contrasting the decadent Eva with the poor family, a contrast which will later prompt him to leave his life as the son of a rich businessman behind.

Lätizia von Febronius

As we have seen, the first depiction of Katharina Zöllner is highly sexualized, yet Christian's wish to help her is free from any sexual attraction towards her. The motif of his incipient sexual abstinence, and thus the loss of his sexuality as a key aspect of his character, is developed further in his relationship with Lätizia von Febronius. This sexual abstinence accompanies quite a radical change in Christian's visual and emotional outlook: his personal and egoistic desires cease to stand at the centre of his actions as he is no longer able to ignore either the feelings of others or life's ugly sides. Hitherto he has been engaged in a number of brief and meaningless affairs which tally with Simmel's notion of human relationships in a modern age. Womanizing was an essential part of his former lifestyle, a symbol of his personal freedom, his power and his status above common moral conventions. In previous circumstances the seduction of a girl like Lätizia would therefore have been a routine matter of no consequence, something which makes his refusal to sleep with her most significant.

The increasing impact of visual experience on Christian's behaviour becomes apparent when he first tries to seduce Lätizia. On this first occasion, his sudden backing off and his disgust find rather curious symbolic expression in the figure of a toad. Christian and Lätizia find themselves in a state of sexual arousal, yet he is prevented from seducing her by the sight of a toad:

> Er zögerte nicht mehr, sich der Beute zu bemächtigen. Da gab es kein Bedenken. Er griff nach ihrer Hand; plötzlich gewahrte er eine Kröte, die mit ekelhafter Langsamkeit über Lätizias weißes Kleid kroch, erst über den unteren Saum, dann gegen die Hüfte empor. Er erblaßte und kehrte sich ab (*CW*, I, p. 52).

It is not clear whether the toad symbolizes sexuality in general, or Christian's desire for the virgin Lätizia in particular. In either case, the toad is seen as a disgusting creature, ugly and slimy, moving towards Lätizia's hips and thus her private parts, as though about to take the virginity symbolized by her white dress. *Hall's Dictionary of Symbols in Art* informs us, for example, that: 'Toads eat the genitalia of a naked female personifying lust'.[79] This rather extreme vision of sexuality as repulsive offers the reader a first hint at Christian's later practice of absolute sexual abstinence. Schäfer's view that Christian is scared of the 'weibliche[s] Prinzip' seems to be mistaken because he is about to reject sexuality in general.[80] It is equally difficult to accept Karlstetter's interpretation of the scene when he writes: 'Der Ekel vor allem Dunkeln, Häßlichen, Schleimigen, der ihm von jeher eigen, läßt ihn Lätizias Reize vergessen. [...] Das Bild des gefühllosen und kalten Menschen [...] bestätigt sich'.[81] As we shall see in the next paragraph, it is precisely Christian's love for Lätizia that does not allow him to sleep with her.

The scene of Christian's second suppression of his desires is further proof of the impact visual experiences have on his behaviour towards others. This time a *mémoire involontaire* is strong enough to defeat his intention of sleeping with Lätizia. It therefore seems to happen against his will when he sends her away again, for even though he has never been more excited by a woman's promise to come secretly to his room at night, something holds him back:

> Aber es war etwas dawider. [...] Es war ein blutüberströmtes Gesicht dawider, an dem die schwarzen Haare klebten, und es war ein vom Wasser aufgedunsenes Gesicht dawider, das vordem schön gewesen war. Es war ein Gesicht dawider voll Haß und Scham, das auf schlechtem Linnen ruhte, und ein anderes, in einer Kofferkammer, mit einer weißen Binde umkleidet. [...] Es war sein Herz dawider. Es war die Liebe dawider, die er für Lätizia empfand (*CW*, I, p. 146).

This rapid flow of images based on the memory of people whom he has either seen publicly humiliated, like Katharina, or whose violent deaths he has witnessed (his lover Adda, who was killed by her own lion; his friend Sir Denis Lay, drowned in the Thames) prevents him from sleeping with her and thus makes him suppress his sexual desires. In fact, he is described as obeying an inner voice that urges him to restrain himself. He thus gradually moves away from the sort of love represented by 'eros' towards the concept of 'agape'. In other words, he leaves the world of sensual pleasures behind in order to live according to a more pure and divine concept of love.[82] The novel as a whole lacks positive depictions of sexuality, which is why it is so significant

79 James Hall, *Dictionary of Symbols in Art* (London: John Murray, 1974), p. 304.

80 Schäfer, *Plaidoyer*, p. 318.

81 Karlstetter, *Bild des Jugendlichen*, p. 59.

82 'Eros' and 'agape' are the two Greek words for love. According to the Swedish theologian Anders Nygren, 'eros' refers to a form of love that is egocentric and based on self-interest and lust while 'agape' is unconditional and self-sacrificing. See Anders Nygren, *Agape and Eros: A Study of the Christian Idea of Love*, 3 vols, trans. by A. G. Herbert (London: Society for Promoting Christian Knowledge, 1932), I, pp. 22–24.

that Christian dissociates love from sex. Moreover, his transformation is taken a step further as even his memory has opened to the misery and pain of others. It is no longer solely concerned with objects of everyday use. His memory can therefore be seen to be mirroring his gradual transformation. For the first time his unselfish love for another person, expressed in his refusal to seduce Lätizia, combined with his diffuse awareness of the human agony around him, comes before the satisfaction of his own needs and desires.

Eva Sorel

The end of Christian's love affair with the dancer Eva Sorel symbolizes the main turning point in his life, which is also expressed in the novel's original published form, namely, in two volumes entitled 'Eva' and 'Ruth'. Eva is the key representative of the life Christian has been living so far, a view that is corroborated by Thomas Mann's analysis of her character:

> Die bedrohliche Ratlosigkeit des international-kapitalistischen Lebens ist bunt und eindringlich gegeben. Seine Spitze, sein höchster Sinn, seine Form der Vergeistigung, die zur Herrschaft gelangt: die Tänzerin. Die Frage nach dem Ziel des Lebens wird schmerzhaft und brennend, während Erzähllust sie mit tausend flirrenden Bildern umspinnt.[83]

Christian is indeed at a loss to understand where life is taking him, yet he knows that the merely sensual love which Eva has to offer can only be a distraction from his inner turmoil. Unfamiliar with the road ahead, Christian knows that parting with Eva means parting with life as a rich young man and thus it can be understood as the end of his former self. Thus the final scene of their relationship marks another step in the development of Christian's perception. Following an incident involving a drunken man who inflicts an injury on Eva's feet, Christian kneels before her holding her feet in his hands. The symbolic act of kneeling is otherwise performed only twice in the novel: at the beginning of his transformation Christian kneels before Frau Kroll; and at the end before the 'Lustmörder' Niels Heinrich. Both times it is a highly significant act and a symbol of spiritual devotion as it traditionally forms a central part in different religious prayer routines. Eva, however, spoils it by deriving a kind of sexual pleasure from it: '[D]aß du vor mir kniest, ist wunderbar, mein süßer Freund' (*CW*, I, p. 311). Moreover, she is impudent enough to press his head down even further. There is thus a strong contrast between this act of crude sexuality and the spirituality that kneeling should

83 Mann, *Tagebücher 1918–1921*, p. 142.

imply. (Similarly, when Johanna Schöntag kneels before Eva it has an air of idolatry because she reveres her like a goddess (*CW*, I, p. 374)). At this point Christian remembers the miserable objects from Frau Kroll's squalid flat and suddenly fails to see Eva's beauty and attractiveness:

> Diese menschenhaften Gebilde, diese Füße einer Tänzerin, Glieder einer geliebten Frau, das Seltenste und Kostbarste der Welt, schienen ihm auf einmal häßlich und abstoßend, und jene niedrigen und armseligen Dinge, [...] waren dagegen schön und verehrenswert. [...] Er begriff [...] daß er, im Wechsel von Gestalt zu Gestalt, die Menschen wohl gesehen und gehört [...], daß es aber dabei sein innigstes Bemühen gewesen, sie noch von sich abzuhalten [...]. Die Frist war verstrichen (*CW*, I, pp. 12–13).

Eva, the most appealing of all women in his world, has lost all charm in his eyes. With her Christian therefore leaves another crucial aspect of his character behind, namely his love for beauty, wealth and comfort.

Karen Engelschall

Instead, Christian is now possessed by what could almost be termed a desire for ugliness. Appreciating a human being, even behind the ugliest shell, will prove one of the main trials on his way to sainthood. It will show whether his altered perception can stand the test in the face of everyday life. Soon after his last encounter with Eva (tellingly described as 'letzte Lockung, letzter Verzicht' (*CW*, I, p. 398)), Christian meets his task in the form of the prostitute Karen Engelschall. He comes across the pregnant streetwalker in a bar where she is being assaulted by her pimp for not earning enough money. However, even though Karen finds herself in the most miserable situation with blood streaming down her face, the narrator immediately prevents us from feeling any sympathy for her. Her cries are referred to as 'viehisch monotone Laute' (*CW*, I, p. 414) and the description of her person is even more drastic: 'Reizloseres, Verwüsteteres als der Anblick, den sie darbot, war kaum zu denken' (*CW*, I, p. 420). Later the narrator goes even further when he portrays her as 'ein Tier mit der Häßlichkeit des zerstörten und verstörten Menschen, eine bösartige Wilde' (*CW*, II, p. 2).

The character of Karen is, therefore, not in line with depictions of prostitution in other literature from around that time. She does not conform to the stereotype of the 'prostitute with a heart of gold' (unlike, say, Shen Te in Brecht's *Der gute Mensch von Sezuan* (1939)); nor is she a 'Madonna of sexual liberation' or a victim of modern urban space, which, as Christiane Schönfeld shows, were common portrayals in Expressionist writing.[84] Instead, as a woman Karen is depicted as repulsive, with no perceivable sexual appeal, in addition to which she is rather dislikeable. However, all these characteristics make her the ideal centre for Christian's new life and he decides to move to Berlin with her. Moreover, his new interest in Karen makes Christian forget all about Eva:

> Das strahlende und königliche Wesen lockte ihn nicht mehr, wenn er an das blutüberströmte Gesicht der Dirne dachte, denn diesem gegenüber empfand er eine Art von Neugier, die mehr und mehr sein ganzes Inneres ausfüllte, so daß nichts daneben Platz hatte (*CW*, I, p. 424).

The depiction of Karen as repellent in body and persona enables the narrator to create sharp contrasts, which are an important narrative tool in this novel. The most significant of the contrasts achieved by means of her character is when Karen asks Christian for his mother's pearl necklace. Frau Wahnschaffe is said to own the most precious pearls in the whole of Europe and ever since Karen has seen her wearing them in a photo, she has been longing for them. Pearls in particular are a long-established symbol of extreme luxury, one of the most famous examples being the legend of Cleopatra, according to which she had pearls dissolved in water in order to drink them. Jewellery (the diamond Ignifer, the pearl necklace and so on) is generally a symbol of power in the novel as it is one of the key symbols of the ruling class. As can be deduced from various entries in the diaries of Harry Graf Kessler, in post-war Germany pearls had become the symbol of a form of Wilhelmine life that had ceased to exist, namely the rule of the aristocracy of wealth and blood. On 31 March 1919, during the revolution in Berlin, Kessler writes:

> Diese Gesellschaftsdamen aus der Vorkriegszeit, Mumien, die ihre Perlen auf alten, vergilbten Hälsen herumtragen, wirken erschreckend im heißen Atem und Blutdurst der Massen, die keine seidenen Vorhänge mehr selbst aus Abendunterhaltungen der besten Kreise ausschließen.[85]

Bearing all this symbolic value in mind, Wassermann creates a stunning contrast here when he has his protagonist give Europe's finest pearls to a syphilitic prostitute. The result is one of those strong images on which the novel depends and which possibly proved to be provocative and uncomfortable to some readers.

Through his time spent with Karen, Christian becomes indifferent to all material matters and yet, even more importantly, also to all matters concerning

84 Christiane Schönfeld, 'Streetwalking the Metropolis: Prostitutes in Expressionism', in *Commodities of Desire: The Prostitute in Modern German Literature*, ed. by Christiane Schönfeld (Rochester, NY: Camden House, 2000), pp. 111–30 (p. 117).

85 Kessler, *Tagebücher 1918–1937*, p. 170.

the human body. A few months previously Christian would have thrown away his coat if a beggar had touched it. Having grown up in a society obsessed with immaculate physical appearance, it proves to be a major challenge for Christian to overcome his strong sense of disgust at any physical aspect of human suffering. Accordingly, when Karen dies he is asked to put his new perception into practice. Although she now strongly resembles a leper, for the first time during their relationship, Christian takes her into his arms, where she dies peacefully: '[E]r verspürte keinen Ekel vor dem riechenden Körper mit den aufgebrochenen Eiterschwären; er umfing sie [...] als sei es gar kein Mensch, sondern ein kleiner Vogel' (*CW*, II, pp. 300–01). This scene closely echoes the legend of St Francis, according to which his greatest victory was when he finally managed to overcome his disgust and embrace a leper.[86] With this experience Christian moves beyond the body and is now in search of the soul. The end of Karen's life also signifies the end of his bodily existence in that he has become indifferent to all aspects of it. The body, hitherto a main concern of his, matters no longer.

Ruth Hoffmann and Her 'Lustmörder'

The last part of Christian's character to remain before he can finally disappear is that of forming human attachments. He has severed all ties with his family, looks after the poor while being penniless himself and practises absolute sexual abstinence. However, he is still emotionally attached to his friends in Berlin, most of all to Ruth Hoffmann. With the introduction of Ruth into the novel and her dramatic death, Wassermann once again creates a great contrast against which Christian's behaviour appears saintly, almost superhuman. Ruth Hoffmann is the sixteen-year-old daughter of an Eastern European Jew who, like so many others, came to Berlin to make his fortune and failed. The character of Ruth offers another positive depiction of an Eastern European Jew, linking her to Monika Olifat in *Zirndorf*. However, unlike Monika, Ruth is an angelic figure and thus another character whose depiction in the novel is exaggerated. Her state of innocence equals that of Caspar Hauser, a similarity which is underlined even further by her association with an element or a spirit. If Karen represents the human body, then Ruth represents nature and the human soul:

> Da war ein reines Element, aufgeschlossen, enthusiastisch, mitlebend, mitschwingend; der Instinkt eines jungen Tieres, das sicher schreitet. [...]

86 Jørgensen, *St. Francis*, p. 33. For a similar scene, see also Gustave Flaubert, 'St Julien l'Hospitalier', in *Trois Contes* (Paris: Gallimard, 1966), pp. 81–131 (pp. 127–29).

> Aus Steinen wuchsen ihr Seelen zu. Sie war befreundet mit Wegen, Türen, Zäunen, Laternen, Ladenschildern. [...] der Mut zum eigenen Herzen gab der Atmosphäre um sie einen bestimmten Charakter wie kräftiger Pflanzengeruch (*CW*, II, p. 165).

The surprising word 'Pflanzengeruch' could even be a reference to St Clare, a saint and female follower of St Francis, who was accustomed to calling herself 'Brother Francis's plant'.[87] Ruth is thus a saintly, spiritual character with no perceivable bodily existence as she has devoted her life to helping the poor and supporting her family. Christian finds a spiritual guide in her and they form a very close relationship which, however, at no point carries any sexual connotations. Instead, she makes him understand that he still has a long way ahead of him: '[Er] fing an zu begreifen, daß er nicht sehen und fühlen konnte' (*CW*, II, p. 168). This means his perception has not yet changed sufficiently as he is still unable fully to see the human being in front of him. When Ruth dies at the hands of Karen's brother, the 'Lustmörder' Niels Heinrich, Christian is faced with the biggest challenge of his life: he has to understand why Niels Heinrich rapes and murders Ruth, the virgin with the eyes of a child.

With its depiction of a 'Lustmord' the novel becomes one of a whole range of works of art engaging with this topic. As Maria Tatar shows, there was a widespread obsession with the theme of 'Lustmord' during the 1920s.[88] Otto Dix and George Grosz filled their canvases with the bodies of mutilated prostitutes; Musil's Moosbrugger and Döblin's Reinhold are shown to murder whores in the most brutal way; and Peter Lorre stars as the child-murderer M. in Fritz Lang's *M. Eine Stadt sucht einen Mörder*. At the same time, there were well-known real-life cases such as Fritz Haarmann and Peter Kürten, who were brought to trial.[89] The fact that *Wahnschaffe* was published in 1919, making it a very early depiction of 'Lustmord', is another proof of Wassermann's acute awareness of social developments as well as the demands of the literary market.

Nevertheless, in this early depiction of the theme, Wassermann departs from the usual order of events as he does not choose a derelict prostitute as the victim but an angelic figure. The contrast between the murderer and his victim could therefore not be greater, highlighting the brutality of the crime. To make

87 Jørgensen, *Saint Francis*, p. 110.

88 Maria Tatar, *Lustmord: Sexual Murder in Weimar Germany* (Princeton: Princeton University Press, 1995).

89 Fritz Haarmann (1879–1925), also known as 'Der Schlächter', was tried and sentenced to death in 1925 for the murder of twenty-four men between the ages of ten and twenty-two. Peter Kürten (1883–1931), also known as the'Vampir von Düsseldorf', was tried and sentenced to death in 1931 for the brutal killings of nine women and children. Kürten's was the most notorious case of the Weimar Years and Fritz Lang's film *M.* is partly based on the story.

matters worse, the novel even confronts the reader with a detailed account by Niels Heinrich of how he raped and murdered the young girl:

> Sie habe die Hände aufgehoben, und er habe bemerkt, daß sie, während er draußen gewesen, die Adern an ihren Handgelenken durchgeschnitten habe. Das Blut sei dick heruntergeronnen. Sie müsse es mit einer Glasscherbe getan haben, die zwischen Mauersteinen gesteckt. Da sei er in helle Tobsucht geraten, wie wenn es drauf und dran gewesen wäre, daß sie ihm einer wegnähme. Er habe sie an den Haaren zu Boden gerissen. Sie habe geschrien. Einen einzigen, langen Schrei. Den Schrei höre er noch jetzt. Glied um Glied, Hauch um Hauch, Zuckung um Zuckung sei sie sein geworden. So nur könne man besitzen; so und nicht anders. Himmels-, Gottes-, Erdenseligkeit (*CW*, II, p. 389).

Afterwards he mutilates her body and cuts off her head, acts which make the crime recognisable as a 'Lustmord'. This unsparing account of a sexual murder contributes to the creation of Christian as a saintly figure. The murder and the confession of the crime are not only the climax of the novel's action but also of Christian's spiritual development. The loss of Ruth has led to the crisis in his life, at the end of which he has become a modern saint. As Karlstetter puts it: 'Ihr [Ruth's] Tod ist es schließlich, der ihn in die schwerste Krise seines Lebens führt, deren Überwindung ihn dann den Weg seiner Bestimmung mit aller Konsequenz ergreifen läßt'.[90] Joeris's claim that with the cruel killing of Ruth 'der Holocaust wie im voraus dargestellt [erscheint]' seems inappropriate, given the unimaginable horrors at that time of the Third Reich.[91] The impression of Christian's strength of character and his sainthood is amplified by another detail in the depiction of the murderer: Niels Heinrich is not insane. Both Christian and the reader are denied the easy way out represented by a deranged character who is not really responsible for his crimes. Leja's interpretation of Niels Heinrich as insane is therefore mistaken.[92] Instead, we are presented with a repellent yet intelligent young man who is fully aware of what he has done. Niels Heinrich simply rejects any common values, prefers a state of violence and lawlessness, and could therefore be understood as a personification of evil. In this context it is important to remember that, in the poem by Cornelius Ermelang about St Francis referred to earlier, God is described as watching equally over the good and the bad. Similarly, Christian is determined to see the human being behind this evil shell.

90 Karlstetter, *Bild*, p. 88.

91 Joeris, *Aspekte*, p. 132.

92 Gabriele Leja, 'Jüdische Gestalten im erzählerischen Werk Jakob Wassermanns', in *Jakob Wassermann: Werk und Wirkung*, pp. 66–98 (p. 95).

What is Dostoevsky Doing Here?

When discussing the final scene between Christian and Niels Heinrich, it is crucial to acknowledge Dostoevsky's influence on Wassermann. It might at first seem arbitrary at this point to bring in Dostoevsky, but a comparison between the ending of *The Idiot* and that of *Wahnschaffe* contributes towards Wassermann-Dostoevsky scholarship and makes the parallels between the two novels immediately recognizable. As Horst-Jürgen Gerigk in particular shows, the influence that Dostoevsky had on other writers is of great significance for the development of twentieth-century literature.[93] Wassermann himself professed:

> Es ist kaum möglich, die Erscheinung eines Schriftstellers wie Dostojewski auf einen äußeren Anstoß hin zu umschreiben oder, was sie für die eigene Existenz bedeutet hat, mit einiger Verlässlichkeit zu fixieren. [...] selten noch ist ein einziger Mann, der nicht Religionsstifter oder Welteroberer war, Veranlasser einer so umfassenden Veränderung der psychischen Situation von Generationen gewesen.[94]

In her dissertation Ruth Richter offers a wide-ranging discussion of the influence Dostoevsky's novels and writing techniques had on Wassermann's work, including *Wahnschaffe*.[95] She points out the striking parallels between Prince Myshkin and Christian, yet fails to mention the parallels between Niels Heinrich and Rogozhin. By contrast she considers Voss to be Christian's opponent and thus Rogozhin's parallel figure, a view which leads her to overlook the considerable similarities between the two novels' final scenes.[96] It is in these scenes that Christian and Myshkin are finally revealed as saints, as they have their last encounters with the two murderers who robbed them of those human beings they loved the most: Ruth and Nastassya Filippovna. In the closing passage in Wassermann's novel, when Christian kneels before Niels Heinrich, the text runs:

> Niels Heinrich, heruntergezogen, sank in die Knie. [...] Und sie knieten, einer vor dem andern. Sich selbst entrissen durch Berührung, gab der Mörder

93 Horst-Jürgen Gerigk, *Ein Meister aus Russland: Beziehungsfelder der Wirkung Dostojewskijs* (Heidelberg: Winter, 2010). See also M. Wegner, 'Europäische Romanentwicklung im 20. Jahrhundert und F.M. Dostojewskij', *Zeitschrift für Slawistik*, 21 (1976), 500–12.

94 Jakob Wassermann, 'Einige allgemeine Bemerkungen über Dostojewski', in *Lebensdienst*, pp. 259–63 (pp. 259–61).

95 Ruth Richter, 'Der Einfluss F. M. Dostojevskijs auf die Werke Jakob Wassermann' (unpublished doctoral thesis, University of Bonn, 1951).

96 Richter, 'Der Einfluss F. M. Dostojevskijs', pp. 19–20.

> seine Schuld dem Menschen, der ihn richtete, ohne zu verdammen. Er war frei. Und auch Christian war frei (*CW*, II, pp. 429–30).

After Rogozhin has confessed his murder to Myshkin and lies down with a fever, the events are described in similar terms:

> Dann streckte der Fürst jedesmal seine zitternde Hand nach ihm aus und berührte leise seinen Kopf, seine Haare, streichelte sie und streichelte seine Wangen ... das war alles was er tun konnte. [...] schließlich beugte er sich wie in bereits völliger Entkräftigung und Verzweiflung nieder auf das Kissen und schmiegte sich mit seinem Gesicht an das bleiche und unbewegte Antlitz Rogoshins. Tränen rannen aus seinen Augen auf Rogoshins Wangen.[97]

In both scenes the worldly institutions of justice are of no consequence as they are, at least in the case of Wassermann, shown to be inefficient and flawed. Jütten therefore rightly concludes that for Wassermann 'das rechte Maß und der rechte Ausgleich [...] einzig vom Individuum selbst zu bestimmen [sind]' while any form of institutionalized justice is rejected.[98] Similarly, Flake's protagonist Lauda arrives at the conclusion that 'Strafe ist Rachsucht der Gesellschaft'.[99] However, in both scenes we have saint-like figures carrying out an act of devotion and compassion in front of one of the lowest members of society and thus accepting such figures as part of themselves. As Lion Feuchtwanger puts it in his review of the novel: 'Wie blättert eine behutsame Hand noch die Ärmsten, Bösesten, Vertiertesten auf, bis auf ihren Kern, bis dahin, wo sie dein Bruder, bis dahin, wo sie Du sind!'[100] This is expressed in their physical contact: as Christian and Niels touch each other for the first time, the two extremes included in human nature become one. 'Christian und Niels verkörpern den Kampf des guten und des bösen Prinzips',[101] is how Jütten describes the dynamics between the two figures; and yet it seems that Christian, who has set out to become the lowest of the low, has finally achieved his aim. He does not defeat Niels Heinrich but recognizes him as part of himself, as human nature is inevitably composed of good and evil and God watches over both.

The novel ends with the disappearance of its protagonist. All that remains of him are legends, according to which he is seen doing good in London's East

97 Fjodor M. Dostojewski, *Der Idiot*, trans. by E. K. Rahsin (Munich: Piper, 1954), p. 935. Rahsin's translation of Dostoevsky's entire oeuvre first appeared between 1905 and 1919, so this is most probably the translation Wassermann would have read.

98 Jütten, *Diskurse*, p. 149.

99 Flake, *Stadt*, p. 216.

100 Lion Feuchtwanger, 'Christian Wahnschaffe', in *Ein Buch nur für meine Freunde* (Frankfurt a. M.: Fischer, 1984), pp. 337–42 (p. 340).

101 Jütten, *Diskurse*, p. 132.

End, New York's China Town or at the scene of a mining accident: always among the poor and as close as possible to human misery. Apart from being a remarkable technique of fictional closure, it is the final moment in Christian's transformation into a modern saint: the transcendence of the self becomes his greatest achievement. He has ceased to be the person he was to the extent that he has even given up his name. The question of what a modern saint actually does is mostly avoided in favour of this spiritual triumph. That Christian's development is now complete is further emphasized when Voss mocks him and is subsequently called 'Judas' by one of Christian's friends (*CW*, II, p. 447). Following this analogy further leads to the conclusion that Christian has now become Christ.

This panorama of multi-faceted pre-war Europe is an ambitious attempt to attain the rank of world literature and marks an important step in Wassermann's writing career. It is a proof of his engagement with other writers and writing traditions, as he tries to assimilate Dostoevsky and offers by far the largest-scale treatment of the Expressionist theme of the 'neuer Mensch'. However, it can also be seen as an attempt to come to terms with the dramatic social and political changes brought about by the events of the War. Wassermann's 'solution' might seem peculiar at first, as he introduces a saintly figure into the modern world, yet unlike other saints Christian has no real followers and founds no movement but tries to be saintly in the context of everyday life. It is this engagement with the ordinary that allows Christian to explore different modes of perception and arrive at the celebration of selflessness expressed in the disappearance of his character. The novel is nevertheless not a rejection of modernity and the changes to which it has led, but rather an attempt to combine modernity with a profound love of humanity. Not to forget the human being in the daily chaos of modern existence and to recognize human nature even in the lowest members of society form one of the novel's central messages.

CHAPTER 4

A World Beyond Hope – the Impossibility of Character in *Der Fall Maurizius* (1928)

Introduction

Wassermann's most famous and most successful novel, even beyond the German-speaking world, *Der Fall Maurizius* (1928) is an open expression of the author's disillusionment since his lifelong mission, namely his struggle against injustice, has failed.[1] Beginning with *Maurizius,* we are therefore confronted with the pessimistic outlook of the late Wassermann who has observed the rise of Nazism in the Weimar Republic and realized that its influence would soon spread to his 'Wahlheimat' Austria. In the last years of his life, as documented in his *Selbstbetrachtungen* (1933), he was left feeling more and more isolated as he feared the rise of a 'Barbarenära' in which art would be of no consequence.[2] Given the general state of society and people's loneliness, alongside their political radicalization with its ever-increasing appeal to the masses, Wassermann has come to consider the project of being a writer an ethical failure. Wassermann's writing is, therefore, no longer informed by the Humanist principle of writing as a means of educating his readers, which Neubauer identifies as a key characteristic of his works.[3] As an artist he has thus lost faith in the possibility of art being an agent for change in a world that is beyond hope:

> Nicht als ob es nicht da und dort Ergriffene gäbe, Reuige und der Verwandlung Fähige, aber am Lauf der Welt ändert sich nichts, am Haß, an der Lüge, am

1 This is Wassermann's only work to have been the basis for a post-war TV production: Theodor Kotulla, *Der Fall Maurizius* (ZDF, 20 September 1981). Tom Appleton informs us that *Der Fall Maurizius* is the biggest success by a German author in the USA thus far, with more than one million copies sold in hardcover during Wassermann's lifetime alone: Jakob Wassermann, *The Maurizius Case* (London: Allen & Unwin, 1930) (Tom Appleton, 'Nachwort', in Jakob Wassermann, *Christoph Columbus: Der Don Quichote des Ozeans* (Munich: DTV, 1992), pp. 217–21.

2 For another example of this pessimism, see also Jakob Wassermann, 'Der Jude in der Kunst' (1932), in *Reden und Schriften,* pp. 157–61.

3 Neubauer, *Schriftsteller*, p. 93.

> Mißverständnis, am Wahn und an der Ungerechtigkeit nichts. […] warum vermag im Bösen ein Einzelner so viel, und im Guten ein Einzelner fast nichts? Es ist in großen und in kleinen Dingen so, das bricht den Mut in uns.[4]

Anticipating his *Selbstbetrachtungen, Maurizius* is Wassermann's bleakest work so far, with very little space for hope to thrive. Esther Schneider-Handschin sees a further indicator for the author's pessimistic mood in his initial consideration of 'Deutsches Inferno' as a more drastic title for the novel.[5] The society depicted in the novel is far beyond the problem of the earlier 'Trägheit des Herzens' and thus, it seems, beyond the possibility of redemption. Gershon Shaked's claim that in his innocence as a victim of society Maurizius offers many parallels to Caspar Hauser is therefore problematic.[6] In the society that Wassermann depicts now, this kind of innocence has indeed become unimaginable. Instead, people are shown to be without compassion as they live in a state of emotional isolation. Schäfer has, therefore, rightly observed that in this novel nobody even seems to have a friend.[7] Characters are callous and remain opaque to each other as they have become incapable of maintaining relationships. Against the background of an ostensible murder mystery, Wassermann unfolds a version of the modern condition that is in many ways a negation of his previous hopes. The author who for so long refused to give up his belief in a better world has now created a searching portrayal of individual and social life which has, almost inevitably, turned into a destructive critique of civilization and an even more pessimistic vision of its future.

Maurizius can in part be understood as a recapitulation of some of the topics that preoccupied Wassermann throughout his career as a writer, most significantly the question of justice and the role of the Jew in an increasingly anti-Semitic society. Alongside the novel's aesthetic merits, these topics have already received considerable discussion in the relevant secondary literature and will therefore be of little importance in this chapter. Instead, this chapter will offer a different reading of the novel in which the Maurizius case retreats into the background to make room for the analysis of Wassermann's portrayal of modern life in relation to his ongoing concern with the depiction of character.[8] Analysis will show that the judicial murder which seemingly

4 Jakob Wassermann, *Selbstbetrachtungen* (Berlin: Fischer, 1933), pp. 105–06.

5 Esther Schneider-Handschin, *Das Bild des Bürgertums in Jakob Wassermanns 'Andergast-Trilogie'* (Bern etc.: Peter Lang, 1990), p. 19.

6 Shaked, 'Fall', p. 109.

7 Schäfer, *Plaidoyer*, p. 53.

8 This approach agrees with Peter de Mendelssohn's view that the novel's concern with questions of justice and guilt is only 'vordergründig' (Peter de Mendelssohn, 'Nachwort', in *Der Fall Maurizius* (Vienna – Munich: Langen Müller, 1981), pp. 541–63 (p. 544).

stands at the centre of the narrative merely serves to frame a work of fiction that is arguably not even a crime novel. This stands in strong opposition to Garrin's claim that despite the 'various digressions and excursions [...] the murder trial remains the core of the novel'.[9] Rather than focusing on the plight of the prisoner Maurizius, this chapter will concentrate on two other aspects of the novel: first, the portrayal of identity as performable and unstable and the impact this has on the human relationships depicted; second, the fact that towards the end of his literary career Wassermann once again returns to the figure of the outsider. After having left that figure behind, Wassermann now presents us with the homosexual Jew Georg Warschauer. He makes this predominantly negative character into a spokesman for an indictment of Western civilization and fails to introduce any contrasting figure to oppose Warschauer's overwhelming cynicism. To use Schäfer's words, the novel therefore becomes a 'beklemmendes Dokument eines von Verzweiflung und Destruktion geprägten Lebensgefühls'.[10]

The novel presents its reader with a curious constellation of characters. First, we have Wolf Freiherr von Andergast, a prosecutor who is made responsible for a judicial murder that was crucial to his professional success. Second, we have the prisoner Leonhart Maurizius, who, in order to protect the woman he thought he loved, namely Anna Jahn, the murderess and sister of his wife Elli, serves a life sentence even though he is innocent. Finally, there is Gregor Waremme, an intellectual of great gifts with promising future prospects who, in order to destroy Maurizius, ruins his own career and commits the perjury that makes this life sentence inevitable. As they are all involved in the crime of incarcerating the wrong man, all three men receive the same punishment: irrespective of actual prison walls, they are all doomed to a life in solitary confinement. This means that after the trial they each begin to lead a life of almost complete social isolation, incapable of maintaining relationships with others. Contrary to a conventional murder mystery, the idea of bringing the actual culprit Anna Jahn to justice is absent from the novel, which is a first indicator that the actual solving of the crime is only of secondary importance.

This Andergast-Waremme-Maurizius triangle embodies a negative version of the disappearance of character which is best described as the disintegration of character. In *Wahnschaffe* the gradual disappearance of the protagonist's persona is depicted as a positive development that leads to modern sainthood; and even in *Laudin und die Seinen*, a novel published as late as 1925, the protagonist's longing for a different self carries positive connotations.[11]

9 Garrin, *Concept*, p. 15.

10 Schäfer, *Plaidoyer*, p. 77.

11 Jakob Wassermann, *Laudin und die Seinen* (Berlin: Fischer, 1925).

Wassermann's take on the question of character in *Der Fall Maurizius*, is, however, far more dismal: character seems to have become impossible, in the sense that none of the main figures is able to maintain a stable identity. Pazi's claim that Wassermann's concept of 'Doppeltsein' is nothing but a masquerade is thus open to question, because 'das wahre "Ich" [...] absolut die Wahl der jeweiligen Identität [beherrscht]'.[12] Instead, the instability of one's identity was for Wassermann one of the negative side effects of the modern condition. Further evidence for his concern with this question can be found in his *Selbstbetrachtungen*, where he writes about:

> [d]ie maßlose Zerrüttung unserer Welt, die sich bei unzähligen Einzelnen in einer bis zur Psychose gesteigerten Existenzangst äußert und eine bis in den Kern jeder Gemeinschaft dringende geistige und moralische Unsicherheit erzeugt hat, ja sogar im Begriff ist, die Fundamente der Persönlichkeit zu untergraben und damit die Idee des Menschentums und die des Gottestums zu stürzen.[13]

As a result of the 'maßlose Zerrüttung unserer Welt', all the novel's main characters have several identities forced onto them by the surrounding circumstances and not necessarily by their own choice. They even serve one another as mirror images. Schneider-Handschin's claim that Wassermann was unwilling to part with traditional narrative styles and thus failed to deal with an increasingly complex reality in his works is thus in need of revision.[14]

As with the previous chapter, one aim here is indeed to refute the claim that Wassermann was an exceedingly traditional, even anti-modern author. Theo Elm, for example, has classified Wassermann among authors such as Franz Werfel or Stefan Zweig, who, 'mit Schicksalsformeln und moralistischem Credo gegen die Moderne die "Welt von Gestern" beschwören'.[15] This portrayal of Wassermann and Werfel as conservative *Bildungsbürger* is unfair in light of the fact that they both retain elements of radical Expressionism, such as the dramatic father-son conflict. The comparison to Zweig's autobiography is uncalled-for since Wassermann's own autobiography, *Mein Weg als Deutscher und Jude*, could not be less nostalgic. Even in those novels that are set in an earlier period, for example *Caspar Hauser*, he offers a critical picture of society and clearly refrains from idealizing the past.

12 Margarita Pazi, 'Die Kraft des Intellekts: Jakob Wassermanns "Der Fall Maurizius"', in *Juden in der Weimarer Republik*, ed. by Julius H. Schoeps and Walter Grab (Stuttgart: Burg, 1986), pp. 61–88 (p. 67).

13 Wassermann, *Selbstbetrachtungen*, p. 17.

14 Schneider-Handschin, *Bild*, pp. 73–74.

15 Elm, 'Talmud', p. 136.

In the midst of this triangle of identities that sometimes seem to collapse into one another stands Etzel Andergast, who is ambitious to solve the Maurizius case, yet soon finds himself drawn into this world of unstable identities. For reasons of structure it is most appropriate to analyse, first, Etzel's relationships with his father and Waremme; and, second, their relationship with Maurizius in order to understand the connections between those characters. That way it will become apparent how the novel's structure supports the depiction of the mirror images which stand at its centre. This analysis will also reveal that the popular image of Etzel as a 'brother' of Agathon Geyer (*Zirndorf*) or even Caspar Hauser (*Caspar*) is in need of revision. Analysis will also show that Martina Landscheidt's description of Etzel as a 'reiner Gerechtigkeitssucher'[16] is as erroneous as Isabelle Classen's claim that Etzel remains free from guilt[17] or Koester's description of him as an 'Idealfigur'.[18] Similarly, it remains doubtful as to whether Etzel really is the purest embodiment of Wassermann's messianic vision, as claimed by Elm.[19] As a result of his altered and more pessimistic outlook, Wassermann is no longer willing, or indeed able, to produce the type of adolescent hero who is an unequivocally positive figure. Until now the figure of the child or adolescent has still been allowed the position of the innocent outsider in Wassermann's writing. The character of Etzel therefore embodies a critical review of this position which adds another layer of significance to it. By this point Etzel is a more apposite expression of the ways in which modern life has impacted on human relationships, as even childhood has ceased to be a space of innocence. Since Etzel's character in *Maurizius* is already understood as bearing traits that can be called negative, it is less surprising that when he returns in *Etzel Andergast* (1931) he is depicted as a dislikeable, fallen hero.

Critical Reception

Given the amount of critical attention *Maurizius* has received compared with Wassermann's other works, it is appropriate to give a brief overview before starting with the analysis. In general critics differ sharply on the aesthetic merits of the novel. In his lengthy critique, Kaspar Schnetzler focuses on elements of style and technique, based on which he aims to defend the novel as

16 Landscheidt, 'Mutmaßungen', p. 25.

17 Isabelle Classen, 'Wider die Todesstrafe: Über Vorlage und Fabel zum *Fall Maurizius*', in *Jakob Wassermann: Werk und Wirkung*, ed. by Rudolf Wolff (Bonn: Bouvier, 1987) pp. 33–46 (p. 43).

18 Koester, *Wassermann*, p. 74.

19 Elm, 'Talmud', p. 135.

an important and ingeniously constructed work of art.[20] By contrast, Marcus Bullock more recently maintains that Wassermann is, in fact, indifferent to any aesthetic consideration.[21] The representation of the legal system in the novel was the main focus of contemporary criticism, as can be deduced from Neubauer's overview. The novel was, indeed, one of the most widely discussed books of the Weimar Republic and even received reviews in publications specializing in questions of law and criminology. Opinions regarding Wassermann's success in depicting the judicial system, as well as the literary merit of the work as a whole, differ greatly. They range from referring to the novel as superficial and 'effekthascherisch' to comparing it to a Greek tragedy. The overall consensus, however, seems to be that Wassermann's depiction exhibits a tendency to be one-sided in its sympathy for the prisoner Maurizius and even 'rechtsfeindlich'.[22] Interestingly, in his diary Schnitzler, who knew Wassermann well, compares *Maurizius* to Arnold Zweig's *Grischa*:

> Lese Arnold Zweigs Grischa. Außerordentlich. Gegen Maurizius gehalten: Wenn man Jacob fragte (in einer Tiefe wo man nicht lügen kann) – Wählen Sie – entweder Justizreform oder neue hundert Auflagen – seine Antwort: Hundert Auflagen. Fragte man Zweig: Ihr Roman verschwindet für ewig – aber Grischa ist gerettet – seine Antwort: Grischa's Rettung! – Und das spürt man natürlich in den Romanen selbst.[23]

In a similar vein, Stephen Garrin considers the trilogy as a whole, focusing on the question of justice and arriving at the result that each volume in the trilogy deals with a different concept of justice: namely judicial, social and moral.[24] Peter de Mendelssohn looks at the genealogy of the novel and offers a comparison to the famous real-life case of Karl Hau that allegedly served as its template. Moreover, he considers the question of whether Warschauer can be seen as an autobiographical figure in the sense that he embodies Wassermann's divided identity as a German and a Jew.[25] Pazi's interpretation shows how the character of Warschauer is used to illustrate Wassermann's failed attempt to assimilate into German society.[26] Similarly, Jütten discusses

20 Kaspar Schnetzler, *Der Fall Maurizius: Jakob Wassermanns Kunst des Erzählens* (Bern: Herbert Lang & Cie, 1968).

21 Marcus Bullock, 'Jakob Wassermann's novel *Der Fall Maurizius* presents the final expression of his views on the relationship of Germans and Jews', in *Yale Companion to Jewish Writing and Thought in German Culture, 1096–1996*, ed. by Sander L. Gilman and Jack Zipes (New Haven and London: Yale University Press, 1997), pp. 471–79.

22 See Neubauer, *Schriftsteller*, pp. 69–77.

23 Schnitzler, *Tagebuch*, IX, 19 June 1928.

24 Garrin, *Concept*, p. 15.

25 Mendelssohn, 'Nachwort', pp. 541–63.

26 Pazi, 'Kraft', pp. 61–88.

the character of Warschauer as an embodiment of the fate of the over-assimilated Jew who wastes all his potential by trying to move from the East to the West.[27] Shaked, too, arrives at the conclusion that Warschauer is without a doubt the Jewish 'shadow' that haunted Wassermann throughout his life.[28] Schneider-Handschin's analysis considers the trilogy as a whole and examines the three works in relation to their own time as well as to their socio-historical context. She presents Wassermann as a member of the 'Bildungsbürgertum'; and the trilogy as an expression of the conservative pessimism of this class as well as Wassermann's cultural criticism and his rejection of processes of modernization.[29] Similarly, Bullock claims the author is a spokesman for the past who is guilty of neglecting philosophical discrimination as his ideology is sustained by pathos instead of a more structured position.[30] Jütten, by contrast, shows that any longing for justice in the novel can be understood as a longing for revenge. Moreover, she reveals that the judicial system is not only immoral but also serves to maintain a bourgeois 'Scheinmoral'.[31] The following analysis will incline towards Jütten's views in the sense that Wassermann will be shown to be a fierce critic of the society in which he lived.

Father and Son

In *Maurizius* childhood is no longer a safe space as Etzel grows up in a world in which maternal tenderness is unavailable and the relationship with his father is largely characterized by its non-existence. When Wolf von Andergast finds out about his wife's adulterous affair he drives her lover into committing suicide and deprives her of any contact with her son. Andergast's relationship with Etzel is essentially the relationship between two actors, pretending to be father and son according to their individual understanding of the role. As a consequence, each knows only the other's interpretation of that role but not the actual person behind it. For Etzel the world of the father is dark, mysterious and ultimately unknowable. Hence he privately starts calling him 'Trismegistos', or 'thrice-greatest', which refers to Hermes Trismegistos, the alleged author of the *Hermetic Corpus*. A combination of the Greek god Hermes and the Egyptian god Thoth, he was given the sobriquet 'thrice-greatest' by the Greeks (*c.* third century BC) because he was believed to be the greatest philosopher, priest and king of his age. When applied to Etzel's situation, this nickname strongly

27 Jütten, *Diskurse*, pp. 251–90.
28 Shaked,'Fall', pp. 94–112.
29 Schneider-Handschin, *Bild*, p. 212.
30 Bullock, 'Wassermann's novel', pp. 471–79.
31 Jütten, *Diskurse*, pp. 251–90.

conveys the fact that he feels overwhelmed and intimidated by his father, yet at the same time it carries satirical connotations, a first hint at the son's growing resistance. However, Garrin's interpretation of the name Trismegistos as 'the monster who has denied the boy of his mother' has missed the point.[32]

Acting has a crucial function in the game of varying identities as it is presented throughout the novel; and Etzel receives his training, so to speak, at home by observing his father. He soon realizes that his father's acting is a means of maintaining a certain distance between them:

> Ihre [Andergast's hand] stumme Beredsamkeit oder ausdrucksvolle Ruhe ließ bisweilen an die Hand eines Schauspielers denken, eines besonders erfahrenen und überlegenen allerdings, der nur strenge und gelassene Charaktere verkörpert und sie wohlerwogen 'spielt', nicht geradezu lebt, sondern eben spielt, um begreiflich zu machen, daß der die Distanz wahrt (*FM*, pp. 15–16).[33]

Etzel is inevitably affected in a negative way by his father's extremely formal and cold behaviour towards him. He not only becomes taciturn and reserved at a very young age but also comes to understand acting as a handy tool when he wants to use other people for his own benefit. He is frequently shown to put on an act with the housekeeper or his grandmother, yet, most importantly, he uses his acting skills in his fight against Waremme, as will be shown later. The reference to Andergast's acting but not living his role is crucial for the understanding of his character. He is unable to live his role because he has neglected his inner life to the extent that it has virtually disappeared. His life is characterized by complete social isolation, with the obvious exception of social obligations resulting from his position in society. Moreover, there is the uncanny exception of his 'lover' Violet Winston, a young American woman whom he met three years earlier and for whom he decided to rent an apartment, in return for which she is obliged to receive him there two or three times a month. Besides Andergast's relationship with Etzel, this secret affair with Violet is the most striking expression of his lack of emotions. The narrator describes Andergast's attraction towards her as follows:

> Sie bot ihm nichts, sie war ihm nichts, denn sie hatte nichts zu geben, sie war selber – nichts. Und eben dieses Nichts brauchte er. [...] Er lebte ja seit zehn Jahren ehelos, und er wußte, daß die Wünsche des Körpers sich auf die Dauer nicht ersticken lassen ohne Gefährdung des geistigen Gleichgewichts (*FM*, p. 218).

Even sexuality is, therefore, nothing but an inevitable physical urge that one has to satisfy, like hunger or thirst, and does not allow people to connect with

32 Garrin, *Concept*, p. 32.

33 For the original edition, see Jakob Wassermann, *Der Fall Maurizius* (Berlin: Fischer, 1928).

each other. Andergast would be unable to share any kind of intimacy with an actual person and therefore refuses to acknowledge Violet as an individual human being. To him she is nothing but a body fulfilling a function. This also becomes apparent when the only conversations they have are meaningless ones about everyday objects. Her stupid blue eyes remind him of nothing, a feature which becomes a source of comfort for Andergast as he has nothing to offer in return. In this version human relationships are therefore reduced to their physical minimum. One of the characters in Klaus Mann's novel *Treffpunkt im Unendlichen* (1932), which is set at around the same time as *Maurizius*, makes a similar observation regarding people's emotional isolation as the one in Wassermann's novel:

> [W]ir könnten uns überhaupt nicht vorstellen, daß der andere wirklich lebt, daß er seinerseits auch ein Ich ist. So gründlich sind wir von einander getrennt. Ich finde, das wäre ja nicht so schlimm, wenn nicht gleichzeitig der eine so auf den anderen angewiesen wäre, zu dem er doch keinen Zugang hat, er kann ihn sich nicht einmal vorstellen, genaugenommen existiert er also gar nicht für ihn. Er braucht etwas, das gar nicht für ihn existiert. So isoliert und dabei so hilfbedürftig zu sein – das ist doch gräßlich; ganz trostlos ist das doch einfach.[34]

Andergast therefore lives in the world physically but without being part of it through relationships with others. Even what would have seemed like inevitable spaces for more profound relationships, namely the family and sexuality, do not prompt Andergast to go beyond his usual reserve.

Following on from the role of perception in *Wahnschaffe*, Andergast's state of isolation is emphasized by his inhibited viewpoint. When he has to greet people in the street he does so with a 'blicklosem Nicken' as he simply refuses to see the world around him: 'Sein steif voran gerichteter Blick nahm an den Bildern der Straße keinen Anteil. Nicht nur das, seine Miene leugnete gleichsam ihre Wirklichkeit' (*FM*, p. 25). Just as he refuses to acknowledge Violet as an individual human being, Andergast also refuses to accept any reality outside himself. In many ways, Andergast is, therefore, unable to see. Instead of relating to other people he prefers to control them and thus turn them into a part of his own reality in which he is in charge. As a result, Andergast becomes the representative of two systems of oppression: that of law and punishment, affecting the prisoner Maurizius; and that of surveillance and control surrounding Etzel. The analysis of the two systems will show how they both have the same effect: Etzel and Maurizius both lose their freedom as they become Andergast's prisoners. This also offers the first significant overlap between the situations of two characters. The narrator even refers to Andergast

34 Klaus Mann, *Treffpunkt im Unendlichen* (Reinbek: Rowohlt, 1981), p. 144.

as Etzel's 'Gefangenenwärter' (*FM*, p. 36) and the world in which the boy lives is described as follows: 'Er lebte zwischen gläsernen Wänden. [...] Es war ein schweigsames System. In der kritischen Lage schienen dann alle Bewohner des Hauses freiwilligen Spionagedienst zu verrichten. Auch Lieferanten, Boten, Briefträger, Amtsdiener waren dem überall spürbaren obersten Willen untertan' (*FM*, p. 13). This system, with its totalitarian structure in which people cannot trust each other, does not differ significantly from the world Maurizius is confined within, for he also lives under constant surveillance and has limited personal freedom.

The other interesting aspect of these systems is their association with specific rooms and, in turn, the relationship between Andergast and these rooms. In the case of the prisoner Maurizius the system of law and punishment is obviously associated with the prison he finds himself in, yet the significance of the jail image does not end there. As can partly be deduced from the above-quoted passage, Etzel not only associates the system of surveillance that surrounds him with the house in which he lives, but also associates the house with his father. In Etzel's view Andergast almost becomes indistinguishable from his house as his presence is perceptible through every object in it: 'Seine [Andergast's] Energien strahlen auf die Sachen über' (*FM*, p. 14). Kaspar Schnetzler also draws our attention to this relationship between people and rooms in the novel: 'Es besteht eine fließende Korrespondenz zwischen Mensch, Raum und Ding. Denn nicht nur prägt der Mensch den Raum, sondern der Raum und das Ding prägen den Menschen. Die Lebensräume geben demnach Auskunft über die Personen, die in ihnen wohnen'.[35] Tellingly, Etzel even looks at his father as if he were 'ein Turm, der keinen Zugang hat, keine Türen, keine Fenster' (*FM*, p. 33). In his son's imagination, Andergast has therefore become a kind of prison tower.

Moreover, Andergast is described as having a hesitant, halting gait, characteristic of people who spend a lot of their time in closed rooms. As a representative of these systems of control Andergast has become the prisoner of these systems, since he is confined to the rooms in which he works so as to deprive others of their freedom. Andergast has spent most of his life locked up in his office and his study at home, from where he has managed these systems of control. His study is described as 'nüchtern und trostlos' (*FM*, p. 227), a room of which there are thousands in every city and which all have the same impact on the men who spend their time in them: 'Sie prägen die Gesichter der Männer, die sich während eines großen Teils ihres Lebens darin aufhalten, sie hauchen ihnen ihre Nüchternheit und Trostlosigkeit ein'

35 Schnetzler, *Kunst*, p. 60.

(*FM*, p. 227). Andergast's case is therefore not unique: he is part of a system in which those who imprison and those who are imprisoned are equally without freedom: 'Zuletzt hat der Hüter selbst keine Freiheit mehr' (*FM*, p. 36). This offers an overlap between Andergast and Maurizius as they have become each other's captives. At the same time, the similarity in their situation may also be a reason for Etzel's strong desire to free Maurizius, as they are both victims of his father.

When Etzel secretly runs away to Berlin in order to solve the crime and free Maurizius, of whose innocence he is immediately convinced once he hears about the case, Andergast's two systems of control begin to fall apart. This is because Etzel does not merely break out of a system of obsessive parental control but also aims to destroy one of his father's greatest achievements as a prosecutor, namely the Maurizius case. As Henry Miller points out: Etzel's 'chivalrous deed is prompted by a spirit of vengeance: he wants to destroy his father's work'.[36] While Jütten arrives at the conclusion that 'Etzels Motivationslage [...] zweideutig [ist]',[37] Shaked even claims that the wish to free himself from his father's authority is indeed Etzel's main source of motivation.[38] Etzel will ultimately reject his father as a parent and as a prosecutor. The consequences of this initial act of rebellion are immediately observable with Andergast, as it is Etzel's disobedience that prompts him to re-engage with the Maurizius case. In the end Etzel not only succeeds in destroying the system of control that has surrounded him for so many years, but his father, too, is left destroyed. Their relationship therefore offers a direct link to the Weimar years, during which, according to Peukert, the battle between the generations was particularly severe and the overall result was a considerable loss of parental authority, especially among the bourgeoisie.[39]

The transformation Andergast undergoes throughout the novel, ending in his collapse, begins with a radical change in his perception. However, contrary to the case of Christian Wahnschaffe, his altered perception proves to have detrimental consequences. Before Etzel leaves, Andergast lacks compassion and interest in his fellow human beings. Situated comfortably within the system, locked up in his office, Andergast is blind to the consequences of his ruthless activity. All he can see in another person is a potential criminal. However, when the system that he has considered invincible is dealt a first blow by Etzel's disappearance, his perception begins to change. As with Christian Wahnschaffe, Andergast's altered perception is initially inspired by several

36 Henry Miller, *Maurizius Forever* (Michigan City, Indiana: Fridtjof-Karla Publications, 1959), p. 6.

37 Jütten, *Diskurse*, p. 275.

38 Shaked, *Macht*, p. 101.

39 See Peukert, *Die Weimarer Republik*, pp. 92, 97.

moments of *mémoires involontaires*. Images of Etzel as a young boy keep appearing in front of his inner eye. Most importantly, though, these images are intertwined with material from the Maurizius case, thus confirming the parallel status that Etzel and the prisoner have for Andergast:

> Es wurde nach und nach angreifend lästig, wie sich die Bilder und Gesichter, die sich aus der Beschäftigung mit dem Proceß ergaben, mit denen aus Etzel's Kindheit vermengten. Es war als hätte er eines jener Opiate eingenommen, die den Willen aufheben und den Geist in zuchtlose Phantasien stürzen (*FM*, p. 165).

These recurring images of Etzel gradually turn into an obsession (*Zwangsvorstellung*), especially as their theme is always the same: the little child is at a loss to understand why his father does not want to spend time with him, thus rejecting his son's love. This image of Etzel becomes a symbol of the life Andergast could have had if he had not been so self-absorbed and refused to interact with other people.

Andergast chooses to replace any emotional attachment by a sense of control which results in severely limited perception. He comes to understand these limits, and even his own lack of perception, in the course of his transformation:

> Niemals in seiner ganzen Praxis war es ihm vorgekommen, daß er die Dinge und Personen sah. Trug vielleicht jener quasi-opiumisierte Zustand daran Schuld, durch den er auch gezwungen war, das vergangene Leben seines Kindes zu sehen, statt, wie er getan, es bloß zu wissen? (*FM*, p. 166).

Through the constant confrontation with this 'film' from Etzel's childhood, Andergast becomes conscious of the extent of his own loneliness, as he does not even know his own son. The implications of the verb 'sehen' here are brought out well by Jütten, who says that Andergast begins 'die Dinge nicht nur zu wissen, sondern zu sehen, d. h. sie in subjektiv-lebendiger Weise zu erfassen'.[40] As we will see later, Andergast is the first of Wassermann's characters to undergo this process of a changing perception, with the result he has to accept that his life is beyond the possibility of change and has been wasted. Altered perception therefore no longer necessarily leads to redemption.

In the novel's final scene Andergast makes a last, desperate attempt to regain control over Etzel as he literally chases his son through the house. However, Etzel violently rejects any bond with his father and thus deals him the final blow: 'Ich will nicht dein Sohn sein' (*FM*, p. 603). Classen has mentioned that the complicated father-son-relationship and Andergast's insanity are typical

40 Jütten, *Diskurse*, p. 273.

Expressionist themes, a point worth exploring in further research.[41] Moreover, this scene offers a point of comparison with Werfel's *Nicht der Mörder, der Ermordete ist schuldig*, in which the reader is also confronted by son and father chasing each other around a table, ending in the latter's collapse.[42]

In our context this scene is significant for two reasons. It adds a physical aspect to the disappearance of Andergast's character through the depiction of his final breakdown. The narrator informs us that there is nothing left but a guilty human being. Moreover, Etzel stands and gazes at his father's 'sich förmlich zersetzende Gesicht' (*FM*, p. 605). His father's face thus almost literally disintegrates. Therefore even Andergast's face has now disappeared to be replaced by a staring mask unable to produce any facial expressions. Neither Andergast nor his prisoner survives the revelation of Maurizius's innocence, though only the latter actually dies while Andergast breaks down into insanity. Andergast's altered perception, his ability to empathize with the people around him and the subsequent disappearance of his old character have led, contrary to the case of Christian Wahnschaffe, to nothing but insanity. This can be seen as a radical departure by Wassermann, expressing his loss of faith in the ability to see as a means to a better world. The notion of Wassermann's break with the idea of altered perception as a means of transforming character will be discussed further in relation to the character of Waremme.

In addition the scene is revealing because of its depiction of Etzel. After he finds out he has fought in vain because Maurizius has already accepted his pardon without demanding rehabilitation, Etzel is in a frenzy and is described by the narrator as follows: 'Das ist nicht mehr der scharmante, beherrschte vernünftige besonnene kleine Etzel, das ist ein Teufel' (*FM*, p. 603). This other, potentially violent, side to Etzel's character is underlined further when he destroys all the furniture in his room and is left with blood streaming down his face: 'Tobsüchtiger Zerstörungstrieb. Raserei der Seele. Von den Schläfen, Wangen, Nase rieselte das Blut' (*FM*, p. 604). This portrayal of an aggressive and uncontrolled Etzel could be understood as a first foreboding of his later development and eventual fall in *Andergast*. Moreover, Garrin's view that 'Etzel wins his struggle: his father must yield and the prisoner is pardoned' misses the actual reasons for the final conflict between father and son.[43] At this point it also becomes clear that Etzel differs considerably from Wassermann's other childlike or adolescent heroes such as Agathon Geyer or Caspar Hauser. The other important feature of this depiction is the fact that

41 Classen, 'Todesstrafe', p. 40.

42 Franz Werfel, *Nicht der Mörder, der Ermordete ist schuldig: Eine Novelle* (Munich: Wolff, 1922), pp. 217–20.

43 Garrin, *Concept*, p. 48.

Etzel is without compassion. Even when his father breaks down in front of him, lying helpless on the floor, he merely watches him instead of trying to help. It is this lack of compassion that separates him more than anything else from Wassermann's previous heroes. As a result the end of the novel offers no space for reconciliation, unlike most of the author's previous works.

Andergast and His Other Prisoner

According to the novel, therefore, a life that has been spent in social isolation is a wasted life. This insight allows us to pursue another overlap between two characters, namely between Andergast and his prisoner Maurizius. As part of his changing perception Andergast comes to understand, in the course of his visits, that he and Maurizius have essentially been living the same life for the last nineteen years. During their conversations the two characters undergo a process of becoming interchangeable at times, something which eventually leads to the disintegration of Andergast's personality. When Andergast visits the prisoner Maurizius in his cell, he is confronted by another version of his own life, one that might be regarded as a mirror image. The most significant moment in this process is when Maurizius recites the speech Andergast gave at his trial nineteen years previously, one that Andergast always considered a masterpiece, yet when he hears it from the lips of the prisoner he suddenly finds it repellent: 'Während er auf den zusammengebückten Sträfling niederschaute, wuchs die Abneigung gegen die eigene, eben aus anderm Mund vernommene Suada bis zu körperlichem Ekel, so daß er schließlich sogar mit einem Brechreiz zu kämpfen hatte und die Zähne konvulsivisch aufeinanderbiß' (*FM*, p. 308). Andergast, the control freak, suddenly looses control over his body. Another parallel between the two characters is the fact that Maurizius, too, has a child he knows hardly anything about; and one cannot be sure that he has actually ever seen his daughter.

Through this confrontation with Maurizius and thus with his own life, Andergast gradually becomes estranged from his own character until the blurring of the two figures leads to the disappearance of his self. It is, therefore, in the prisoner's presence that Andergast begins to doubt the stability of his self: 'Oder war nur in ihm etwas morsch, das Gefüge seines Ich geborsten?' (*FM*, p. 308). As a side effect of this process, Andergast even begins to use the same gestures as Maurizius (*FM*, p. 469) and soon after he begins to feel as if 'der feste Kern seiner Persönlichkeit [...] auseinander geronnen [wäre]' (*FM*, p. 470). Through this process the agony of the prisoner becomes his own as a consequence of which he decides to free him immediately. At the same time, Andergast's own character has disappeared and agony is all that is left to him:

he has alienated even his closest family members (his son and his own mother) and his work as a prosecutor now strikes him as meaningless. Just before his final breakdown and his subsequent insanity, Andergast exists only in relation to Maurizius. He searches the streets at night filled with the desire to run into him, as if he were trying to retrieve his personality that way. Andergast has, in fact, ceased to exist in any other way: 'Es hat Abende und Nächte gegeben, in denen sich Herr von Andergast wie ein alter ego des Sträflings Maurizius erschienen ist. Eingemauert im Haus der Erinnerungen' (*FM*, p. 591). He has thus become the prisoner's second self.

This episode also shows how the novel's formal properties, in this case the use of doubling structures, help to highlight Wassermann's concern with the instability or disintegration of character. He therefore uses an established literary tool to create an atmosphere of uncertainty and collapse which at times leaves even the reader confused and bewildered.[44] Wassermann here makes a more strategic use of the novel's formal properties than in his previous works, making it clear that *Maurizius* is more strictly composed in terms of its narrative frame. Within this frame, he creates, through the doubling structures, a well-planned chaos. In Wassermann's version some characters thus become indistinguishable from each other, from their own as well as the reader's perspective, leaving little room for anything like an individual identity. The structural concept of using mirroring figures intrigued Wassermann to the extent that he continued to explore it throughout his trilogy.

Etzel and Warschauer – Father and Son Revisited

The other key relationship portrayed in the novel is the one between Etzel and Gregor Waremme, alias Georg Warschauer. Like no other figure in the novel, Waremme embodies the instability of character in a modern world with all its possibilities and downsides, as he comprises various lives, characters and names in one person. By constantly putting on an act or performing, Warschauer challenges Etzel to do the same and thus lures him into a game of false identities that remains ultimately unsolvable, thus confirming one of the main assertions of the novel, namely that truth can never be unearthed. Even when Etzel has his final moment of 'success', that is, Warschauer's confession, it is undermined by the fact that it is largely motivated not by Etzel's arguments but by the love of a middle-aged man for a teenage boy. This constellation is prefigured in Wassermann's novella

44 For further examples of doubling, see Andrew J. Webber, *The Doppelgänger. Double Visions in German Literature* (Oxford: Clarendon, 1996).

Aufruhr um den Junker Ernst (1926), in which the Erzbischof falls in love with his young adversary Ernst.[45]

When Etzel finally meets Georg Warschauer in Berlin, the character of Gregor Waremme has long disappeared and lives only in the memory of others. Through the accounts of individuals involved in the Maurizius case, Etzel and the reader have been made familiar with a figure who is not the same as the man he now encounters in Berlin. 'Nicht zu glauben, wenn man denkt, was er damals war und was er heute ist' (*FM*, p. 108): these are the words Maurizius senior uses when he talks about Warschauer. Most characters in the novel are indeed at a loss to grasp the Waremme's personality fully, for he is not a real character but a *persona* created by Warschauer in order to hide his Jewishness. The figure of Waremme thus becomes a fictitious construct invented by a character in a novel. This is not only an intensely complex structure; it also makes room for seemingly endless possibilities: 'Alles, was über ihn ausgesagt wurde, war genau so richtig wie das Gegenteil davon' (*FM*, pp. 180–81). Warschauer is thus given the chance constantly to re-invent himself, which makes him Wassermann's most modern character in the sense that identity has here become nothing more than a performance. Elizabeth Boa argues that it is a characteristic of the post-modern that 'the gap between being and performing disappears', a description which, as we shall see in the following, can equally be applied to the character of Warschauer. Moreover, with him we also find that 'behind the mask there is only another mask as identities are constantly re-negotiated within the field of power'.[46]

Acting therefore also becomes the key to the relationship between Warschauer and Etzel, offering a first parallel to the latter's relationship with his father. In order to be able to confront his adversary, Etzel thus also creates a new identity for himself. On arriving in Berlin he changes his name to Edgar Mohl and soon after discovers that these new surroundings allow him to adopt a different persona. However, this soon becomes more than just a game:

> Er war ja ohnehin ein Doppelter, Edgar Mohl und Etzel Andergast, und er spielte Doppeltsein, um sich bei der strengen Verrichtung, der er sich unterzogen, ein bisschen mit sich selber zu amüsieren, den einen gegen den anderen zu hetzen, den einen am anderen zu messen, allein immer ferner rückte E. Andergast, der doch der eigentliche Körper war, indes E. Mohl, der Schatten, an prahlerischer Leiblichkeit zunahm und auf seinen gefährlichen Wegen keine Einrede duldete (*FM*, pp. 251–52).

45 Jakob Wassermann, *Aufruhr um den Junker Ernst* (Berlin: Fischer, 1926).

46 Elizabeth Boa, 'Aping and Parroting: Imitative Performance in Goethe's *Die Wahlverwandtschaften*', in *Performance and Performativity in German Cultural Studies*, ed. by Lucia Ruprecht and others (Bern: Peter Lang, 2003), pp. 21–41 (pp. 24–25).

The notion that Edgar Mohl becomes a dominant other self is confirmed later, when Etzel realises that Etzel Andergast would never have been able to confront Warschauer (*FM*, p. 341). Through his relationship with Warschauer, Etzel thus experiences the modern uncertainty of character as he goes through a process of losing his initial self. At the same time he also sees the advantages of a different identity as it allows him to behave in ways that Etzel Andergast, despite his putting on an act for his own benefit, would never have dared to do. The way he behaves towards his father in the final scene can be understood as proof that he finds himself unable to return fully to the character of Etzel once he leaves Berlin. As Etzel tries to fight Warschauer with his own weapons, the latter inevitably becomes his teacher, as he cannot help but learn from this master in the art of deception.

Etzel's relationship with Warschauer strongly resembles that with his own father as it is also characterized by a lack of honesty and the desire to control and dominate each other. Moreover, Etzel and Warschauer are both aware that what they see of each other is always a most questionable performance. However, although it is relatively easy to distinguish between Etzel's two identities, it is impossible to discern anything like the 'real' Warschauer, for he always plays 'Komödie' and comes across as an exaggerated figure like an actor on stage. This means he does not even pretend to make his performance a credible one but rather creates another level of uncertainty by acting openly. This is underlined further by his frequently referring to himself as an actor, a practice which brings us to the question of their intentions. Although Etzel's intention is clear from the beginning, namely to make Warschauer confess his perjury and prove that Maurizius is innocent, that of his opponent is at first less obvious. As will be discussed in the second part of this chapter, Warschauer becomes a spokesman for a destructive critique of civilization, a negative version of Christian Wahnschaffe, which is why he can only laugh at Etzel's hot-headed pursuit of justice. However, if Etzel's ideas and struggles are merely ridiculous to Warschauer, why does he spend all this time with Etzel, eventually make his confession and admitting his own guilt? Why does Etzel have a certain power over a man who is depicted as intimidating and hence strongly resembles the double-character of Coppelius from Hoffmann's story *Der Sandmann*?

To begin with, Warschauer knows his perjury is no longer punishable. However, more importantly, it his homosexuality that comes between him and the role he acts out in front of Etzel. Although Warschauer's violent infatuation with Anna Jahn could be understood as part of his identity as Waremme, his homosexuality is the only genuine trait in his character. After all, heterosexuality is a standard part of social performance whereas homosexuality, at the time, was unconventional, even punishable, and therefore not something he would deliberately have made a part of his identity. James W. Jones informs us:

> Until 1851, Prussian law punished 'widernatürliche Unzucht' between two males, or between man and animal, with a prison sentence of from six months to four years and 'zeitige Untersagung der Ausübung bürgerlichen Ehrenrechte.' By the time of German unification, when Prussian law was extended to all German states, this prohibition, codified in Paragraph 175, spoke of a prison sentence, without specifying a length of time, and stated 'auch kann Verlust der bürgerlichen Ehrenrechte erkannt werden.'[47]

The negative attitude towards his homosexuality is corroborated by the fact that, as Waremme, he was involved in 'eine homosexuelle Affäre, in die einige junge Adelige eines vornehmen Korps verstrickt sind' (*FM*, p. 192) and was very keen to hide it. His sexuality is, therefore, the only aspect of his life beyond his control and it is this infatuation with young men that ties him to Etzel. This aspect of Warschauer's character is therefore of far greater significance than Schäfer's description of it as a 'fragwürdig-trübe, homoerotisch geprägte Faszination eines finsteren Charakters' would suggest.[48]

In the course of their relationship, Warschauer finds himself increasingly attracted towards Etzel. Their relationship resembles the male-male bonds between an adolescent boy and an adult man that were allegedly[49] formed in Ancient Greece and became a standard prop in the depiction of homosexuality during the first decades of the twentieth century.[50] The adult man often takes on the role of the mentor, something which could also be said of the relationship between Warschauer and Etzel. Moreover, in their case there are numerous references to his 'Betastungsversuche' (*FM*, p. 268), his caressing and kissing of Etzel, and to the boy, acting the part of Edgar Mohl, who tolerates them in order to achieve his aims, thus highlighting the homoerotic nature of their relationship. In a rare moment we are given access to Warschauer's feelings towards Etzel, which are described as follows: 'Wahrhaftig, der Gedanke eines Verrückten oder eines Teufels, im Hinblick darauf, daß die bloße physische Nähe des Knaben ihm manchmal eine ähnlich zwitterhafte Empfindung verursachte wie die Berührung eines Pfirsichs, der in der Sonne gelegen hat' (*FM*, p. 337). The image of the peach is clearly eroticized as the skin of that fruit is, more generally, often compared to particularly beautiful, young human skin. That it is described as warm in this example further emphasizes its association with a human being and thus with Etzel. Moreover, it also

47 Jones, '*Third Sex*', p. 45.

48 Schäfer, *Plaidoyer*, p. 150.

49 W. Daniel Wilson claims the idea of 'Knabenliebe' is one of the greatest modern misunderstandings since the Greeks only had sexual relationships with men of at least eighteen years of age (W. Daniel Wilson, *Goethe Männer Knabe*, trans. by Angela Steidele (Berlin: Insel, 2012), pp. 14–39.

50 Jones, '*Third Sex*', p. 193.

symbolizes the temptation of the 'forbidden fruit'. The word 'zwitterhaft' could either point to a bisexual tendency within Warschauer or, more likely, refer to the twofold nature of his feelings for Etzel. On the one hand, he feels a strong sexual attraction towards him, while on the other he has paternal feelings for him and will on occasion refer to him as the son he never had.

From Etzel's perspective there can hardly be a doubt about Warschauer's sexual feelings for him, as the latter openly talks about his 'Passion' (*FM*, p. 554) for his young friend. Moreover, Warschauer sometimes almost woos Etzel as one might do with a potential lover: for instance, when he treats him to hot chocolate or takes him out to concerts. In their final scene together, it is therefore the unexpected sight of Etzel's body that prompts Warschauer to admit his perjury rather than the boy's insistence on the importance of justice. Moreover, it seems as if Etzel, aware of Warschauer's infatuation, stages things accordingly. He makes Warschauer visit him at home in his bedroom because he is ill. When he finds himself unable to convince his adversary with his arguments he takes to pretending to have an attack of fever in the course of which Warschauer undresses him in order to apply a wet pack. Warschauer's reaction is described as follows:

> Als er den nackten Jünglingsleib vor sich sah, versank Warschauer in starre Betrachtung. [...] Er sah aus wie ein Verhexter, der ein Gebet angefangen hat und nicht weiter weiß. [...] Er streichelte die Schulter, den Rücken, die Hüfte des schönen, schlanken Körpers, dabei klapperten ihm die Zähne (*FM*, p. 548).

For Warschauer this is undoubtedly a moment of sexual fulfilment and the description of him as bewitched is another hint that his sexuality is the only aspect of his personality which is beyond his control. Even the account of Etzel's feelings points towards a kind of climax, which he experiences after Warschauer has made his confession: 'Etzel umkrampfte mit beiden Händen Warschauers Rechte. Er glitt auf das Bett zurück, ohne die Hand des Mannes loszulassen. Es war wie eine Glücksbetäubung. In leidenschaftlicher Begierde bohrte er den Blick in die wasserblassen Augen' (*FM*, p. 549).

In this scene Etzel is described as unsure about whether or not he is acting, but from the quotation above it is clear that the sexual satisfaction both characters derive from this scene is mutual. For a moment they have both lost control over their constructed identities and, at least partly, given in to their sexual urges. This final scene adds another layer of ambiguity to the state of Etzel's feelings for Warschauer. Hitherto, he has accepted previous moments of tenderness in a cold and reserved manner, as though he considered them a necessary sacrifice, whereas in the final scene he seems to reciprocate Warschauer's feelings. In any case, it shows that Warschauer remains unconcerned by Etzel's political claims and that the boy only reaches his heart in the sense that the older man develops romantic desires for him. In his interpretation of their relationship, Garrin is clearly unaware of these subtleties: 'That Waremme is also capable of human feelings, we see in his relation to Etzel. Despite the fact that the boy is his adversary, he likes him and cares for him when he is ill. Moreover, he respects his youthful idealism'.[51]

At the same time Etzel cannot help being influenced by Warschauer's misanthropic way of seeing the world. This clearly manifests itself in the boy's lack of compassion as he even wishes he could torture Warschauer in order to extract his answers from him:

> denn nichts ist ihm geheuer an Waremme, nichts liebt er an ihm, nichts macht ihn weich, stimmt ihn versöhnlich, am liebsten möchte er ihn gebunden vor sich sehen und ihn mit glühenden Eisen in der Hand zwingen zu gestehen: Ja oder nein (*FM*, p. 352).

Despite the erotic connotations of this fantasy it is the fact that Etzel would accept this violation of basic human rights that makes the initial motivation behind his quest for justice and a better world appear questionable. It actually confirms one of Warschauer's pessimistic views, namely, that fighting for justice can never be anything but an egoistic pursuit (*FM*, p. 543). To him, Etzel is merely one of many rebellious run-away boys and thus nothing but a 'Modeerscheinung'.

This element of selfishness in Etzel's undertaking receives further confirmation when he admits he has never cared about the suffering of Maurizius senior: 'Der Alte, an dem lag mir nichts, der ließ mich eigentlich kalt, eigentlich haßte ich ihn sogar mit seinem Begnadigungsgesuch' (*FM*, p. 540). All this conveys the impression that Etzel is, to a considerable extent, fighting for his own satisfaction, which mainly derives from the destruction of his father's work, even more so when he falls into a frenzy on finding out his father has essentially made the same discovery as he has: Waremme's perjury. He has thus not been able to defeat his father. As Edgar Mohl, Etzel develops a demonic element within himself in order to confront Warschauer, to whom he refers as Satan, yet he is unable to free himself entirely from this other self and in the final scene is himself referred to as the devil by the narrator.

Etzel is, therefore, a more complex, less likeable figure than some of Wassermann's previous adolescent figures, yet it remains doubtful whether this justifies Miller's view:

> There is something monstrous about Etzel Andergast: he is fascinatingly attractive and repellent at the same time. He stands for the new type of youth which made possible the advent and sway of an Adolf Hitler. He might even

51 Garrin, *Concept*, p. 40.

> be regarded as an embryonic Hitler. He is the 'murderer of the soul,' to use the language of his victims.[52]

While Etzel certainly stands for a 'new type of youth', the idea of comparing him to Hitler at first seems absurd, especially as he is, for instance, shown to help his Jewish fellow-pupil Rosenau and at one point his teacher Raff wonders whether Etzel himself is Jewish. Moreover, Etzel has a very critical mind and is a loner, characteristics which hardly predestine him to become the member of a mass movement such as the 'Hitlerjugend'. Nevertheless, in *Andergast* we are presented with a different Etzel who lacks a sense of direction in his life, becomes a member of various youth movements and is, at least for a while, a passionate follower of the radical political leader Jürgen Lorriner. Etzel is also repeatedly shown to express the longing for a 'Führer' in his life. Nevertheless, it would certainly be reading too much into this character if one were to understand him as foreshadowing the horrors of the Third Reich. Rather, it could be said that, through his engagement with this 'new type', Wassermann could not help but create a more ambiguous figure. Moreover, Etzel is a more appropriate expression of the reality with which the author was confronted.

The Return of the Outsider

In the final part of this chapter we shall look at how, in one of his final novels, Wassermann stages the return of the outsider in order to arrive at an almost overwhelming critique of Western values and civilization. Moreover, Georg Warschauer, the outsider he presents to us, is doubly so. Following Hans Mayer's arguments, put forward in *Außenseiter* (1975), Warschauer can be understood as an existential outsider because of his Jewishness and as a sexual one because of his homosexuality. Mayer defines the difference between the two as follows:

> Die jüdische Identitätskrise inmitten der aufklärerischen bürgerlichen Gesellschaft befällt den einzelnen als Teil einer Gemeinsamkeit. Das Außenseitertum wird nicht individuell begründet wie beim Homosexuellen, sondern generell: durch das Judesein. [...] Der angebliche 'Selbsthaß' beweist bloß, daß Aufklärung gescheitert ist und daß man es erkannt hat.[53]

Warschauer's pessimism and misanthropy can therefore be seen as the result of his failure to leave behind the state of living forever in-between and his realization that it will forever be impossible to do so. In what follows we shall

52 Miller, *Maurizius Forever*, p. 11.

53 Mayer, *Außenseiter*, p. 421.

see how Warschauer's attempts to change his status in society can be regarded as almost 'classical' tales or performances by an outsider, a feature which will allow us to link them to other such performances. After the analysis of Warschauer's status as a double outsider we shall move on to Wassermann's failure to provide any opposition to this figure and how he instead makes the 'negative' character the most intriguing one in the entire novel, a surprising development in his writing. Eventually it will become apparent that this new empathy with the unlikable outsider comes to symbolize a new level of resignation on the part of the author, who has lost all faith in ever ceasing to be an outsider himself. Towards the end of his life Wassermann writes about his failure to become an accepted member of society: 'Ich war eine sogenannte umstrittene Erscheinung, und für viele bin ich es geblieben'.[54]

It is appropriate to begin the discussion of Warschauer's way of dealing with his Jewishness with a quotation from Elizabeth Boa informing us about one crucial function of performance in modern society:

> In modernising society, performance no longer showed forth a divinely sanctioned order but conveyed rather the divide between the projected role and marked players mimicking their unmarked betters. Bourgeois pretending to be gentilhommes are joined in the nation state by Jews pretending to be German.[55]

One of these Jews pretending to be German is Warschauer. By becoming the Catholic nationalist Gregor Waremme he fulfils his most ardent wish: in the eyes of the world he ceases to be a Jew. From an early point he has understood that if he continues to live life as an Eastern European Jew, he will never be able to make use of his extraordinary intellectual potential. That, at least, is his version of this situation, for it never becomes quite clear whether he is really highly gifted or this is just what he makes people believe. In any case, he embraces the possibilities that performance offers in order to change his life, no matter how challenging this might be:

> Aber ich [Warschauer] war ein Schauspieler, ich mußte spielen, und wenn ich nicht mit vollendeter Kunst, mit der letzten Hingabe spielte, so konnt ich einpacken. [...] Jede ungewöhnliche Geistes- und Charakterleistung beruht auf einer sublimierten Verwandlungskunst [...]. Halten Sie [Mohl] sich doch vor Augen, welche Wissensgebiete ich zu beherrschen hatte (*FM*, pp. 356–57).

At this point a brief discussion of the concept of Jewish self-hatred, as defined by Theodor Lessing in relation to the depiction of Warschauer, is needed. In *Der jüdische Selbsthaß* (1930) Lessing mentions that he could

54 Wassermann, *Selbstbetrachtungen*, p. 40.

55 Boa, 'Aping', p. 24.

also trace Jewish self-hatred in the works of Wassermann, but refrains from doing so.[56] According to Lessing, this form of self-hatred can be found in any minority but the Jewish people serve as the perfect example to develop his theory.[57] Lessing argues that the Jewish people were the first in the history of mankind always to blame themselves: 'Auf die Frage: "Warum liebt man uns nicht?" antwortete seit alters die jüdische Lehre: "*Weil wir schuldig sind*"'.[58] This strong sense of guilt was combined with the sheer, endless suffering of the Jewish people, which had two significant consequences: Jews began to think of themselves as inferior and at the same time they thought of their oppressors as superior and tried to be like them:

> Denn der in Kampf und Leid gestellte Mensch wird die Tat und den Täter, das Handeln und den Händler immer für *höher* erachten, denn alle Seher und Träumer. Und der Jude war immer in den Kampf gestellt. Er kann nicht wie Blume und Kind Dankbarkeit fordern schon dafür, daß er da ist und schön ist. Er muß '*Werte*' schaffen, um vor sich und anderen gerechtfertigt dazustehen. Und so über sich hinausgetrieben und aus sich herausgefallen, wurde er sich selber wertlos, bis ein grauenhaftes Zerrbild entstand, jenem Händler gleich, der, verdorbene Ware verkaufend, seiner Kundschaft zuruft: 'Glauben Sie mir, meine *Ware* ist gut; *ich* stinke.'[59]

Lessing goes on to show the different possible reactions that are available to the Jew who is forced to hate his origins, his parents and himself. They all prove to be self-destructive, yet one of them, namely assimilation, offers a description of Warschauer's fate. The assimilated Jew succeeds at every act of mimicry and eventually becomes 'one of the others'. In fact, he becomes even more of a German and a Christian than most German people. However, Lessing considers this a form of suicide: 'Du gingst den Weg des Selbstmordes zu Glück und Ruhm'.[60] The Jew who tries to cease being a Jew can never be himself and is forced to put on an act: 'Er wirbt um Achtung, er bettelt um Liebe. Er offenbart sich nicht, sondern vermummt sich. Er gibt sich nicht, sondern schauspielert'.[61] Warschauer thus chooses performance as a means of overcoming his Jewishness, which makes his case a typical example of Jewish self-hatred as described by Lessing.

However, most interesting is that the character of Warschauer strongly resembles one of Lessing's showcases, namely Maximilian Harden.[62] Lessing

56 Lessing, *Der Jüdische Selbsthass* (Munich: Matthes und Seitz, 1984), p. 42.
57 Lessing, *Der Jüdische Selbsthass*, p. 27.
58 Lessing, *Der Jüdische Selbsthass*, p. 13.
59 Lessing, *Der Jüdische Selbsthass*, pp. 36–37.
60 Lessing, *Der Jüdische Selbsthass*, p. 50.
61 Lessing, *Der Jüdische Selbsthass*, p. 117.
62 On Harden, see also Helga Neumann, *Maximilian Harden (1861–1927): Ein unerschrockener deutsch-jüdischer Kritiker und Publizist* (Würzburg: Königshausen and Neumann, 2003).

informs us that Maximilian Harden was the pseudonym of Felix Ernst Witkowski, the son of a Jewish silk merchant from Berlin. As a young man Harden joined a group of actors and was, amongst other things, known for his good looks: 'Er hatte strahlende blaue Augen und ein mädchenhaftes Köpfchen in blonden Locken'.[63] Similarly, Warschauer is described as having been 'blessed' with hair that is 'germanisch blond' and a face that is indeed 'unorientalisch' (*FM*, p. 349). Warschauer also used to be an actor on stage. Warschauer and Harden are both described as fervent nationalists and patriots. While Warschauer acts the role of the devoted Catholic, Waremme, who dreams of a 'Europa [...] unter deutscher Hegemonie' (*FM*, p. 351) and organizes a 'Konferenz der Vaterlandsfreunde', Harden is referred to as the 'gehätschelte[n] Publizist[en] des alten konservativen Preußen'.[64] Both figures are shown to be hugely influential: Waremme is in touch with the Kaiser and the Vatican and Harden is considered one of the most powerful figures in Wilhelmine Germany:

> Harden schloß sich nie einer Partei an, aber alle Parteien umwarben ihn. Er hatte kein Amt, aber alle Ämter lauschten auf ihn. Er verschmähte Titel und Orden, aber die Träger der besten Namen und Titel zitterten vor seinem Urteil.[65]

Warschauer also never accepts titles and positions. The fact that he is revealed to be homosexual while Harden was the one who (as we shall see later) famously accused Eulenburg and Moltke of being homosexual could indeed be read as a criticism of Harden's behaviour at the time. After World War I the previous fame of both figures is forgotten and they both return to their Jewish identity. However, while Warschauer does so of his own accord, Harden is made a Jew once more by the rise of racial anti-Semitism in Germany. The actual extent of Warschauer's return to his Jewishness, however, remains unclear. Moreover, his eventual plan of returning to the East seems more like a moment of defeat than a positive moment of reconciliation with his roots, as portrayed by Jütten.[66]

While Warschauer therefore succeeds in turning most of his character into a performance, he struggles to do so when it comes to his sexuality. Throughout the novel it seems that sexuality is the one urge that defies all performance as even a character like Andergast cannot help but follow his sexual urges. As part of his identity as Waremme, Warschauer is keen to create the image of the 'Weiberheld' and, as we can deduce from the accounts of other characters, he makes most

63 Lessing, *Selbsthass*, p. 171.
64 Lessing, *Selbsthass*, p. 175.
65 Lessing, *Selbsthass*, p. 170.
66 Jütten, *Diskurse*, p. 287.

people believe that he is just that. However, the two sexual encounters of his that are described in the novel seem to tell a rather different story.

The first of Warschauer's sexual encounters is his alleged rape of Anna Jahn. By creating the identity of the German patriot Waremme, who supports the idea of a war against France, Warschauer also tries to conform to a certain kind of masculinity. David Prickett informs us that there was a:

> more general crisis of masculinity (including hetero- and homosexual, and anything in between these polarities) with the rise of modernism at the turn of the century. As early as Germany's victory over France in 1871, the ideal male is the strong male, who is pure, hardened, and uniformed. The new German Empire defines itself vis-à-vis these strong young men; indeed, it is suggested that Germany's victory over France as well as its very existence depends solely on such men.[67]

In order to make his performance as Waremme complete, Warschauer therefore needs to emphasize his manliness. Apart from disseminating the image of himself as a 'Weiberheld', he also feels that to have a woman permanently by his side would make things even more complete. It is no surprise, therefore, that he chooses Anna Jahn for this role, a woman he refers to as the 'deutsche Helena'. By choosing a 'Helena', he identifies himself with the archetypically German figure of Faust, thus giving himself an even more German air, appropriating one of German culture's most important myths. However, Anna refuses him because, as Waremme puts it, 'Sie spürte das fremde Blut' (*FM*, p. 367). Apart, then, from being xenophobic she is also to a certain extent aware of his performance, which seems to indicate that Warschauer's other identity is not credible enough to allow him to engage in a genuine relationship.

However, Warschauer's desire to possess Anna does not stop there. During one of his conversations with Andergast, Maurizius claims that Waremme confessed to him that he raped Anna when she was seventeen years old. However, this allegation is never actually confirmed by either Warschauer or Anna. Moreover, the scene of the confession is staged in a most theatrical way and we cannot be sure whether or not it is simply part of the invented character of Waremme. However, the image he creates for himself as a womanizer is certainly of far greater significance than Och allows when he describes it as among Warschauer's 'dämonisch-diabolische Züge'.[68] Whatever the case, the circumstances surrounding this rape are

67 David James Prickett, 'Envisioning the Homosexual: Gender Performance, Photography, and the Modernist Homosexual Aesthetic', in *Performance and Performativity*, pp. 177–201 (p. 181).

68 Och, 'Ahasver', p. 120.

of interest. Anna and Waremme both participate in a theatre production in Cologne. After the performance Waremme brings her the news that her brother Erwin has died 'in einem Gefecht in Südfrankreich' (*FM*, p. 434).[69] While Waremme tries to comfort her, he becomes 'stürmisch' and subsequently rapes her. The assault hus takes place in a theatre, a space of false identities where things happen without actually happening in reality. The theatrical aspect of this rape is further emphasized when, for his first 'confession' of it, Waremme recites Shakespeare's *Measure for Measure,* Act II, scene 4, in which Angelo tries to force Isabella to sleep with him. As Isabella is a nun and has taken a vow of chastity there is a barrier between her and Angelo which could be understood as analogous to the racial barrier between Waremme and Anna.

The other interesting aspect of this rape is that it takes place immediately after the news of the death of Anna's brother as a German soldier who, according to the ideal of masculinity at the time, would have been considered most manly and heroic. In this light it almost seems as if the rape were less an expression of Waremme's desire for Anna than his desperate attempt to complete the image of himself as strong and manly. Moreoever, Gilman informs us that towards the end of the nineteenth century there was an 'increasingly intense anti-Semitic critique of the Jewish body as inherently unfit for military service'.[70] At the same time the rape can also be understood as the desire of the Jewish man for an Aryan woman, as well as the attempt to defy the image of the effeminate Jewish body. In his analysis of their relationship, Henry Regensteiner fails to draw the conclusion that Waremme's attraction to Anna Jahn is, in fact, an essential part of what he refers to as the outsider's 'tortured quest for complete acceptance in the German cultural orbit'.[71]

The novel's other sexual encounter involving Warschauer is the previously mentioned homosexual affair involving young aristocrats, which brings us to the idea of understanding Warschauer's story as an almost classical tale of a homosexual double life. According to Mayer, the desire of the homosexual man to appear very manly was a reaction to being forced to hide his true desires from the world: '[D]ie sodomitische Diaspora [lebt] im Zustand der Nichtidentität: [...] Dem jüdischen Selbsthaß korrespondiert der Selbsthaß

69 In the original edition it reads 'Südwestafrika', which is the only difference between the editions. The word 'Südfrankreich' in the later editions might, therefore, just be a mistake and not a change Wassermann made himself (Jakob Wassermann, *Der Fall Maurizius* (Berlin: Fischer, 1928), p. 414.

70 Sander Gilman, *The Jew's Body* (New York, London: Routledge, 1991), p. 42.

71 Henry Regensteiner, 'The Obsessive Personality in Jakob Wassermann's Novel *Der Fall Maurizius*', *Literature and Psychology*, 14 (1964), 106–16 (p. 114).

des Homosexuellen. [...] Der Sodomit im Zwang des Doppellebens wendet sich angewidert ab von den "Tunten"'.[72] The reason it would have been so crucial for a man like Waremme, who was pursuing a partly political career, to pass as heterosexual was that the revelation of a man's homosexuality 'was likely to ruin one's career and the possibilities of a prison term were nothing less than real in the Germany of the early 1900s'.[73] Moreover, the public exposure of homosexuals was a prominent tool for the elimination of a (political) opponent; or, as Mayer puts it: 'Päderastie war stets ein polemisches Argument'.[74] The discovery of a man's homosexuality was a tool exploited for political purposes by the bourgeoisie in their fight against the aristocracy and likewise by the Socialists against the bourgeoisie. The case of Philipp zu Eulenburg[75] was probably the most famous during the Wilhelmine era. Moreover, ever since the exposure in 1902 of Europe's richest man at the time, Friedrich Alfred Krupp, as a homosexual by the Social Democratic Party newspaper *Vorwärts*, the public had greatly enjoyed reading about such stories in the press, suggesting there was an actual market for them.

Wassermann tells a similar story of homosexuality that had to be hidden at all costs for political reasons:

> [K]ürzlich [hat sich] wiederum eine neue Skandalgeschichte an seinen Namen geheftet, eine homosexuelle Affäre, in die einige junge Adelige eines vornehmen Korps verstrickt sind und die zu unterdrücken seine Gönner sich mit allen Kräften bemühen. (Es gelang ihnen aber doch nicht ganz, ein sozialistisches Blatt brachte, vorläufig ohne Namensnennung, einen ziemlich alarmierenden Artikel (*FM*, p. 192).

In *Maurizius* Wassermann thus portrays a scenario that comes very close to events that actually took place by showing how the Socialist press used the disclosure of their opponents' sexual preferences as a political weapon. Even though Warschauer's homosexuality also functions as a metaphor for his Otherness, Wassermann offers an insight into the lives of homosexuals before 1914. In this context it seems noteworthy that Magnus Hirschfeld, a prominent advocate for the rights of homosexuals, was among Wassermann's acquaintances in Berlin.[76]

72 Mayer, *Außenseiter*, pp. 182–83.

73 Jones, '*Third Sex*', p. 272.

74 Jones, '*Third Sex*', p. 182.

75 Philip zu Eulenberg (1847–1921) found himself at the heart of a homosexual scandal in 1907. A politician and diplomat, Eulenberg had homosexual relations with members of the Kaiser's inner circle. In 1906 Harden published an article accusing Eulenberg of having an affair with a senior French diplomat which led to a number of trials involving high-ranking members of the German Imperial Army and the aristocracy.

76 Müller-Kampel, *Collage*, p. 213.

The depiction of Warschauer's desperate desire to hide his homosexuality can be linked to the atmosphere of constant fear in which homosexuals were forced to live; and even more to the witch-hunt which followed the Harden-Eulenburg-Moltke trials (1907–09) and in the course of which the number of 'arrests for acts against Paragraph 175 doubled from 1907–1912 in Germany'.[77] Moreover, there is a long list of homosexuals who committed suicide due to blackmail or fear of discovery. Warschauer's emigration to the USA can ultimately also be linked to his homosexuality, for, as Jones informs us, fictional homosexual characters would frequently be portrayed as leaving for the New World in order to find freedom from persecution.[78] In *Die Schlafwandler*, for instance, Hermann Broch also portrays the plight of the homosexual man in the figure of the wealthy business man Eduard von Bertrand. He also travels the world yet eventually commits suicide becase his homosexuality has been made public, around the same time as the Moltke trials took place.[79] It would therefore be mistaken to consider Warschauer's homosexuality as a mere device to underline the monstrosity of his character, as in the studies by Blankenagel and Landscheidt.[80]

Warschauer thus lives in constant fear of either his Jewishness or his homosexuality being discovered and it is only in his relationship with Etzel that he reveals these two aspects of his identity. Etzel is the only character in the novel to whom Warschauer talks openly about his Jewishness, but only after first making sure that he is not an anti-Semite: '"Haben Sie mit Juden verkehrt, Mohl?" – "Und ob. Bei uns gibt's Juden die Menge." – "Hatten Sie jüdische Kameraden?" – "Auch." – "Also keine prinzipielle Gegnerschaft?" [...] "Schön. Das wollt ich wissen"' (*FM*, p. 344). The notion of Warschauer's confession can thus be understood to go beyond the mere confession of his perjury. In fact, his relationship with Etzel can be seen as a continuing process of confession during which he admits to being Jewish as well as indirectly owning up to the fact that he is homosexual. This idea of a multilayered confession also allows us to attribute another motive to Warschauer's prolonged interest in Etzel, namely, that a confession always offers a moment of relief and liberation. In *The History of Sexuality*, Foucault writes that 'Western man has become a confessing animal'.[81] In other words, since the Middle Ages the confession has become 'one of the West's most highly valued techniques for producing

77 Jones, '*Third Sex*', p. 107.

78 Jones, '*Third Sex*', p. 196.

79 Hermann Broch, *Die Schlafwandler* (Frankfurt a.M.: Suhrkamp, 1994).

80 Blankenagel, *Writings*, p. 276; and Landscheidt, 'Mutmassungen', p. 22.

81 Michel Foucault, *The Will to Knowledge: The History of Sexuality*, I, *An Introduction*, trans. by Robert Hurley (London: Penguin, 1998), p. 59. For the French original see Michel Foucault, *Histoire de la sexualité. La volonté de savoir*, 3 vols (Paris: Gallimard, 1976), I.

truth'.[82] For our context it is important that Foucault describes the confession as 'a ritual in which the expression alone, independently of its external consequences, produces intrinsic modifications in the person who articulates it: it exonerates, redeems, and purifies him; it unburdens him of his wrongs, liberates him, and promises salvation'.[83] Moreover, Foucault sheds light on the power relationship between the confessing subject and the listener and comes to the conclusion that 'the agency of domination does not reside in the one who speaks (for it is he who is constrained), but in the one who listens and says nothing'.[84] The confessing subject depends on the listener for his or her confession. When applied to the relationship between Warschauer and Etzel, this principle makes the attachment of the middle-aged man to the teenage boy even more plausible: Warschauer depends on Etzel for his confession, not so much, though, for the confession of his perjury, as for that of his Jewishness and, indirectly, that of his homosexuality.

Nonetheless, despite this eventual confession Warschauer's failure to become an accepted member of society leaves him an unalterable misanthropist. The following claim by Classen is therefore mistaken: 'Etzel erweckt den verlogenen Waremme schließlich durch das Geständnis der Wahrheit zu neuem Leben und setzt Gefühle und Verantwortungsbewußtsein in ihm frei'.[85] Warschauer is in some ways a negative version of Christian Wahnschaffe, as he undergoes similar experiences but with a very different outcome. Most importantly, Warschauer represents a reversal of the idea of perception as the means of transforming a character, as portrayed in *Wahnschaffe*. Whilst being able to see and understand the suffering of the people around him leads to insanity in the case of Andergast, it leads to utter indifference and egocentrism in the case of Warschauer. His refusal to engage with his perception finds an expression in the dark glasses he wears almost constantly; moreover, his eyes are frequently referred to as pale or even dead. Lindemann-Luiken's interpretation of these glasses as a symbol of coldness does not, therefore, take the importance of perception into consideration.[86]

However, unlike with any of Wassermann's previous characters, this state of not seeing the world around him is based on a conscious decision. Like Christian Wahnschaffe, Warschauer has seen it all: he has spent ten years in America, mostly in Chicago and mostly among the poor and deprived masses. He has witnessed the horrors of the abattoirs, people's domestic

82 Foucault, *The Will to Knowledge*, I, p. 59.
83 Foucault, *The Will to Knowledge*, I, p. 62.
84 Foucault, *The Will to Knowledge*, I, p. 62.
85 Classen, 'Todesstrafe', p. 37.
86 See Lindemann-Luiken, *Auswirkungen*, p. 147.

misery, the injustice of the judicial system and the racist treatment of immigrants and of African Americans, as exemplified in the account of the violent death of his friend Joshua Cooper. Warschauer therefore becomes, as Bing rightly observes, a representative of contemporary America.[87] The fact that Warschauer spent most of his time in Chicago is not only significant because Wassermann himself visited the city during his trip to America in 1928, but also because of that city's cultural significance. At the time Chicago was considered by many to be the low point of ruthless capitalism because its wealth was based on a gigantic meat industry, and thus the slaughter of animals on a hitherto unknown scale. As a consequence, Warschauer confronts Etzel with a drastic description of the life in this city:

> Bedrängte Gegenwart, so dicht beim Sterben zahlloser Kreatur [...] aus den riesigen Hallen und Speichern schwelt der süßliche Blutdunst auf, ständiges Blutgewölk brütet über der ganzen Stadt, die Kleider der Menschen riechen nach Blut, ihre Betten und ihre Kirchen, ihre Stuben, nach Blut schmecken ihre Speisen, ihre Weine, ihre Küsse (*FM*, p. 379).

Using Chicago as one of the symbols of the horrors embedded in modern life, places Wassermann in the context of such authors as Upton Sinclair and his novel *The Jungle* (1906) or Brecht and his play *Die heilige Johanna der Schlachthöfe* (1929), for which Sinclair's novel was a source. Blankenagel takes offence at this depiction of America as prejudiced and narrow-minded, thus failing to see the further discourse in which Wassermann is engaging.[88] Moreover, his horrifying experiences in the New World not only make Warschauer one of Wassermann's most modern characters but also come across as a bleak vision of Europe's future. Tellingly, only a few years later Wassermann himself refers to Europe as a 'von Menschenblut triefendes Schlachthaus' and declares that the idea of Europe has become a 'unhaltbar gewordene Fiktion'.[89]

Warschauer's experiences do not lead, as in the case of Christian Wahnschaffe, to an altered perception and thus to the desire to bring about change. Instead they lead to the refusal on Warschauer's part to engage with the world around him:

> Das Auge, das sieht, ist ein Regulativ für das Herz, das leidet. Da die meisten Menschen mit Blindheit geschlagen sind, leiden sie desto mehr. Der Sehende wird kalt. Eine grausame Wahrheit, aber wärs keine, wie könnten wir, Sie und ich, jeden Morgen aus dem Bett steigen und wieder das Hemd und die Strümpfe

87 Bing, *Wassermann*, p. 266.

88 Blankenagel, *Writings*, p. 276.

89 Wassermann, *Selbstbetrachtungen*, pp. 100, 107.

> anziehn und wieder die Zeitung lesen und wieder zu Frau Bobike wandeln? Wie wäre das möglich? Und was mich betrifft, ich leide ausschließlich an mir selber. An andern leiden, das ist Schwindel (*FM*, p. 382).

Warschauer has seen the world, recognized it for what it is and as a result arrives at a rejection of Western civilization. Full of contempt, he considers it to be beyond change and all the big words such as religion, humanity and charity are nothing but the 'aufgeklebten Zettel in einer Kurpfuscher-Apotheke' (*FM*, p. 335). In his opinion, stupidity and greed are the only motives that actually prompt human beings to act; and once he had realized this, he chooses a life of complete solitude which prevents him from being afflicted with this unpleasant human condition. He shows a strong lack of belief in compassion or even the idea of justice, claiming that justice can never be possible because human beings are neither interested in it nor capable of it. Like Wahnschaffe, Warschauer disappears at the end of the novel, without, however, the positive connotations of the earlier novel. Warschauer decides to leave the 'hiesige Bühne' and to return to Upper Silesia 'gen Osten, gen Osten' (*FM*, p. 554) allegedly to look after a daughter he has not seen for twenty-three years. His aim is, therefore, not to go into the world and bring about change, but instead to retreat from a world that grants him nothing but the status of an outsider and does not allow him to be the man he wants to be.

Schneider-Handschin argues that Warschauer fails to draw further conclusions from his experiences: 'Mit dem Aufzählen von Beispielen endet Warschauer-Waremmes Kritik und Auflehnung'.[90] While this is certainly true, it is unfair to accuse Wassermann of not providing concrete solutions to the social problems of his time as it is not a novelist's task to do so. Critics have failed to understand the significance of the mere existence in one of Wassermann's novels of a character like Warschauer, whose most fascinating aspect is the fact that his pessimism and misanthropy remain largely unrefuted. Not only is there no moment of reconciliation or optimism in the end, but Etzel's opposition to Warschauer's views is of no consequence. Wassermann has found no way of countering his own creation; instead, he is overwhelmed, as well as intrigued, by this outburst of pessimism, which, given his previous works, can be seen as the strongest indicator yet that Wassermann had lost faith in his previous mission. Only a year later, in his biography of Christopher Columbus, Wassermann even reiterates the idea that the project of human civilization has been a failure:

> Ohne einen gewissen Mut und ohne Resignation kann man die Vergangenheit des menschlichen Geschlechts nicht als das erkennen, was sie ist: eine

90 Schneider-Handschin, *Bild des Bürgertums*, p. 52.

> ununterbrochene Kette von Unrecht, Übervorteilung, Diebstahl, Gewalttat und Morde. Dies sind nur vierhundert und etliche Jahre [since Columbus's discovery of the New World and the ensuing atrocities]. Ich kann mir eine Geistesstimmung denken, die seufzend zu dem Schluß gelangt: es könnte, mit nur geringen Variationen, auch gestern gewesen sein.[91]

At this point the connection between Warschauer's criticism and the novel as a whole becomes clear. As we have seen, the novel offers a depiction of society as composed of isolated individuals who are no longer capable of forming genuine relationships with one another. Society has ultimately become dysfunctional, with its individual members left fighting for themselves. In this context the function of Warschauer's critique is to show that this state of injustice results from this utter lack of empathy and is thus an innate human condition. Moreover, by referring to injustices that have taken place in the past, such as the crimes committed by European colonizers in Africa (*FM*, p. 544), he reveals the hypocrisy behind the idea of positive development that is the result of human civilization. Instead, he demonstrates that a constant line of misery and inequality can be traced from the beginnings of Western civilization up to the present. Most importantly, the figure of Warschauer not only shows that the current state of society is more than just a momentary phase but also crushes all hopes for a better future. Warschauer has lived in the New World for ten years and arrives at the conclusion that life over there is even worse than in Europe. The state of affairs in America here functions as an indicator of the negative developments that will also affect Europe but with a time-lag of a few years. With his description of the living conditions and general state of emotional depletion in America, Warschauer arrives at a bleak vision of Europe's future. Unlike the other characters in the novel, Warschauer is, therefore, fully aware of the state in which society finds itself as well as the future that lies ahead. It could be said that Warschauer and the narrator both arrive at the same conclusions, the former by analysing society and the other by depicting it, yet Warschauer's reaction to this knowledge is one of passive acceptance. As he puts it: 'Der Sehende wird kalt' (*FM*, p. 382). When he, as a negative mirror image of Christian Wahnschaffe, also disappears at the end of the novel, this is not accompanied by an air of optimism and self-sacrifice. Instead it is, so far, the greatest moment of defeat in Wassermann's writing.

91 Wassermann, *Columbus*, p. 114.

CHAPTER 5

Who Am I? – On Male-Male Relationships and the End of the Text in *Etzel Andergast* (1931) and *Joseph Kerkhovens dritte Existenz* (1934)

Introduction

The analysis of the two remaining novels in the so-called 'Andergast Trilogy', *Etzel Andergast* (1931) and *Joseph Kerkhovens dritte Existenz* (1934), is intended to show how, in their depiction of male-male relationships, these two novels can be understood as a continuation of *Maurizius*. At first sight the two subsequent novels do not seem to have much in common with *Maurizius* since there is no continuous narrative apart from the reappearance of its protagonist Etzel Andergast, who is, however, several years older and altogether a different character. Garrin's view that Etzel's reappearance alone 'ties the three works together' is not satisfactory.[1] It is therefore necessary to illustrate how these three novels are linked thematically in order to determine whether the term trilogy is indeed suitable, a notion that has been vehemently rejected by Peter de Mendelssohn.[2] This question is even more important in the light of Wassermann's tendency to have characters reappear in novels that are otherwise unrelated, as with Eva Sorel, who is portrayed as a child in *Das Gänsemännchen* and reappears as an adult in *Christian Wahnschaffe*. To enable a comparison with the findings from the previous chapter, the portrayal and development of character will stand at the centre of the examination again. Analysis will show how Wassermann started off with a negative version of the disappearance of character in *Maurizius* but arrives, just before the end of his own life, at a most remarkable statement as *Joseph Kerkhovens dritte Existenz* draws to a close, namely the demand for the disappearance of the text. In a similar vein to *Wahnschaffe*, in which the fading away of character carried positive connotations, Wassermann now depicts the vanishing of Kerkhoven's precious manuscript as a necessary sacrifice for the benefit of humanity.

1 Garrin, *Concept*, p. 14.

2 Peter de Mendelssohn, 'Jakob Wassermanns letztes Werk', in *Joseph Kerkhovens dritte Existenz* (Munich: DTV, 1989), pp. 531–59 (p. 531).

Even though the two later novels confront us with stronger female characters than those in *Maurizius*, the analysis will focus predominantly on the male-male relationships portrayed in the two novels. This focus is justified since feminist criticism has by now already dealt thoroughly with the female characters.[3] The examination will illustrate how, through the depiction of these, by now symbolic, father-and-son relationships, Wassermann arrives at various critical pictures of German society before World War I as well as during the Weimar Republic. Adopting the viewpoint of various characters, Wassermann keeps re-visiting those different periods, thus allowing very different perspectives on them. Moreover, linking those periods through these male-male relationships corresponds to Peukert's view that many of the things we are used to associating with the Weimar years actually have their roots in the Wilhelmine era.[4] While he is not interested in actual politics, Wassermann is keen to explore the psychological forces at work through his analyses of different forms of, mostly failed, male bonding. This repeated surveying of the same periods from different perspectives can be understood as a link not only between the three novels but also between their individual parts. This will in particular help us to understand how the seemingly unconnected first part of *Andergast*, that is, 'Joseph Kerkhoven – Die Vor-Welt', can indeed be linked to the rest of the novel through more than just the reappearance of characters.

This first part of *Andergast* tells the story of the homosexual industrialist and explorer Johann Irlen, who witnesses the disintegration of his friend Otto Kapeller's personality and thus of the world he used to know on the eve of the Great War. Through the actions of this outsider figure the question of what a human character actually is becomes the centre of attention, culminating in Irlen's attempt to make himself part of Joseph Kerkhoven's character. At the same time the relationship between the two men serves as an illustration of a possible relationship between pre- and post-war Germany.

In the second part, Kerkhoven becomes the third father in Etzel's life and, as with his predecessors Wolf von Andergast and Georg Warschauer, this 'son' Etzel will seek to destroy him. This time, however, Etzel himself is left destroyed by a life that does not allow him to reconcile his polar longings for order and rebellion, for a father and for the latter's destruction. Etzel refuses to give people more of himself than a merely superficial performance which eventually, with striking parallels to the case of his actual father Andergast, leads to his self-destruction. Garrin's claim that 'Etzel's personality differs substantially from that of his father' will therefore be proven wrong.[5] At

3 Schäfer, *Plaidoyer*.
4 Peukert, *Die Weimarer Republik*, pp. 27, 166.
5 Garrin, *Concept*, p. 35.

the same time, Etzel is shown to be a typical child of his time and thus a representative of the troubled youth of the Weimar Republic. This becomes most apparent when Etzel, who lacks a sense of direction in his life, falls into the trap of political radicalism and, for a short while, follows the radical political leader Jürgen Lorriner. Moreover, in his function as a representative of Weimar youth culture, the figure of Etzel can also be read as a 'kalte persona', as described by Helmut Lethen,[6] and thus as a critique of a certain understanding of 'Neue Sachlichkeit'.[7]

Kerkhoven depicts the title character's life after the catastrophe of Etzel's betrayal. Even though the latter is absent from this novel, it remains a searching portrayal of the relationship between the older generation, now represented by Kerkhoven, and the contemporary one. Wassermann investigates whether the destructive forces he considers 'zeittypisch' (as represented by Etzel and Herzog's first wife Ganna) can be tamed by spiritual means. Moreover, we are confronted with the question of whether the previous generation already contains these destructive and anarchic forces, merely projecting them onto the younger generation. Geraint Vaughan Jones has, therefore, rightly pointed out that the character of Kerkhoven embodies Wassermann's 'philosophical search' once humanism has seemingly become insufficient.[8] More generally, *Kerkhoven* is dominated by the figures of Kerkhoven and the novelist Alexander Herzog; and, to an even stronger degree than in the case of Andergast and Maurizius in *Maurizius*, we see these two characters merge into one person. This construction is complicated even further by the fact that, in the character of Herzog, Wassermann seemingly introduces himself into his own work, the implications of which will be part of the analysis. This is of particular importance since towards the end of the novel Kerkhoven and Herzog, in what seems like a combined effort, eventually destroy the dying Kerkhoven's manuscript, which was to be his final masterpiece. The disappearance of the text, as well as Wassermann's own involvement in its destruction, will be discussed as the final moment in Wassermann's life as a writer.

6 Helmut Lethen, *Verhaltenslehren der Kälte: Lebensversuche zwischen den Kriegen* (Frankfurt a. M.: Suhrkamp, 1994), pp. 53–133.

7 'Neue Sachlichkeit' is probably best thought of as a new attitude that evolved during the Weimar Years in Germany and found different forms of expression in music, the arts and literature. Sometimes decried as an Americanism, it aimed at a depiction of society, relationships, technology and other things that was free from illusions and sentiment in favour of objectivity. Notoriously difficult to define, 'Neue Sachlichkeit' ought not to be thought of as a homogenous movement.

8 Geraint Vaughan Jones, 'Jakob Wassermann's "Joseph Kerkhovens Dritte Existenz": Its Philosophy and Structure', *German Life and Letters*, 3 (1949/1950), pp. 169–85 (pp. 169, 174).

Wassermann and His 'Gestalt'

Before discussing the relationship between the two figures of Kerkhoven and Irlen, it is necessary to give a brief account of Wassermann's notion of character and 'Gestalt', otherwise the subsequent experiment of literally making Irlen a part of Kerkhoven's character might seem incomprehensible and even absurd. Moreover, Neubauer has rightly observed that 'Form und Gestalt' are essential to the understanding of Wassermann's work.[9] In this context it is necessary to refer to Wassermann's concept of 'Gestalt', as presented in his speech entitled 'Rede über die Gestalt' (1924), since it is inextricably linked with his conception of character.

Reaching far beyond being a mere question of style or narrative technique, the depiction of character is, for Wassermann, always also a portrayal of that figure's historical and social context. The state of a character therefore becomes a measure for the general state of society. According to Wassermann, a 'Gestalt' can have its origins in history, religion or any form of art, even music or architecture. These 'Gestalten' literary or historical examples, which include Hamlet, Werther, Robespierre and Richard the Lionheart, have, over the centuries, become independent of criticism and opinions and live on as guiding authorities that we treasure. Charles Dickens was the last artist to create 'Gestalten' that could represent an entire epoch. As a myth the 'Gestalt' survives the passing of time and thus satisfies our 'Sehnsucht nach Gesetzmäßigkeit und nach dem Bilde'.[10] Moreover, the 'Gestalt', through representing an entire epoch, transmits knowledge to people that would otherwise require considerable study and thus teaches them how to see. This is what Wassermann refers to as the transformation of individuals through fantasy. A life without these 'Gestalten' would lead to barbarism because people would be devoid of true guidance.

Nonetheless, the 'Gestalt' has become increasingly rare, without people noticing the danger that lies in this development. The state of society justifies Wassermann's opinion because nowadays the word, and thus the worst enemy of the 'Gestalt', holds sway. It is the word in its most negative form that:

> von Rednertribünen rast, die Völker in Parteien zersplittert, Meinung gegen Meinung peitscht, um jeden in seiner Meinung grausam und dünkelhaft zu machen, Starre des Vorurteils zur Auszeichnung erhebt, Neid, Gier, Verkennung, Verbitterung, Ruhelosigkeit, ja Raub und Mord durch lügenhafte Manifeste legitimiert und Mißtrauen sät zwischen Stämmen, Brüdern und Freunden.[11]

9 Neubauer, *Schriftsteller*, p. 123.

10 Jakob Wassermann, 'Rede über die Gestalt', in *Lebensdienst*, pp. 347–83 (p. 363).

11 Wassermann, 'Rede über die Gestalt', p. 378.

Since the 'Gestalt' functions as a 'Spiegel und Deuter [der Zeit]',[12] the absence of this most complete form of character is alarming. Wassermann is, therefore, aware that the distinct and rounded figures known from classical fiction are no longer feasible because the state of society does not allow them to be created or appreciated. Instead, the characters in his final novels have become more porous, which also means they can influence each other in extraordinary ways. Poeschel has, therefore, rightly remarked that: 'Die Flächen ihrer [Wassermann's Gestalten] Körperlichkeit sind nicht ihre Grenzen. Sie sind nicht in einem statuenhaften Umriß beschlossen'.[13]

Concerned with the difficulties of characterization, Wassermann undertakes the experiment of making one persona become part of another and thus stretches the boundaries of the concept of character in ways hitherto unprecedented in his writing. The curious incident of Irlen becoming a part of Kerkhoven, which will shortly be examined in detail, is therefore best understood as a reaction to a crisis of character as Wassermann perceived it and the subsequent search for a new form of 'Gestalt'. This development of character is also mirrored in the overall form of the three novels. Mendelssohn has shown that while *Maurizius* is still narrated in the traditional form of the novel, this form is already crumbling in *Andergast*, only to fall apart completely in *Kerkhoven*: 'Von einer Struktur, einer Komposition im herkömmlichen Sinn will der Dichter hier kaum mehr etwas wissen, sie ist ihm unwichtig, nebensächlich geworden. [...] Die Kunstform war zerbrochen, das Leben hatte sie ihm zerschlagen'.[14] The notion of Wassermann as a traditional narrator therefore cannot be applied to his late works. Just as with the traditional 'Gestalt', form has also become impossible for Wassermann. Mendelssohn uses these different stages in the development of form as an argument against the notion of the trilogy, yet seen in the context of the development of Wassermann's characters it is more plausible to consider these changing narrative styles as part of one process rather than as a dividing line between the novels. Garrin's view that 'the last volume [of the trilogy] falls apart structurally' is therefore also rather limited.[15]

Johann Irlen – the End of a Generation

With Irlen, Wassermann has once again chosen the figure of a homosexual outsider who has travelled the world to be a spokesman for the failure of Western

12 Wassermann, 'Rede über die Gestalt', p. 382.

13 Poeschel, *Wassermann*, p. 94.

14 Mendelssohn, 'Letztes Werk', p. 549.

15 Garrin, *Concept*, p. 14.

civilization. This time, however, in contrast to Warschauer, he is a member of the higher classes, a former officer, and the continent he has explored is Africa instead of America. What is more important is that this failure of human civilization is mainly pinned down to two concrete examples, namely the First World War and the history of colonization. The reasons given for the end of Irlen's career as an officer offer interesting parallels to the engagement with homosexuality during the Wilhelmine era in *Maurizius*. Irlen was forced to resign from his position in 1907, which, as we have seen in the previous chapter, was the year in which the Eulenburg-Moltke trials began. The narrator describes the incident as follows: 'Seine freundschaftlichen Beziehungen zu einem Prinzen des kaiserlichen Hauses lieferte einer Kamarilla, die schon längst auf der Lauer lag, die gewünschten Waffen. Er musste den Abschied nehmen' (*EA*, p. 15).[16] Even though this is not a direct mention of his homosexuality, it strongly implies his involvement in an affair which, as James W. Jones tells us, turned into a 'massive anti-homosexual witchhunt throughout Germany in which aristocrats, government officials, and military officers all became suspect'.[17] Many were then made to resign from their positions. As with Warschauer, Wassermann thus demonstrates once more how homosexuality was exploited as a tool to eliminate political opponents. In this light another quotation is revealing: 'Er [Irlen] gehörte zu der kleinen Zahl von Offizieren, die, voller Ahnung, vor dem Einbruch der schamlosen Phrase mit allen ihren Folgen in schmerzlichem Ekel zurückwichen' (*EA*, p.14). The fact that he could foretell the outcome of this affair could be read as another indicator of his own involvement. His career, similarly to that of Warschauer, has thus been ruined by his having been in a homosexual affair or the fear of its discovery. A further hint at his homosexuality can be seen in a reflexion made later in the novel by Marie, his nephew's wife, who comes to understand that as a woman she is 'doppelt reizlos für ihn' (*EA*, p. 32).

The depiction of this affair is followed by an account of Irlen's relationship with Otto Kapeller, the son of an industrial tycoon. Otto is clearly rendered as a homosexual; Schneider-Handschin even compares him to Friedrich Alfred Krupp, who was Europe's richest man at the time and committed suicide in 1902 over the public exposure of his homosexuality. There are obvious parallels between Krupp and Kapeller: the ancestors of both were simple blacksmiths; both chose a secret place where their homosexuality could pass without notice; and both were without mercy in the face of labour

16 For the original edition see Jakob Wassermann, *Etzel Andergast* (Berlin: Fischer, 1931).
17 Jones, '*Third Sex*', p. 104.

strikes.[18] Moreover, Wassermann makes use of a common stereotype in the depiction of homosexuals by presenting Otto as an artistic figure.[19] This becomes apparent in Irlen's report of his first encounter with the young man:

> Er saß am Klavier und spielte Debussy. Ich habe nie einen jungen Menschen von einschmeichelnderem Wesen gesehen. Schlank, mit einem stählernen Körper, lächerlich blond, lächerlich hübsch. Er gab sich ohne jedes Zaudern in meine Hand [...]. Es überwältigte mich. Hauptsächlich das eine, daß er in mir immer das Gefühl zu erwecken verstand, ich hätte ihm bis jetzt gefehlt (*EA*, p. 121).

Irlen is obviously smitten with the young man, whom he also describes as a poet unaware of his gift. Otto soon becomes his favourite friend, as a consequence of which Irlen eventually accepts the offer to work for the company of Otto's father so that the young man could always have him by his side.

However, after the sudden death of Otto's father their relationship is soon disrupted. Otto's character turns out to be unstable and he becomes a tyrant at home and indulges in the above-mentioned homosexual affairs. This development leads Irlen to the following observation: 'Ich erlebe eine Metamorphose, die meine Anschauungen über die Konstanz jener Summe von Eigenschaften, die wir Charakter nennen, gründlich über den Haufen wirft' (*EA*, p. 17). However, this disappointment not only has severe implications on a personal level, but gains a much wider significance, since Irlen considers Otto to be representative of his generation. This generation, as Irlen comes to understand, is devoid of ideals and far removed from what he considers reality. Irlen's attempt to shape Otto according to his own ideas could, in this context, therefore be understood to symbolize the fact that that Irlen's generation has lost control over the younger. Otto is gradually revealed as a figure without shape and substance and as another actor of everyday life. Once Otto is burdened with too much wealth and responsibility, Irlen becomes aware how 'die Stützen seiner [Otto's] Persönlichkeit [...] wie Brückenpfeiler unter dem Druck von Treibeis [wankten]' (*EA*, p. 125).

Otto thus plays a double role in Irlen's life as he represents the next generation that is decadent and out of control and also lets him down as a lover. This homoerotic attachment to Otto becomes clear during one of their final scenes when Otto, in a moment of jealousy, tearfully accuses Irlen of having an affair with his sister. Irlen's reply could not be clearer: 'absurd absurd ... als wäre ich dem Edelsten meiner Natur untreu geworden und hätte ihn damit in heillose innere Verwirrung gestürzt. Absurd' (*EA*, p. 133). This lovers'

18 Schneider-Handschin, *Bild*, p. 94.

19 Jones, '*Third Sex*', p. 271.

tale, which is at the same time a story of two conflicting generations, comes to an end when Irlen shoots Otto in a duel after the latter has insulted him in public. The duel, which the workers at Otto's factory aptly consider an 'in-die-Knie-Brechen vor den verknöcherten Ehrbegriffen seiner Kaste' (*EA*, p. 17), seems like an outdated and desperate attempt by Irlen to re-establish a form of sense and order among a generation that, in his opinion, has long forgotten the way back 'aus dem Schein in die Wirklichkeit' (*EA*, p. 136).

The duel prompts Irlen to go on an expedition to the Congo and reconsider his entire existence. Life as he knew it has become questionable since he feels the significance of his generation to be fading. The description of his experiences in Africa strongly resembles those accounts given in Wassermann's biography of the explorer Henry Morton Stanley, which was published in 1932, only one year after *Etzel Andergast*. Among the many parallels between the two figures, the most striking are that both are depicted as outsiders and that both have homoerotic relationships with indigenous African men. In Irlen's case it is his strong attachment to the figure of the handsome Ngaljema, while Stanley, according to Wassermann, 'periodenweise der Knabenliebe gehuldigt hat'.[20] Moreover, most importantly, Wassermann arrives in both works at a fierce condemnation of European civilization and its supposed merits by shedding a light on the agonies that Europe inflicted on the African continent. After a description of the cruelties committed by the Arab ivory traders in Africa, Irlen arrives at even more damning conclusions regarding Europe's involvement:

> [D]as christliche Europa hat ihnen nichts vorzuwerfen, da es doch dreihundert Jahre lang mit schwarzem Menschenfleisch geschachert und sich bereichert hat, Europa und Amerika, das ihm über den Kopf gewachsen ist, sie sind eines Geistes. [...] Europa ist der Mord, seine Religion, seine Praktiken, seine Zivilisation, jedes für sich, alle zusammen (*EA*, p. 168).

This criticism clearly refers to the slave trade in Africa and to the notorious exploitation of the Belgian Congo and can be understood as a direct follow-up to *Maurizius*, in which Warschauer utters similar views condemning Western civilization. Through this direct confrontation between his civilized world and the 'savage' surroundings of Africa, Irlen comes to see that Europe is sick and that the indigenous Africans are actually superior to the so-called civilized Europeans. The views expressed here can be linked to an increasingly widespread critique of colonialism which, for example, can also be found in Wassermann's contemporary Ödön von Horváth, who, even though taking a more humorous tone, arrives at a similar critique in the conversation between Schmitz and Kobler in his novel *Der ewige Spießer* (1930):

20 Jakob Wassermann, *Bula Matari: Das Leben Stanleys* (Berlin: Fischer, 1932), pp. 229–30.

> Und glaubens mir, wenn man die armen Neger nicht so schamlos ausbeuten tät, wäre das der Fall, denn dann wären ja alle Kolonialprodukte unerschwinglich teuer, weil dann halt die Plantagenbesitzer auch gleich das Tausendfache verdienen wollten – glaubens mir, mein sehr Verehrter, wir Weißen sind die größten Bestien.[21]

A few years earlier and close to the time in which this part of *Andergast* is set, Thomas Mann, in his *Betrachtungen eines Unpolitischen*, also arrives at a fierce condemnation of the slave trade as well as of British involvement in India.[22] Admittedly, though, Mann's main aim here is to denounce British hypocrisy.

On his return to Europe in 1913, Irlen immediately realizes that Europe, with Germany as its 'Herzvolk', is confronted by the dangers of war. Unlike Warschauer, he decides to intervene, an act which cures him of his last remaining illusion: the importance of the individual in a growing mass society. Irlen describes the initial purpose of his expedition to Africa as follows:

> Es handelte sich darum, einmal aus den sämtlichen Hüllen und Schalen herauszuschlüpfen, in die die Existenz innerhalb einer so tyrannisch-gleichmacherischen Lebensform wie die unsere uns einschnürt. Wir haben uns ja verloren. Einen großen Blickwinkel aus großer Weite zu finden, darum ging's (*EA*, p. 169).

The experience makes Irlen reconsider his views on Western civilization as well as his former world with its ideals. His belief in human agency, however, remains firm, an attitude which characterizes him, in the narrator's view, as belonging to the 'old' Wilhelmine world. Even though Irlen finds himself in the final stages of the African sleeping sickness, he decides to travel to London and thus sacrifice the remainder of his life in order to prevent the war. However, he achieves nothing more than a few conversations in gentlemen's clubs. The narrator refers to this as an 'Akt stoischer Selbstverleugnung [...], [der] sich auf ein tiefes, bei einem solchen Kopf beinahe unbegreifliches Mißverstehen dessen gründete, was persönlicher Einsatz und private Initiative am Gang welthistorischer Geschehnisse zu ändern vermögen' (*EA*, p. 209). This experience leads him to the conclusion that his entire life has been futile and that he lives in a society in which the impact of the individual does not matter: 'Aber eine Folge hätte sein müssen, irgendeine, die allerkleinste. Nein, keine' (*EA*, p. 222). Unable to live in a society in which the individual must remain an outsider unless he or she becomes part of a bigger group or movement, Irlen decides to take his own life.

21 Ödön von Horváth, *Der ewige Spießer*, ed. by Traugott Krischke (Frankfurt a.M: Suhrkamp, 2001), p. 198.

22 Thomas Mann, *Betrachtungen*, pp. 366–69.

Irlen's world, his ideals and eventually his self are thus shown to be crumbling. This state is further emphasized by his suffering from the African sleeping sickness, which affects his nervous system. His situation is described as follows:

> Dadurch hörte das Leben auf, ein Gefüge zu sein, es zerstückt sich in eine Summe einzelner Sekunden und Augenblicke als wären sämtliche Buchstaben eines Dramas durcheinander geschüttelt und man hätte an Stelle einer geistbestimmten Form einen Haufen von hundertausend Alphabeten vor sich (*EA*, p. 101).

Irlen's life is losing its definite shape, something which marks the end not only of his character but also of his era, since in the two novels 'shapelessness' becomes one of the main characteristics of life in Germany after 1918. Goldmann captures this mood when, in 1929, he writes that life has become a 'zusammenhangloses Sein'.[23]

In order to highlight Irlen's function as a representative of the Wilhelmine era, it is important to point out some of the parallels between Irlen and Wassermann's friend, the industrialist, politician and writer Walther Rathenau. Elisabeth Albanis has argued that Irlen can be understood as a fictional representation of Rathenau, who also served as the model for Paul Arnheim in Musil's *Der Mann ohne Eigenschaften*. Irlen can therefore be understood as a 'typical member of the industrial bourgeoisie'.[24] Albanis, however, instead of understanding Irlen as a homosexual character, infers that his status 'as a lonely figure on the periphery of society [...] strongly suggests that he is supposed to be interpreted as having a Jewish identity'.[25] However, it is more intriguing to understand this replacement of the original Jewish figure by a homosexual one as another parallel Wassermann is drawing between the status of Jews and homosexuals as both standing outside society. Even though much of her interpretation is based on this aspect of Jewishness, Albanis nevertheless shows many other parallels between the two figures. Rathenau, like Irlen, travelled to Africa; and both characters are described as 'exclusive, well-connected, a patron of the arts, easily infatuated with all things foreign, a man of political ambitions as well as a dangerous thinker'.[26] Irlen and Rathenau both suffer from their relationship to Germany as they try to rescue a nation that does not want to be saved by them. Another parallel can be seen in Rathenau's close friendship with Maximilan Harden, which ended with Rathenau challenging

23 Goldmann, *Wassermann*, p. 7.

24 Elisabeth Albanis, 'Jakob Wassermann's Memorial to Walther Rathenau in *Etzel Andergast*', *German Life and Letters*, 50 (1997), 18–35 (p. 19).

25 Albanis, 'Memorial to Walther Rathenau', 19.

26 Albanis, 'Jakob Wassermann's Memorial', 20.

the latter to a duel. The description of Irlen in the novel strongly resembles that of Rathenau which Wassermann published as an obituary in 1922.[27] Moreover, Lindemann-Luiken has rightly observed that for Wassermann the assassination of Rathenau equalled an 'emotionale Katastrophe',[28] which makes it even more plausible that he felt the need to write about it. In this light it is difficult to accept Garrin's claim that the relationship between Irlen and Kerkhoven is 'a fictional account of the author and Hugo von Hofmannsthal'.[29]

Irlen and Kerkhoven – Generations Unite

If Irlen can therefore be understood as a representative of the Wilhelmine era, then Kerkhoven has to be understood as a representative of the succeeding generation. With a life taken over by work, Kerkhoven becomes Wassermann's most archetypal representative of modern daily life. Stuck in a wearisome routine and an unhappy marriage, Kerkhoven lives in a state of 'Selbstauslöschung' (*EA*, p. 49) which arguably means he does not live at all. It is only through his friendship with Irlen that he becomes aware of his loneliness, which Irlen considers 'ein Merkmal der Zeit' (*EA*, p. 45). Irlen thus also comes to see Kerkhoven, who lives a life devoid of love and friendship, as representing a new era and cannot resist the temptation to try and shape Kerkhoven, who inspires 'eine Art Lenker- und Entdeckerfreude' (*EA*, p. 58) in him. Convinced of Kerkhoven's talent, Irlen wants him to leave his old self and thus his unhappy existence behind in order to embrace his true vocation, namely to become a 'Seelenarzt'. With the depiction of Kerkhoven's transformation in the first part of the novel, Wassermann goes far beyond the instability of character shown in *Maurizius*. As already suggested by the title of his last novel, *Kerkhoven*, Wassermann here advances a theory according to which individuals carry within themselves various identities or existences that emerge at different points in their lives. The analysis of Kerkhoven's transformation will show that these existences are not to be understood as phases but as far more substantial changes in the life of an individual.

One of the difficulties in writing about the figure of Kerkhoven is that he seems to have become the narrator's primary example for illustrating his belief that 'die Fiktion eines fest umrissenen Charakters' (*EA*, p. 107) has become increasingly hard to maintain. The character of Kerkhoven is therefore notoriously difficult to grasp. In fact, this corresponds to the initial lines in *Andergast*, in which the narrator admits that the characters he is trying to

27 Jakob Wassermann, 'Zu Walther Rathenaus Tod', in *Lebensdienst*, pp. 23–30.

28 Lindemann-Luiken, *Auswirkungen*, p. 29.

29 Garrin, *Concept*, p. 65.

depict are indeed so complex that 'ich schlechterdings daran verzweifle, im einzelnen zu Bild und Figur zu gelangen. Ich muß mich damit abfinden, selbst auf die Gefahr hin, daß mir das Chaos über dem Kopf zusammenschlägt' (*EA*, p. 9). Wassermann, who has repeatedly been criticized for creating dominant, even patronizing narrators,[30] here presents us with a narrator who is uncertain of his own task. This signifies another radical departure in Wassermann's writing, one reflected throughout the novel. The most important aspect of Kerkhoven's character in its first part is, however, his transformation from a mere physician into the 'Seelenarzt' with whom the reader is confronted throughout the rest of the trilogy. In a conversation with Irlen, Kerkhoven reveals why, so far, he has not been able to achieve any great results in the field of medicine: 'Es fehlt mir das Doppelte, das die großen Leute haben, der innere Dual. [...] wenn ich dich noch in mir hätte, Johann. Als Komplement sozusagen ... Unser Herrgott hat mich nicht fertig gemacht. Was mir fehlt, das bist du' (*EA*, p. 110). Kerkhoven's character is, therefore, incomplete, almost one-dimensional, and Irlen considers it a mere question of willpower to change it.

The final scene between Irlen and Kerkhoven is the most significant because Kerkhoven's transformation is described in vivid terms with a strong magical element. Moreover, it marks the beginning of Wassermann's most significant approach towards a more synthetic understanding of spirituality. Kerkhoven is described as a person who 'durch eine Art Zauberei veranlaßt worden ist, aus dem Rahmen seiner Persönlichkeit herauszutreten und für eine Weile auch, halb körperlos gleichsam, in diesem Zustand zu verbleiben' (*EA*, p. 220). Irlen has asked Kerkhoven to assist him with his suicide by providing him with a lethal mixture. For a while there are two Kerkhovens in the room, fighting over the 'right' decision: 'Ja, da sind sie also alle beide da, der Mann der Barmherzigkeit und der Mann der Gerechtigkeit. Sie liegen sich in den Haaren' (*EA*, p. 223). Since Kerkhoven finds himself unable to reach a decision, Irlen reminds him of his wish to possess 'das Doppelte', that is, to make Irlen a part of himself.

Irlen eventually convinces Kerkhoven by telling him about the Parsis' belief in 'Fravashis':

> Sie sind ein Teil der menschlichen Seele, doch vom Körper unabhängige Wesen. Es heißt, daß sie in einem der Vernichtung preisgegebenen Körper nicht verweilen können, sie gehen heraus. Sie sind nicht vernichtbar wie das Gewissen und das Bewußtsein, [...] sie sind auch nicht auf ein und denselben Leib angewiesen, sie dürfen sich eine andere Behausung suchen, vorausgesetzt, daß sie einem Reinen gehört. Wenn sie das tun, ist es ein freiwilliges Opfer. [...]

30 Neubauer, *Schriftsteller*, p. 179.

> So hat jedes lebende Wesen einen Fravashi, aber es gibt Auserwählte, die haben auch zwei, sogar drei. Merkwürdig, nicht? (*EA*, p. 225).

The 'Fravashis' are part of the novel's eclectic use of religious imagery, one which seems to indicate that any form of religiosity or spirituality is relevant in the search for a better future and will become even more apparent in Kerkhoven's final search for spiritual fulfilment. In this context Mendelssohn has suggested the useful term 'gesamtreligiöse Ebene' to describe Kerkhoven's later state of mind.[31] Joeris also observes that towards the end of his life Wassermann was aiming for a 'übergeschichtliche Sicht der Dinge. [...] Die Werte der Humanität und der Liebe erlangen einen unbedingten Vorrang'.[32] The refusal to prioritize one particular religion is formulated around the same time and in much stronger terms in his 'Rede an die studentische Jugend', in which Wassermann claims: 'Solcherart entstehen dann Kreuzzüge, Hexen- und Ketzergerichte, Bürgerkrieg und Terror, Chauvinismus und Nationalismus, immer mit der Berufung auf den Tempel, der die Stätte des einzigen wahren Gottes sei, während die Anhänger aller andern Götter erschlagen werden müßten'.[33] This stands in strong opposition to Joeris's other claim that Wassermann conceded to the Jewish religion and people a 'Führungsanspruch' due to them having suffered for so long and to their messianism.[34]

At this point Kerkhoven finally understands that Irlen is, at least partly, sacrificing himself for the physician's sake, thus becoming the complementary part of Kerkhoven's soul. The idea of sacrifice could be seen as standing at the centre of this transformation. Once implanted into Kerkhoven's system, it becomes the guiding principle in his life, in particular towards the end of *Kerkhoven*. In the five weeks between Irlen's death and the outbreak of World War I, Kerkhoven undergoes a development 'als erlösche in gewissen Abständen die Wirklichkeit in ihm' (*EA*, p. 226). However, the narrator claims that the phenomenon cannot be explained in merely scientific terms, as the human soul is more than just a few chemical reactions. Instead, it is said that Kerkhoven embarks on a journey from which he returns a different man with almost supernatural powers. Wassermann thus experiments with the idea of allowing his otherwise realistic characters to experience supernatural influences, as well as allowing them to have more than one existence. Moreover, in its strange spirituality this scene allows another connection to

31 Mendelssohn, 'Letztes Werk', p. 534.

32 Joeris, *Aspekte*, 25.

33 Jakob Wassermann, 'Rede an die Studentische Jugend über das Leben im Geiste: Zum Goethetag 1932', *Die Neue Rundschau*, 43 (1932), 529–46 (p. 539).

34 See Joeris, *Aspekte*, p. 33.

Hesse's work as it is also reminiscent of the ending of *Demian*, in which the dead title character is said to have become a part of Emil Sinclair:

> Aber wenn ich [Sinclair] manchmal den Schlüssel finde und ganz in mich selbst hinuntersteige, da wo im dunkeln Spiegel die Schicksalsbilder schlummern, dann brauche ich mich nur über den schwarzen Spiegel zu neigen und sehe mein eigenes Bild, das nun ganz Ihm [Demian] gleicht, Ihm, meinem Freund und Führer.[35]

Following his final encounter with Irlen, Kerkhoven is thus endowed with a mysterious power over other people's souls that will soon turn him into one of the most sought-after doctors in Berlin. In his function as a 'Seelenarzt', Kerkhoven will attempt to counterbalance the effect that life in the city of Berlin has on many people while at the same time being devoured by the endless demands of the city's masses. Symbolically speaking, the dying 'old' age has thus left Kerkhoven with the task of shaping the new era after the collapse, which he will unsuccessfully attempt in his relationship with Etzel Andergast.

Etzel and Kerkhoven – the Impossible Son

The beginning of the second part of the novel, entitled 'Etzel Andergast – Die Mit-Welt', is set fourteen years later and thus in the later stages of the Weimar Republic. Tellingly, Kerkhoven has also moved to Berlin and thus to the centre of this new era. From this point onwards, the trilogy as a whole, especially the figure of Kerkhoven, can be understood as an attempt to come to terms with a world that ceased to make sense a long time ago. This becomes apparent in Kerkhoven's relationship with Etzel Andergast but also in his function as a physician; even though he does not recount events in the first person, Kerkhoven becomes the focalizer of the novel. It is through his eyes that Wassermann draws his most intriguing picture of life in Germany towards the end of the Weimar Republic. However, in his review, Alfred Döblin makes the following important observation:

> [E]s ist nicht seine [Wassermann's] Art, über die Feststellung hinaus zu Entscheidungen und Entschlüssen vorzustossen, er liebt es Spannungen zu belassen, zu verschleiern und zu besänftigen. [...] Ist dies nun aber eine Auseinandersetzung mit der Zeit? Der "Politische" von heute wird sagen: nein. Aber unter Zeit und Zeit ist Verschiedenes zu verstehen.[36]

35 Hesse, 'Demian', p. 365.

36 Alfred Döblin, 'Jakob Wassermanns letztes Buch', *Die Sammlung*, 10 (1933/34), 517–23 (pp. 518–19).

It would, therefore, indeed be a futile pursuit to look for solutions to specific political or social problems in these two novels; rather, they ought to be understood as Wassermann's version of the later stages of the Weimar Republic.

According to the narrator, the years between 1914 and 1928 have changed 'das Bild der Menschheit' (*EA*, p. 237), and the body of the individual, in this case Kerkhoven's, would have changed accordingly. Hence the narrator makes it clear that we are no longer dealing with the same person since the 'I' can no longer be considered a stable entity:

> Nur die Wand des Körpers macht, daß das Fließende nicht zerfließt, und auch sie ist nicht viel fester als der Schatten, den sie wirft, Membran, das sich hart wehren muß gegen den Andrang des Fließenden. Eigentlich ist es allein die Idee von Gesicht und Form, die dem Vergehen trotzt, deswegen bist du dir in jedem Spiegel einen Augenblick lang grausig unbekannt, und dein geheimnisvoller Schreck darüber ist nichts anderes als die jäh aufblitzende Erkenntnis der Illusion, der du dich über dein Ichsein unaufhörlich hingibst (*EA*, p. 237).

This is one of Wassermann's most drastic statements to date, going far beyond his previously depicted instability of character. Wassermann thus says not only that the body is in constant change but also that the self has become more unstable since 1914. The state of the self could therefore be understood as a mirror of the severe changes in society brought about by the Great War and thus as an illustration of Wassermann's theory concerning the 'Gestalt'.

This refutation of the concept of 'I', underlined even more by his addressing his reader directly, corresponds to views expressed by Ernst Mach in *Die Analyse der Empfindungen und das Verhältnis des Physischen zum Psychischen* (1886). Mach famously proclaimed 'Das *Ich* ist unrettbar'[37] and:

> maintained that consciousness consisted of sensations, and that the self which received these sensations was simply a complex of feelings, moods and memories, attached to a body. By changing only gradually, this complex gives the illusion of permanence; but in fact there is no permanent, substantial self underlying the flux of sensations.[38]

These ideas were then developed further by Hermann Bahr, who uses the notion that reality is in constant flux.[39] Wassermann can therefore be seen as responding to this important modern discourse. Franz Werfel's *Blasphemie*

37 Ernst Mach, *Die Analyse der Empfindungen und das Verhältnis des Physischen zum Psychischen*, 2nd edn. (Jena: Gustav Fischer, 1900), p. 17.

38 Robertson, 'Modernism', p. 163.

39 Robertson, 'Modernism', p. 163.

eines Irren (1914) serves as another example from literature in which a similar view is expressed: 'Ich zu sagen ist immer ein Versprechen, das man nicht halten kann'.[40] Broch's *Schlafwandler* also needs to be mentioned in this context as a major attempt to explore this crisis of the self across several decades of German history and by means of various characters. In the third book the shell-shocked soldier Gödicke experiences a 'Sturm, der die Teile seines Ichs durcheinanderrüttelte'.[41] In the first book Joachim von Pasenow realises 'daß er der verschwimmenden und verfließenden Masse des Lebens nicht mehr habhaft zu werden vermochte und daß er immer rascher und immer tiefer in ire Hirngespinste glitt, und alles war unsicher geworden'.[42] Towards the end of the novel Hanna Wendling feels her 'I' to be transcending her body 'als werde ihr Ich nicht durch ihre Haut begrenzt'.[43] The main characters in the trilogy are therefore constantly driven by a sense of having lost themselves and are, as a consequence, unable to establish who they really are. In this situation Kerkhoven comes to play a double role since, as a physician, he diagnoses the maladies of the time in which he lives while at the same time he cannot help being affected by them. In this context it is also important to consider the symbolic value of the figure of the physician, who in modern fiction has often replaced that of the priest.[44] Wassermann emphasizes this link through his choice of the name 'Kerkhoven' because in Dutch 'Kerk' means church. The physician as witness of modern life is not an arbitrary choice therefore as throughout the novel Kerkhoven will always fulfil several functions: observer, physician and 'Seelsorger'.

When Etzel and Kerkhoven finally meet in Chapter 9, they are immediately drawn towards each other, even though with his reappearance Etzel has turned into an even more problematic character. This time the relationship between the younger man and the older mentor figure is free from the homoerotic tendencies that dominated the relationship between Etzel and Warschauer. At the centre of the relationship between these two stands the wish to overcome their individual forms of isolation: Kerkhoven, as a mirror image of his time, is a modern workaholic and thus finds himself isolated from his private self; while Etzel, as another mirror image from the same time, suffers from a form of deliberate emotional isolation brought about by the traumatic events of his youth: 'Er konnte keinen brauchen, der

40 Franz Werfel, 'Blasphemie eines Irren', in *Die Schwarze Messe – Erzählungen*, ed. by Knut Beck (Frankfurt a. M.: Fischer, 1989), pp. 99–107 (p. 101).

41 Broch, *Schlafwandler*, p. 486.

42 Broch, *Schlafwandler*, p. 128.

43 Broch, *Schlafwandler*, p. 613.

44 For other examples, see Franz Kafka's *Ein Landarzt* (1917), Henrik Ibsen's *The Wild Duck* (1884) and Arthur Schnitzler's *Paracelsus* (1898).

den eisernen Tresor aufsprengte, um die unter Verschluß gesetzte Seele zu beäugen' (*EA*, p. 255). Etzel is therefore characterized as a representative of a time in which, as Helmut Lethen puts it, 'Entfremdungs-Kälte der "Gesellschaft" als Lebenselixier denkbar wird'.[45] As Broch comments: '[der Mensch ist] unfähig seine Einsamkeit zu sprengen'.[46]

With Kerkhoven as a member of his father's generation, it is therefore even more surprising that he immediately inspires the following thoughts and feelings in Etzel:

> Sich ihm [Kerkhoven] anzuvertrauen war ein Gedanke, der nicht ohne weiteres von der Hand zu weisen war. [...] Nicht ausgeschlossen, daß er, mit diesen Hexenmeister-Augen, zu sehen imstande war, was keiner sah, wenigstens keiner von denen, die, jenseits der Wendekreise, in der verderblichen Zone des Erfolgs und der Geschäfte wohnten: die Fetten, die Beruhigten, die Aktionäre, die Gesetzeshüter (*EA*, p. 278).

For Etzel, Kerkhoven thus becomes an alternative father figure, embodying the possibility of reconciliation with the generation of his own father Wolf von Andergast, with whom he had lived in a state of constant confrontation. This is also the first indicator of the view, propounded throughout the novel, that underneath the rebellion of the younger generation lies the unfulfillable longing for order and reconciliation. Here Hofmannsthal's influence, which Wassermann acknowledges in his 'Rede an die studentische Jugend', becomes palpable. In 'Das Schrifttum als geistiger Raum der Nation' Hofmannsthal writes: 'Denn nicht Freiheit ist es, was sie [youth] zu suchen aus sind, sondern Bindung'.[47] At the same time, Etzel assumes the role of a son for Kerkhoven in that the latter hopes that by curing Etzel he will be able to have a positive impact on this lost generation of German youth:

> In den Raum der bedrohten Vitalität und des zynischen Sterbens, in dem Kerkhoven bisweilen zumute war, als sei alle Jugend von einem Wundmal gezeichnet und wehre sich immer weniger gegen den Tod und immer mehr gegen das Leben, das heißt gegen das Leben-Sollen, gegen das Sein als solches (vielleicht kennt die Geschichte kein schwereres Verhängnis, sagte er sich), trat nun mit einem Mal dieser Etzel Andergast (*EA*, p. 283).

The story of Etzel and Kerkhoven can thus be understood as a tale of two conflicting generations whose failure to be reunited ends in catastrophe. It is at the same time an investigation into the limits of paternal authority as well

45 Lethen, *Verhaltenslehren*, p. 9.

46 Broch, *Schlafwandler*, p. 551.

47 Hugo von Hofmannsthal, 'Das Schrifttum als geistiger Raum der Nation', in *Die Berührung der Sphären* (Berlin: Fischer, 1931), pp. 422–43 (p. 438).

as an attempt to understand the paradox surrounding the figure of the son, namely the desire and the inability to be led.

Etzel, to whom the narrator refers as a child of his time, thus stands at the centre of Kerkhoven's endeavours to come to terms with the fate of Germany's youth. In the course of his analysis of Etzel's character, Kerkhoven may not always draw a favourable picture of him but he is never without sympathy. This means that even though Wassermann's depiction of Germany's youth can at times be drastic, it is never condemning and therefore reflects his own engagement with that youth. On Wassermann's importance amongst the younger generation Leydecker remarks: 'Wassermann's global appeal seems to have been particularly strong to young people, with the effect he had on the younger generation of the 1920s being likened to Hermann Hesse's significance for the hippy generation of the 1960s'.[48] Towards the end of his life, as mentioned in his 'Rede an die Studentische Jugend', Wassermann received and replied to numerous letters from distressed young people seeking advice.[49] He was thus highly aware of their severe crisis: 'In Deutschland allein gibt es momentan ungefähr sechs Millionen junge Menschen ohne jede tragfähige Lebensgrundlage. [...] [I]ch spreche von Hoffnungslosen [...]. Das Dasein bietet ihnen überhaupt keinen Anreiz mehr'.[50] Despite this awareness of their plight, Wassermann refuses to lend them his unbridled sympathy. Instead, he seeks to explore the tensions between the two generations at conflict without necessarily taking sides:

> Nicht jeder Vierzigjährige ist schon darum ein Verbrecher und Idiot, weil er zwanzig Jahre älter ist als du, nicht jeder Fünfzig- und Sechzigjährige ein Rückschrittler und Feind, nicht jeder Vater ein Narr und jeder Sohn ein Held und Märtyrer.[51]

This approach is also reflected in *Andergast*. In the course of the trilogy, Wassermann therefore moves from a rather classical father-son-conflict, with the father as a predominantly negative figure in *Maurizius*, to a more complex, searching portrayal of it in *Andergast*. This strong interest in the fate of the younger generation as embodied in the character of Etzel stands in strong opposition to Mendelssohn's claim that *Andergast* is really only concerned with Kerkhoven's personal development.[52]

Apart from another way of looking at the father-son dynamic, the figure of Etzel also embodies a critique of the 'neusachliche' concept of character,

48 Leydecker, 'Case', p. 85.
49 Wassermann, 'Rede an die Studentische Jugend', p. 534.
50 Wassermann, 'Rede an die Studentische Jugend', p. 530.
51 Wassermann, 'Rede an die Studentische Jugend', p. 544.
52 Mendelssohn, 'Letztes Werk', pp. 531–32.

especially since the novel was written at a time when writers and intellectuals had largely begun to reject 'Neue Sachlichkeit'. Even though, as David Midgley has shown, 'Neue Sachlichkeit' is a term that is notoriously difficult to use,[53] it is nevertheless rewarding to point out some of the parallels between the figure of Etzel and that of the 'kalte persona' as presented by Lethen. Lethen argues that between 1910 and 1930 avant-garde movements were fascinated by the 'Gestalt mit der einfachen Kontur'[54] and thus with the 'Gestalt eines morbiden Subjekts ohne seelische Tiefengliederung, dessen Bewegungsraum weder durch Interventionen der Moral noch durch die Stimme des Gewissens eingeschränkt wird'.[55] In strong opposition to Expressionism this 'kalte persona' refrains from any form of radical expression, makes no confessions and rejects the idea of authenticity. Rather, this 'Kult der Sachlichkeit' finds itself in favour of the idea of acting as the basis for a character: '[D]ie Stimme des Schauspielers tönt durch die vors Gesicht gehaltene Scheibe, das Ich ist selbstmächtig erst im Bewußtsein dessen, was nach außen tritt'.[56] This concept of character denies the existence of a significant inner life and thus the need for psychological insight, a denial which stands in strong opposition to Wassermann's psychological approach.

Tellingly, Kerkhoven's initial impression of Etzel strongly resembles the depiction of Etzel as an actor of everyday life in *Maurizius*:

> Allmählich kam er zur Vorstellung eines Menschen mit zwei oder drei Existenzen, der in jeder Umgebung sogleich deren Farbe annimmt, sich wie alle andern äußert und es in der Kunst der Anähnlichung bis zur Vollendung gebracht hat, ohne den Selbstwillen zu verlieren und auf Entschlußfreiheit zu verzichten (*EA*, p. 289).

Etzel thus continues to live the life he first led during his time in Berlin as a teenager. He spends time in all sorts of social circles thanks to his various identities without, however, revealing anything about himself and thus shows himself to be following in Warschauer's footsteps. It is Kerkhoven's fatal wish to discover the soul behind this facade. Only when it is too late are they both compelled to realize that there is no such thing. Etzel's stubborn refusal to talk about his inner self will eventually be explained by the lack of it. This can be read as a critique of the kind of 'neusachliche' literature which depicts a subject that is 'bis zu dem Punkt gepanzert, wo es nur noch Leere birgt'.[57]

53 David Midgley, *Writing Weimar: Critical Realism in German Literature 1918–1933* (Oxford: Oxford University Press, 2000), pp. 14–59.

54 Lethen, *Verhaltenslehren*, p. 53.

55 Lethen, *Verhaltenslehren*, p. 66.

56 Lethen, *Verhaltenslehren*, p. 60.

57 Lethen, *Verhaltenslehren*, p. 42.

In the course of a long conversation with Kerkhoven, Etzel's biography is revealed to be a typical one for a member of his generation. However, Etzel's uncommonly high level of self-awareness and self-analysis prevents his story from turning into a somewhat naive or innocent account of the life of a young man. He begins the story of his life after the Maurizius case by talking about the broken relationship with his parents. His reasons for failing to build up a relationship with his mother are most revealing:

> Die Mutter war ihm zu sehr Fleisch damals. Sie roch nach Fleisch und Blut. Sie hatte Haare in den Achselhöhlen. Es war aus seinem Hirn nicht wegzudenken, daß sie mit ihm geschlafen hatte, mit ihm, dem Vater, Trismegistos, vor achtzehn Jahren, vielleicht an einem genau zu bestimmenden Tag (*EA*, p. 320).

Apart from the obvious Oedipal connotations, which have been pointed out by Regina Schäfer,[58] this quotation is particularly interesting as a means of characterizing Etzel's perception. He is unable to see anything above and beyond the actual object in front of him. Consequently his mother is not idealized in any way: she is nothing but a human being made of flesh who slept with his father in order to conceive him. Since Etzel's perception is limited to an unfeeling realism he is unable to see anything else in her and refers to himself as a 'fühlloses Mißgebilde' (*EA*, p. 320). This means that Etzel is able to see and analyse the world in great detail but unable to feel it. In Wassermann's view, therefore, the dilemma of Etzel and his generation is linked to over-analytical and unfeeling perception. This description of Etzel could be read as a further attack on a certain outlook associated with 'Neue Sachlichkeit', whose 'unifying feature, in the German context, is not so much a new style as a way of looking at things which [...] vehemently repudiates the theoretical, intellectual, holistic pretensions of Expressionism'.[59] With the figure of Etzel it is therefore this 'new perception of the human environment'[60] that Wassermann is criticizing.

As he had before with Christian Wahnschaffe, in *Andergast* Wassermann sends another protagonist off to Berlin who breaks with his upper-class family and whose perception of the world is problematic. For a while Etzel also lives among the poor and deprived in Berlin. On the comparison between those two protagonists Schäfer writes: 'Der Preis für den Schritt von symbolischer Überhöhung zur Authentizität ist das folgerichtige Scheitern einer nur mehr menschlichen Mission'.[61] The experience therefore only adds to Etzel's general state of disillusionment since it is no longer clear where victims and guilt are to be found in this society:

58 Schäfer, *Plaidoyer*, pp. 79–124.
59 Midgley, *Writing Weimar*, p. 26.
60 Midgley, *Writing Weimar*, p. 30.
61 Schäfer, *Plaidoyer*, p. 310.

> Er hat sich gewissenhaft bemüht, sie zu ergründen, all diese Existenz außerhalb des Gesetzes und am Rande der bürgerlichen Welt. Er hat keine klare Scheidung gefunden. Wo endet Verhängnis, Mißwirtschaft, Schwäche des Systems, und wo beginnt die Verantwortlichkeit derer, die die Opfer sind? [...] Überall Schuld; bedenkt man's genau, wird die Schuld Allschuld, ist also nicht mehr zu fassen und zerstiebt. [...] hier ist nichts zu holen für dich, [...] es ist ein abfaulendes Stück der Welt, da vergeudest du nur die Zeit (*EA*, p. 340).

This quotation signifies another important development in Wassermann's writing and thought: not only is his protagonist without hope and illusions, but the world around him is moving towards a state of chaos in which victims can no longer be told apart from perpetrators. Even with Warschauer this division is still intact and enables him to position himself outside society. For Etzel such positioning is no longer possible as he struggles to form an opinion about the world around him, let alone to find a place in it. As a consequence, he finds it impossible to dedicate himself to a regular job or to pursue his education: '[E]in Ganzes wird nicht verlangt, ein Ganzes kann nicht geleistet werden' (*EA*, p. 334). This new state of blurred boundaries offers another point of comparison with Broch's *Schlafwandler*, in which August Esch's world is described as one in which 'die Grenze zwischen Wirklichkeit und Unwirklichkeit [...] nirgends deutlich zu erkennen [ist]'.[62]

In this state of self-loss and chaos, in a world where paternal authority has broken down, Etzel tries out two different solutions at the heart of which stands the same desire. He becomes entangled with various youth movements and devotes himself to his master Kerkhoven. Both times his motivation is the same:

> Wie sollte er, Etzel Andergast, führen, der selber so dringend der Führung bedarf, der geradezu *der* Mensch ist, der ohne Führer verloren ist? Träumt er sich doch zuzeiten einen imaginären Wächter oder Lenker an seine Seite, einen herrlich-überlegenen und unvergleichlich weisen, wie ihm zu Sinn ist. Als müsse er sich ohne den glatt hinlegen und seine Adern in den Erdboden verströmen lassen, als Zeichen nur, als Opfer. Wie in so vielen ist auch in ihm die verzehrende Sehnsucht nach Führerschaft (*EA*, p. 348).

As Lethen puts it: 'Das desorientierte Subjekt bedurfte der "äußeren Stimme", die sagte, wo es langging'.[63] Given the quotation above, it is obviously tempting to draw a connection to the events immediately following the time in which the novel is set, namely the Third Reich and the role played in it by youth movements. However, it is more rewarding to analyse Etzel's relationship with his 'Meister' and show how he is indeed beyond the 'Führerschaft' he so

62 Broch, *Schlafwandler*, p. 413.
63 Lethen, *Verhaltenslehren*, p. 64.

strongly desires. Etzel's attempt to destroy his 'Meister' and thus his 'Führer' contradicts Miller's view that young people like Etzel made possible the rise of Fascism in Germany.[64] Tellingly, Broch diagnoses the same 'Sehnsucht nach dem Führer'; to him, however, it is born out of people's awareness of their loneliness and the 'kreatürliche Angst' resulting from it.[65]

Etzel and Lorriner – the Plight of the Leader

At this point a brief discussion will be useful of Etzel's involvement with these youth movements through an examination of his relationship with the young political leader Jürgen Lorriner. Both can be seen as typical representatives of Weimar youth or, as Peukert has described it, the 'überflüssige Generation' who were particularly prone to political radicalization.[66] At the centre of the portrayal of the relationship between Etzel and Lorriner stands the complex power structure that evolves between the admirer and the admired as well as Wassermann's general rejection of utopian 'Gemeinschaftsideale' that do not take human nature into account. Their story seems like an illustration of Wassermann's insight 'daß man mit Menschen kein Paradies errichten kann'.[67] With the depiction of Etzel's increasing and potentially unsatisfiable demands and Lorriner's despair at being unable to meet them, Wassermann offers a sympathetic insight into the trials and tribulations of the young demagogue. Tellingly, the story of Lorriner ends with his final breakdown into insanity.

An entire chapter is dedicated to that story and the narrator is acutely conscious of how he wants to tell it. He refuses to offer an account of Lorriner's gradual development but, rather, wants to show how the two destinies of Lorriner and Etzel are linked:

> Ich müßte mich sonst in einem nur seelisch und geistig vorhandenen Raum ohne alle anschaulichen Elemente mit den Bedingtheiten und schwankenden Ergebnisse [*sic*] psychologischer Untersuchung begnügen. Entwicklung, was ist das überhaupt; erschöpfte Form, jeder Aufriß ist wesentlicher, nichts wird Gleichnis in ihr, eine scheinbare Breite der Welt soll das Bild der Welt ersetzen, und an Stelle der lebendigen Figur, die rund ist und etwas bedeutet, tritt das lähmende Nacheinander in der Zeit. Das hört sich an wie eine Ästhetik, ist aber nur die einfache Erfahrung von der geschehenen Veränderung unserer aufnehmenden Sinne (*EA*, p. 360).

64 Miller, *Maurizius*, p. 11.
65 Broch, *Schlafwandler*, p. 714.
66 See Peukert, *Die Weimarer Republik*, pp. 30, 100.
67 Wassermann, 'Rede an die studentische Jugend', p. 539.

The narrator thus consciously tries to adapt to his readers' altered perception by refraining from using psychological insights into his characters or narrating events chronologically. The refusal to talk about a figure's development can be linked back to the refusal to believe in human personality as one clear and identifiable entity. The narrator here suggests that since characters are unstable and constantly changing, with people having several existences, it would be a futile pursuit to trace their development. Instead, one could gain more insights into an individual and the world around him or her by showing some of their significant moments or 'Bilder'.

After having been disappointed by his father as well as by another important father figure, Lorriner begins to seek power over other people as a compensation for the love he never received at home. Lorriner serves as another illustration for Wassermann's above-mentioned theory that the revolt of young people is an expression of their natural longing for a 'Lebensmitte' (*EA*, p. 371). Lorriner participates in various revolutions at home and abroad. His good looks, coldness and fanaticism make him the ideal demagogue and he soon becomes a leader of the young masses. Any idealist pretensions are immediately defeated by the fact that to him it does not matter much whether he is planning a revolt in the name of Communism or Fascism since his main source of motivation is his personal hatred of the world. The narrator makes it clear that Lorriner is not an original thinker or a modern saint but merely the product of the general despair around him.

When Lorriner meets Etzel, he at first enjoys the feeling of being needed by him but soon feels overwhelmed:

> Das Merkwürdige ist nur, daß sich der Gefundene dann als der Gesuchte fühlt und mit all seinen Kräften bestrebt ist, das ideale Bild zu sein und den Rahmen auszufüllen, der gewöhnlich zu groß für ihn ist; er reckt und streckt sich, und manchmal wächst er in der Tat über sich hinaus, bis er unter der seelischen Anstrengung zusammenbricht. In der Gläubigkeit der Jünger liegt eine gewaltige Tyrannei (*EA*, p. 370).

Wassermann is therefore not interested in portraying the radical leader as a 'seducer' but, on the contrary, intends to show that he has to serve as the foil for his followers' personal projections. This is exemplified in his relationship with Etzel, who for a long time refuses to give Lorriner up even though he knows the latter has betrayed his cause and is altogether a rather deplorable human being. Etzel makes a mistake that is typical of young people: 'daß sie ihr Wunschbild so leidenschaftlich in sich verwirklichen, daß sie die äußere Wirklichkeit fast nicht mehr sehen' (*EA*, p. 380). It becomes even worse when Etzel finally has to realize that Lorriner is not who he wanted him to be and seeks to punish him for it. At this point his 'love' for Lorriner becomes comparable to his later obsession with Kerkhoven's wife Marie since he makes both of them suffer for not conforming to his image of them. Etzel's expectations are high as he is looking for someone to be like the three men in the fiery furnace (Daniel, 1–3) who sang hymns while they were burnt to death. Etzel is thus revealed to be every bit as extreme as his leader. When he finds out that Lorriner is involved in the loss of important documents he pursues him with a relentlessness comparable to that of his father until Lorriner finally admits it.

When Lorriner unsuccessfully tries to start another revolt in Berlin, Etzel's personal disappointment provokes Lorriner into assaulting him:

> Also den feurigen Ofen, das ist ein unbrauchbares Möbel, den wollen wir jetzt mal in die Rumpelkammer stellen, Lorriner. [...] Sehe ein, daß es schlauer ist, in der Direktionskanzlei zu hocken und mit dem Federhalter zu kämpfen als selber auf die Barrikaden zu steigen. Eklige Sache. Kann dir das nachfühlen. Bluten sollen die anderen (*EA*, p. 402).

After these words Lorriner almost kills Etzel with a knuckleduster; and when this last desperate attempt to regain control fails and Etzel once again confronts him with his inauthenticity as a leader, he breaks down into insanity. Etzel has thus at the very least contributed to the destruction of yet another father figure whose eventual breakdown strongly resembles his own father's mental collapse. The youth movements are thus shown to rebel against paternal authority of any kind, even against their own leaders. Moreover, the depiction of this form of violence corresponds to Peukert's findings that for some young people violence served as a means to compensate for their 'Ohnmachtserfahrungen'.[68]

It is therefore Etzel's disappointment in these various youth movements around him, political as well as non-political, and in particular in his relationship with Lorriner that drives him into the arms of Kerkhoven and even prompts him to start living with the 'Seelenarzt', the only person in whom Etzel can still believe:

> Es gibt nicht soviel verehrenswerte Leute. Kerkhoven, ja der. Aber Kerkhoven war der Meister, die große Ausnahme, an ihm konnte überhaupt nichts und niemand gemessen werden. Er konnte aber nicht der Einzige sein, [...] es mußten doch ein paar übrigbleiben, an die man sich außerdem halten konnte, die nicht versagten, sich nicht untreu wurden, deren Sein und Tun sich nicht als Humbug herausstellte, wenn man es unter die Lupe nahm (*EA*, p. 429).

Wassermann thus portrays a conscious return to the father figure in a world where any attempts at creating an urban family made up of other young people have failed.

68 Peukert, *Die Weimarer Republik*, p. 100.

Etzel and Kerkhoven – the Catastrophe

In the course of their relationship Kerkhoven is shown to be unable to act according to his main assumption about the younger generation:

> Kerkhoven glaubte erkannt zu haben, daß das, was die Psychologen und Zeitkritiker Krankheit der Jugend nannten, verschlagene Sehnsucht nach Gehorsam und Befehl war [...]. In ihrem Innern haßten und fürchteten sie eine Freiheit, die sie zu einer erbarmungslosen Einsamkeit verurteilte (*EA*, pp. 465–66).

His experiment to provide Etzel with regular employment as his assistant and to offer him a home fails when Etzel embarks on an affair with Marie and afterwards disappears. It remains unclear why Etzel would in the long run refuse this offer and in addition betray his master. The main reason seems to be that, despite his great concern for Etzel, Kerkhoven never ceases to see some kind of guinea-pig in him: 'Wenn er dieses außergewöhnliche Individuum quasi sicherstellte; es [...] dem blinden Zugriff des Schicksals entzog [...]. [H]atte er dann nicht Ersprießlicheres geleistet als wenn er Hunderten und Hunderten von bereits Gebrochenen und zu Boden Getretenen half (*EA*, p. 462). The fact that even the narrator refuses to comment on this line of thought indicates his disapproval.

Kerkhoven, who lives estranged from his own two sons – he often does not see them for many weeks – fails, like Etzel's own father, to establish an emotional bond with him. There are even parallels in the names Etzel has chosen for them: Trismegistos and 'Meister' both seem to describe a superior being to which Etzel owes respect but not necessarily love. Even though Kerkhoven could nevertheless be described as a father figure to Etzel, it would still be a mistake to see Etzel as occupying the place of a son in Kerkhoven's life since the latter's attachment to Etzel is always driven by a clear purpose. Etzel is to become his means of reforming the younger generation since he is going to turn Etzel into the heir to his own thoughts, a 'Spiegel [...] für das eigene Ich' (*EA*, p. 462). It is this lack of emotional commitment on Kerkhoven's side that prevents the reconciliation between the two generations. The father is, therefore, shown to be as cold as the son. Moreover, this coldness also stands at the centre of Etzel's affair with Marie as they give to each other what they could not have from Kerkhoven. Etzel even admits in a conversation with Marie: 'manchmal glaub' ich fast, ich hab' dich ihm nur weggenommen, um herauszubringen, ob er ein Herz hat wie andere Menschen' (*EA*, p. 582).

Etzel's affair with Marie helps to illustrate how Kerkhoven has been isolated by the demands of his profession. In this context Etzel functions as a peculiar mirror image since he begins to fulfil his master's marital duties based on what seems like an order from Kerkhoven himself. Tellingly, it is the fact that Etzel always has time for Marie that initially makes him attractive in her eyes. Kerkhoven's relationship with time, on the contrary, is rather different: 'Dann hat ihn allmählich die Zeit verschluckt, denselben Mann, aufgefressen Glied für Glied hat ihn die Zeit, deren Herr und Gebieter er war, fort ist er, zum Schatten ist er geworden' (*EA*, p. 507). Broch also comments on this development by pointing out that after losing their faith, all that is left to people is 'die Unterwerfung unter den Einzelwert, der zu seinem Berufe geworden ist, nichts bleibt ihm übrig als zur Funktion dieses Wertes zu werden – ein Berufsmensch'.[69] Kerkhoven, now the slave of his watch, had previously also wooed Marie with the free gift of his time whereas now he can only dedicate ten minutes of his day to her. In order to find relief from his guilty conscience, he more or less orders Etzel to look after Marie in order for her to be 'betreut' (*EA*, p. 510). From this point onwards, Etzel becomes Kerkhoven's full-time replacement as he now engages in a sexual relationship with the latter's wife. This rather uncanny exchange of character is completed when Etzel immediately takes to Marie's children and quickly becomes a father figure to them. At first he feels no remorse because, in his understanding, Kerkhoven has long thought of this option and hovers above them as the 'gewährende Gottheit' (*EA*, p. 539).

At first glance, the outcome of Etzel's final attempt to destroy yet another father figure, his beloved master, looks greatly similar to the last scene between Etzel and his father in *Maurizius*: Kerkhoven breaks down in tears and Etzel simply disappears. However, this time it is the father figure who survives and the son who wipes himself out. Moreover, this time his attack is also aimed at the mother figure. At the beginning of the penultimate chapter the narrator prepares the reader for the 'new' Etzel with whom he or she will be confronted:

> Es ist ein anderer Etzel, der uns entgegentritt, nicht mehr der Freundesfreund, nicht mehr der erglühte Jünger, nicht mehr der Gerechtigkeitssucher, [...] ein anderes Bild ist es, ein anderer Mensch, und der Weg, den er geht, ist so finster, wie ein Menschenweg nur sein kann (*EA*, p. 543).

In addition the narrator suggests 'der Sturz der Engel' (*EA*, p. 542) as an alternative title for the chapter, something which seems to imply that for Etzel all the hopes he attached to that new generation have come to an end. Nevertheless, Etzel and Kerkhoven are both granted a moment of vital insight into their lives. They are both made to experience a clash of realities, which means they both have to realize their reality is at odds with the one they suddenly notice around them. The theme of conflicting realities is continued

69 Broch, *Schlafwandler*, pp. 498–99.

into the final novel with the depiction of the relationship between Ganna and Alexander Herzog.

Etzel's moment of insight makes him understand that his second existence has been dominated by his own guilt since he underwent a metamorphosis: the former seeker of justice has been perverted in a world where guilt seems inevitable: '[A]uf einmal verwandelt sich das Unrecht, das vor seinen Augen geschieht und das aus der Welt zu schaffen er sich geboren wähnte, in Unrecht, das er selbst begeht, [...] er begreift die Unabwendbarkeit der Schuld (*EA*, p. 601). Given Etzel's previous identity, this is a major insight and the process is intensified even further when he comes to understand the nature of his own guilt. Like his father he has refused to acknowledge any reality but his own and like him he has almost destroyed the woman he loves. When Marie finally agrees to marry Etzel in a moment of great despair he suddenly comes to realise his own guilt. Tellingly, only a few moments before he disappears forever from Marie's life, Etzel's face, like that of his father, seems to disappear and she screams: 'Was ist? Ich seh dein Gesicht nicht!' (*EA*, p. 587). The voice Etzel hears inside could have been heard by his father, too, who was equally driven by the desire to control others: 'Das Licht einer Blendlaterne blitzt auf und erleuchtet die Tiefen. Der ungeheure Schatten steht da und spricht: Eine Menschenseele so weit treiben heißt sich in die Verdammnis stürzen, Etzel Andergast' (*EA*, p. 587). The 'Blendlaterne' is significant here because in *Maurizius* it is the symbol of the young Etzel's endeavours to find justice by bringing light into the dark. At the same time it refers to the hypocrisy of an avant-garde that, according to Lethen, identifies with the fallen angel Lucifer (in the novel Etzel is frequently referred to as a devil): '[D]er wie ein Blitz aus dem Himmel gefallene Engel erhebt auch als Fürst der Finsternis immer noch den Anspruch, "Lichtbringer" zu sein'.[70] Moreover, this strong resemblance to his own father as well as his attempt to replace Kerkhoven corresponds to the view that the concept of 'Neue Sachlichkeit' signifies a return of the father. Lethen informs us that many critics consider the '"Kult der Sachlichkeit" und "Kälte" eine Kompensation der verlorenen Vaterinstanz und in den Verhaltenslehren der Diskretion die Arbeitsteilung der patriarchalischen Gesellschaft'.[71] Wassermann therefore suggests that the concept of 'Neue Sachlichkeit' had to fail as a revolution because it is just another mirror image of, and therefore not radically different from, the world of the father.

However, Etzel's guilt does not end there since he feels equally responsible for the ensuing breakdown of his master. Wassermann makes Etzel witness the collapse of another 'father' but this time with a very different outcome. After

70 Lethen, *Verhaltenslehren*, p. 122.

71 Lethen, *Verhaltenslehren*, p. 69.

a long phase of denial, Kerkhoven finally has to accept that his reality has also been at odds with the one around him and that Etzel and Marie have indeed betrayed him: 'Endlich weiß Kerkhoven. Endlich sieht er. [...] [D]aß es [Marie's affair with Etzel] eine geile und verräterische Wirklichkeit war, indes er blind vertrauensvoll daneben gelebt hat' (*EA*, p. 599). Once again Etzel stands and watches the breakdown of a mighty father figure: 'Er muß zusehen, wie der Meister hinsinkt. Zusehen, wie er den Kopf auf einen Stuhl legt und heult. Der Meister heult' (*EA*, p. 599). This time, however, his habitual coldness fails him and Etzel is unable to re-experience the moment of triumph at his own father's downfall: 'Kalt überläuft es den Etzel Andergast. So kalt wie er gewesen ist, so kalt überläuft es ihn' (*EA*, p. 599). Etzel is thus made to experience the coldness he has hitherto shown towards others in order to demonstrate that the ideal of a cold conduct cannot or should not be lived.

After a short period of aimless wandering Etzel returns to the house of his mother, in whose company he also spends the transitional phase between his first and his second existences. As an apparent result of his experiences with Kerkhoven and Marie, Etzel is reunited with his mother and the two live in perfect harmony. Moreover, Garrin's claim that the novel ends 'on a negative note'[72] is misleading as it is clearly optimistic about Etzel's future: 'Das Haus ist ein Grab im Schnee. Mit einer abgelebten Wirklichkeit ist er [Etzel] in das Grab hineingestorben, mit einer neuen wird er aus ihm auferstehen' (*EA*, p. 608). These final words not only suggest a kind of happy ending but also – since he will be resurrected – hint at Etzel's positive development in the near future. Most importantly, however, the younger generation, even though damaged in the process, has triumphed over the father. After all, the reader is at this point provided with no further information regarding Kerkhoven's destiny. It is only at the beginning of *Kerkhoven* that we find out Etzel has disappeared to Moscow and Kerkhoven has recovered from his breakdown. The character representing the younger generation has therefore been more or less annihilated while the father figure is about to enter his third existence. In his final novel Wassermann thus abandons his initial attempt to present the reader with a reformed representative of the younger generation and instead focuses predominantly on the destiny of the older, and thus his own, generation. Döblin's interpretation of this step is of great interest:

> Wassermann lässt es sich nicht nehmen, sich mit etwas auseinander zu setzen, womit er täglich umgeht, nämlich: mit sich. Keine schlechte Aufgabe, und sie wäre manchem der Herren, die sich mit den Weltideen beschäftigen, zu wünschen. Die Zeit, das bin zunächst einmal "ich".[73]

72 Garrin, *Concept*, p. 61.
73 Döblin, 'Letztes Buch', p. 519.

Wassermann's subsequent preoccupation with himself is therefore best understood as a concern about the times he was living in.

Kerkhovens dritte Existenz

Wassermann's final novel is a most curious work and since he died before he could subject it to a final revision, it is best understood as a final draft rather than the actual finished book, especially because Wassermann was a notorious editor of his own work. Neubauer tells us: 'Was auf ihn [Wassermann] oberflächlich oder unfertig wirkte, wurde eliminiert – selbst nach aufwendigster Arbeit'.[74] Published posthumously by Querido in 1934, the work has received very little critical attention. Its middle section has, however, recently been translated into English by Michael Hofmann and published under the title *My First Wife*.[75] This middle part, which can be understood as a novel within a novel, adds to the curious nature of the work as a whole. In it, Wassermann retreats into a concern not only with his own generation but with himself in a most literal way: the depiction of the marriage and divorce of Ganna and Alexander Herzog in the middle section, entitled 'Ganna oder die Wahnwelt', is a detailed description of Wassermann's own marriage to his first wife Julie Speyer. Schäfer has shown that, excepting a few variations, it is a highly accurate and easily recognizable part of the author's own life.[76] Wassermann thus introduces himself, only very thinly disguised, into his own novel, yet he does not stop there since towards the end Alexander Herzog and Joseph Kerkhoven at times become indistinguishable from each other. He thus becomes one with his fictional creation. Most importantly, however, it is Herzog who loses Kerkhoven's manuscript and thus brings about the most significant disappearance of the closing text. For the rest of this chapter we shall thereforealso consider the implications of Wassermann's decision to introduce himself in this way into his final novel.

In order to create a situation in which characters can function as mirror images, the first part of the novel is mostly concerned with the depiction of Kerkhoven and Marie's marriage after the catastrophe that is her affair with Etzel. Their marriage has been disrupted by Etzel, while that of Alexander and Bettina has been shaken up by Herzog's first wife Ganna. In both cases we are, therefore, dealing with a third, obsessive character as the intruder. If we accept that the novel's middle section is an account of Wassermann's

74 Neubauer, *Schriftsteller*, p. 9.

75 Jakob Wassermann, *My First Wife*, trans. by Michael Hofmann (London: Penguin, 2012).

76 Schäfer, *Plaidoyer*, pp. 163–201.

own marriages, then Herzog represents Wassermann, Ganna represents Julie Speyer and Bettina Herzog represents Marta Karlweis. We can, however, see a first and significant blurring of boundaries between the 'real' and the fictional in the portrayal of Marie's affair with Etzel, for it was Wassermann's second wife Marta Karlweis who apparently had an affair with her husband's assistant Hans Aufricht,[77] a man to whom Schnitzler refers as Wassermann's 'Eckermännchen'.[78] Similarly, though he has many affairs with other women, Alexander Herzog, Wassermann's fictional mirror image, does not have an affair with his sister-in-law. Wassermann himself, however, did have an affair with his sister-in-law Agnes Speyer.[79] In the novel Wassermann's private experience is thus dealt with in two different narrative strands.[80] By referring to such details I do not seek to contest the view that 'Ganna oder die Wahnwelt' is largely based on Wassermann's own life, but it is important to bear in mind that he was driven by narrative as well as moral considerations (his two wives were still alive at the time) and that we have to accept his version of events as slightly polished. Wassermann thus draws on his own life for material but adapts it in accordance with aesthetic and narrative considerations. However, Mendelssohn's view that *Kerkhoven* is not even to be called a novel but rather a piece of autobiographical writing goes a step too far.[81]

The topic of delusion (*Wahn*) stands at the centre of *Kerkhoven* and proves to be one of the main links between the lives and works of Kerkhoven and Herzog. Both men are writing a book about this topic: a scientific account in Kerkhoven's case and a form of autobiography in Herzog's. However, only Herzog's account becomes part of the novel, a fact which will be discussed in more detail later in this chapter. From the title of Kerkhoven's book, *Pathologie der Wahnvorstellungen und ihr Einfluß auf Religion, Gesellschaftsform und Gesetzgebung*, it can be inferred that delusion is thought of as a universal pathology and thus another negative diagnosis regarding the times and state of society as a whole. In terms of tone and mood this strongly resembles Broch's diagnostic question, asked in 'Zerfall der Werte': 'Sind wir wahnsinnig, weil wir nicht wahnsinnig geworden sind?'[82] Kerkhoven himself is no exception to this general delusion since he is initially obsessed with the idea of seeking

77 According to Mendelssohn there can be little doubt about this affair, especially since Karlweis and Aufricht emigrated together to the USA (Mendelssohn 'Letztes Werk', p. 545).

78 Entry for 21 December 1924, in Schnitzler, *Tagebuch*, VIII (1995), *1923–1926*, p. 215.

79 Schnitzler's diaries are an invaluable source of information, documenting in detail Wassermann's affair with Agnes Speyer.

80 Schäfer, *Plaidoyer*, p. 251.

81 Mendelssohn, 'Wassermanns letztes Werk', p. 532.

82 Broch, *Schlafwandler*, p. 419.

revenge on his rival Etzel: 'Bemüht, das Wesen der Wahnvorstellungen zu erforschen und sie tiefer zu erfassen, als es bis jetzt geschehen war, stieß er auf eine verderbliche, an der sein eigenes Gehirn erkrankt war. [...] Er lechzte nach Genugtuung in irgendeiner Form' (*JK*, p. 35).[83] He follows his urge to find Etzel only to discover that the latter has disappeared without a trace to Russia and he finds himself on a futile odyssey: 'Jagd nach einem Schatten. [...] Er ist vor Dir bis ans Ende der Welt geflohen' (*JK*, p. 39). It is, however, not the insight into Etzel's defeat that frees Kerkhoven from his delusion but the sight of Etzel's mother Sophia, whom Kerkhoven watches secretly as she prays in a church. It is this image of the kneeling mother that enables him to grant Etzel absolution and thus free himself from his delusion: 'Die kniende Mutter hatte ihn entsühnt' (*JK*, p. 41). This unscientific solution to a seemingly scientific problem paves the way for the question as to whether destructive forces can be tamed by spiritual means.

With the disappearance of Kerkhoven's manuscript at the end of the novel, the scientific approach will ultimately be rejected in favour of a more spiritual or even mystical way of looking at the problem. According to Schneider-Handschin, this eventual rejection of the scientific method forms part of Wassermann's cultural pessimism:

> Es ist unverkennbar, dass Wassermann auf die konservative Kulturkritik, die sich Modernisierungsprozessen in Wissenschaft, Technik und politischer Organisation widersetzte, fixiert blieb, was ihn von realistischen, zukunftsweisenden Lösungen abschnitt und zumindest teilweise, seine als persönliches Scheitern empfundene Wirkungslosigkeit erklärt.[84]

While there is beyond doubt an element of cultural pessimism in Wassermann's late writing, it would be unfair not to look beyond that, especially since a pessimistic outlook seemed almost inevitable for him in the early 1930s. It is therefore important to examine what Wassermann tries to achieve with his portrayal of character in this novel, regardless of whether or not he succeeds in providing a convincing result. Mendelssohn agrees with the view of the novel as an imperfect yet intriguing piece of art.[85] With his description of Kerkhoven's gradual loss of faith in modern medical science as well as his gradual merge with Herzog's character, Wassermann attempts to depict a fusion of science and literature. Even though this attempt might at times appear flawed, looking at the ways in which he tries to achieve this is a more fruitful approach to the novel than dismissing it as the work of a

83 For the original edition see Jakob Wassermann, *Joseph Kerkhovens dritte Existenz* (Amsterdam: Querido, 1934).

84 Schneider-Handschin, *Bild*, p. 212.

85 Mendelssohn, 'Letztes Werk', p. 531.

frustrated 'Bildungsbürger' or, as Schäfer does, as a 'mißglückte Synthese von Ratio, Wissenschaft, Unfug und Glauben'.[86]

The idea of mirror images and situations is crucial to the idea of the fusion of science and literature that dominates the novel. It also allows us to link it to *Maurizius*, in which the idea of mirror images is equally important. In order to prepare for merging with another character, and as a solution to his personal crisis, Kerkhoven decides to join an excursion to the island of Java. After Warschauer in *Maurizius* and Irlen in *Andergast,* we are confronted by yet another European man in crisis who travels overseas with the aim of resolving his issues. The insights regarding the self gained by Kerkhoven on the tropical island strongly resemble those expressed by Irlen: 'Der europäische Mensch des zwanzigsten Jahrhunderts ist in sein Ich hineinerstarrt wie die Spinne in den Bernstein' *(JK*, p. 43). Similarly to Warschauer, Kerkhoven arrives at the conclusion that the state of European civilization is deplorable, with its people largely unhappy. Nevertheless, even though his stay on the island encourages him to abandon even more the concept of a fixed human personality, his altered understanding of Western civilization does not, as with Warschauer, lead to a state of misanthropic nihilism. Instead, Kerkhoven is fuelled with the desire to change the way we look at science and medicine in particular. Once again, Wassermann lets a character undergo similar experiences, yet with a very different outcome. The fact that this time he has chosen the figure of a scientist is highly significant and can be understood as a departure from the radical pessimism expressed in *Maurizius*.

Mirror Images and their Function

After Kerkhoven's return from Java, he settles with his family in the south of Germany, where he opens his small sanatorium. This farewell to Berlin as the capital of modern Germany is obviously significant. In the context of the novel it symbolizes a retreat from the overwhelming masses in the city to a renewed concern with the individual. The endless number of patients in Berlin did not allow Kerkhoven actually to help a single one, something which he hopes to achieve now. The episodes following his return, until he starts to focus mainly on Herzog, can easily seem arbitrary and irrelevant to the rest of the plot. They could, however, also be understood as further mirror images that help to connect *Kerkhoven* to the other two novels in the trilogy, as well as a means of preparing the reader for the Ganna episode and the idea of a fusion of rational and more irrational elements. Moreover, Döblin found a convincing image to describe the function of these episodes:

86 Schäfer, *Plaidoyer*, p. 306.

> Die Nebenfiguren, die scheinbar von außen hereinschneien, werden instinktiv mit größter Sicherheit an ihren Ort gebracht. Und da sind sie auf einmal keine Anekdoten, Episoden, sondern lösen sich von einer Phrase des Hauptthemas ab und umspielen das Hauptthema in einer charakteristischen Weise.[87]

The first episode in question is that of Kerkhoven's patient Martin Mordann, who is modelled on the real-life character of Maximilian Harden.[88] The earlier claim that the figure of Warschauer in *Maurizius* can be understood as a reaction to the Harden trials is not diminished by this second representation. It rather confirms Wassermann's prolonged interest in this persona, especially since this depiction of Harden cannot be called accurate either.[89] In the novel the character of Mordann, who is mortally ill when he arrives at the sanatorium, serves two discernible purposes. As a former celebrity, Mordann is an easily recognizable representative of pre-war Wilhelmine Germany, even if people have now forgotten about him: '[N]ur noch die Maske von ihm [war] vorhanden, das Gespenst von ihm' (*JK*, p. 89). By now Mordann is nothing but a self-obsessed anachronism who therefore helps to contrast his 'old' views with Kerkhoven's new ones. Mordann is not only an obvious representation of the 'Literat', a figure Wassermann has a long history of criticizing,[90] but is also shown to be a purely rational figure who is so ignorant of the divine that Kerkhoven refers to him as the 'Gottesfeind' (*JK*, p. 133) and arrives at the conclusion that this is not a life worth saving.

As a rational thinker Mordann wants to hear nothing about Kerkhoven's unconventional or even mystical thoughts and experiments: 'Ich [Mordann] höre ordentlich, wie sich der heilige Darwin und der heilige Häckel im Grab umdrehen. Hochmoderne Nebelfabrikation der mystisch erleuchteten Wissenschaftler, die auf das Göttliche schlagen und ihre Zauberkunststückchen meinen' (*JK*, p. 128). He also refers to the sanatorium as a 'metaphysischen Luftkurort' and to Kerkhoven's work as 'Hokuspokus' (*JK*, p. 128). In this context it is most significant that Kerkhoven claims in conversation with Mordann: 'Wir stehen in verschiedenen Zeitaltern und sprechen verschiedene Sprachen zueinander' (*JK*, p. 128). Mordann's derogatory rational and secular views are thus dismissed as belonging to a former era which ended in human catastrophe, namely the First World War. At this point the novel suggests that these views have been tried and failed, which is why new views and solutions are necessary.

87 Döblin,'Letztes Buch', p. 522.

88 Harry F. Young, *Maximilian Harden, Censor Germaniae: The Critic in Opposition from Bismarck to the Rise of Nazism* (The Hague: Nijhoff 1959), p. 2.

89 Mendelssohn, 'Letztes Werk', p. 551.

90 Wassermann, 'Der Literat'.

Broch also dedicates several passages of *Schlafwandler* to the conflict between the rational and the irrational and deplores the gradual loss of the divine ever since the the Middle Ages. Wassermann and Broch both therefore describe the purely rational as a dangerous element in modern life and thought. In the characters of Esch and Joachim von Pasenow, Broch moreover shows, similarly to Wassermann, that a return to traditional forms of religion has become equally impossible. The most striking parallel, however, is that both Broch and Wassermann suggest that this modern obsession with the rational has led to a form of irrationalism which is destructive and out of control. Broch writes:

> Furchtbarer Spiegel, furchtbares Echo der zum Absoluten durchbrechenden Ratio! Ihrer Strenge irdisches Widerspiel wird zum Zwang und zur stummen Gewalt, und die rationale Unmittelbarkeit ihres göttlichen Zieles wird zur Unmittelbarkeit des Irrationalen, das den Menschen zu widerwillig stummem Gehorsam überwältigt hat, ihre unendliche Fragekette wird zur eingliedrigen des Irrationalen, das nicht mehr fragt, sondern nur noch handelt, eine Gemeinschaft zersprengend, die es nicht mehr gibt, da sie ohne Kraft, doch voll des bösen Willens sich selbst im Blut ersäuft und in Giftgasen erstickt.[91]

The other even more significant aspect of Mordann's character is his obsession with the idea of completing his autobiography before his death in order to clear his reputation. Kerkhoven shows himself to be highly critical of this desire, which he identifies as a delusion:

> Diese gellenden Worte [...]. Sie enthüllten ihm [...] den Wahn des Tributs; den Wahn von papierener Unsterblichkeit; den Wahn von der Dauer des gedruckten Worts, von der Dauer des bloßen Namens, als stünde dahinter wirkliches Werk und wirkliche Tat und nicht leerer Schall, nicht eitler Machtrausch [...]. Denkwürdige Zeit, die ein solches Menschengebilde hervorgebracht hatte (*JK*, p. 135).

The idea of lasting fame based on written words is thus set aside in favour of the deed or other more palpable achievements. Since Kerkhoven fails, or refuses, to prolong Mordann's life, the latter dies without having written his book and the reader is confronted with the first failure of the text. Moreover, Mordann burns one of his most treasured possessions, the compromising letters of an aristocrat (presumably another reference to the Eulenburg affair), which he has been meaning to publish, and thus destroys a significant set of manuscripts before they can be used. The figure of Mordann therefore prepares the reader for the idea that some texts are better left unwritten, as well as for the failure and disappearance of a text that will dominate the end of the novel.

91 Broch, *Schlafwandler*, p. 713.

The other episode dominating the interval between Kerkhoven's return and the Ganna chapter is the story of Selma and Karl Imst, his lover Jeanne Mallery and Kerkhoven's patient Emilie Thirriot, who is a psychic medium. Imst and Jeanne have been sentenced to life behind bars for poisoning Imst's wife Selma with arsenic. One of Kerkhoven's employees, the nurse Wys-Wiggers, happens to be related to Karl Imst and informs Kerkhoven and Marie about the case. Marie is immediately convinced of the couple's innocence, which again reminds Kerkhoven of a similar case: 'In gewisser Weise erinnerte es ihn an die erstaunliche Entschleierung der Unschuld jenes Leonhart Maurizius, der neunzehn Jahre im Zuchthaus gesessen und dem der sechzehnjährige Andergast zum Befreier geworden war' (*JK*, p. 102). Even more importantly, Marie, who from now on devotes all her time to the case, in this way experiences a connection to her former lover Etzel:

> Dabei empfand sie es als eine schier unheimliche Fügung, daß sie gleichsam das Kernerlebnis des Menschen übernahm, der ihr einst zum Schicksal geworden war und sie aus einer Träumerin zu einer Wachen gemacht hatte [...]. Ohne daß er es gewollt und gemeint freilich, aber als Träger der Bestimmung (*JK*, p. 110).

Thus Wassermann not only establishes a clear link with the previous two novels but also adds another layer of meaning to the catastrophe that Marie's adulterous affair has turned out to be.

This episode serves in two more ways as a mirror image. To begin with we are confronted by yet another marriage destroyed by an adulterous love affair. Moreover, we are confronted by a wife who is comparable to Ganna Herzog. Selma is described as equally demonic, destructive and deluded as Ganna; and she even stages her own suicide to make it look as if her husband and his lover had murdered her. What matters most, though, is Kerkhoven's reaction to this case since it paves the way for how we are to read and understand the story of Ganna and her husband. Asked by Jeanne whether Selma's deed would still allow people to think of Selma as a human being, Kerkhoven replies:

> [I]n der Hinsicht darf man nicht knausern. Sehen Sie, meine Liebe, jeder von uns ist in jedem Augenblick gleich fähig zum Guten und zum Schlechten. Wir wissen nicht einmal immer, ob es gut oder schlecht war, was wir getan haben (*JK*, p. 418).

In conversation with Marie, Kerkhoven even considers Selma's suicide to be an act of greatness and marvels at it. The depiction of human delusion, even in its wildest and most damaging forms, is therefore not aimed at a condemnation of these people. Instead, Wassermann explores their world without necessarily passing judgement on them. This becomes even more noteworthy when we take Joseph Roth's interpretation of the novel into account. According to Roth, Wassermann's portrayal of delusion is not just about exploring psychological issues but is also to be understood as a critique of his time.[92] The idea of delusion therefore becomes a means for Wassermann to understand and explore the world in which he lived. This notion will be discussed in more detail in connection with the Ganna section.

The other way in which the Imst episode serves as a mirror image is in its fusion of rational and irrational elements. This is because the case is eventually solved by means of the visions of a 'fünfundvierzigjährige, schwer irritierte, beinahe unzurechnungsfähige Frau' (*JK*, p. 102), that is, Emilie Thirriot. Her visions enable her to see what actually happened on the night before Selma died, namely that Selma poisoned herself. The mistake made by a flawed legal system is thus set right by the visions of a psychic medium. This case is used as another example to dismiss a rational approach to life, since only a narrowly rational person would consider this a supernatural phenomenon:

> übernatürlich im Sinn der Ratio-Menschen und der Zwei-mal-zwei-ist-vier-Leute, die noch immer in banaler Zweifelsucht belächeln und zu leugnen bestrebt sind, was ein Mann wie Kerkhoven, zur Genüge belehrt über die Ausweitbarkeit der menschlichen Seelenkräfte, längst nicht mehr zu den Wundern rechnete (*JK*, p. 114).

For Wassermann, the patron saint of the fusion of scientific and more spiritual beliefs – in the novel as well as in real life – was the Swiss-Russian neuropathologist Constantin von Monakow (1853–1930).[93] Several of Monakow's publications can be found in Wassermann's private library.[94] Moreover, Schneider-Handschin tells us that Wassermann met Monakow in Zurich just before the latter's death.[95] Wassermann therefore aptly begins his chapter on 'Wahn' with a reference to the death of Kerkhoven's friend in Zurich, the 'große[r] Gelehrte' and director of the 'hirnanatomische[s] Institut' (*JK*, p. 139), a reference which makes him easily identifiable as Monakow. The narrator even offers a summary of the scientist's view of the human body:

> Da war denn der menschliche Leib, bewegt und regiert von einem allbeständigen, im wahrsten Sinne oberen Geist oder Organwesen, keine mehr oder minder

92 Joseph Roth, 'Wassermanns letzter Roman', in Joseph Roth, *Werke*, ed. by Hermann Kesten, 4 vols (Cologne: Kiepenheuer & Witsch, 1976), IV, pp. 428–31 (p. 428).

93 For a short biography of Monakow, see Jones, 'Kerkhoven', p. 180.

94 See Wassermann's private library in the Stadtbibliothek Nuremberg. The remains of Wassermann's library from his villa in Aussee were bought by the Stadtbiliothek in 1966 and comprise 2,798 volumes.

95 Schneider-Handschin, *Bild*, p. 141.

> vollkommene Maschine mehr, kein vitalistischer Automat, kein bloßes Produkt chemischer Bindungen und Reaktionen, sondern weit darüber hinaus [...] ein in das große All-Leben gewobenes und der Ewigkeit angehörendes, ja von ihr unzertrennliches Kräftezentrum, das [...] zusammengehalten wurde durch die Liebe (*JK*, p. 140).

In his essay Jones clearly shows further parallels between Monakow's writings and Kerkhoven's spiritual search. Moreover, Jones explains Monakow's theory in some detail; a brief summary will therefore be sufficient at this point. In his later years Monakow became increasingly interested in biological philosophy and as part of it he devised the theory of the toxic origin of mental disorder. At the centre of Monakow's later theory stands 'syneidesis or "biological conscience"', which Jones describes as:

> the automatic principle of regulation in the biological world protecting the organism from danger and constituting the urge towards wholeness and balance and the restoration when damaged. [...] This urge towards self-perpetuation is perceived at every level of life, physical and psychical, and has its source in the hormé or basic urge which gives unity and purpose to the organism.[96]

This hormic urge therefore stands at the centre of all individual and collective life, as it is the only protection against disintegration. Religion is a necessary part of this urge, which also means that it derives from the bio-psychological structure of the organism. In the context of the novel it is important that Monakow believed his theories to be metaphysical rather than merely scientific and that he used them in the treatment of mental illnesses. Monakow considered mental illness to be the result of a 'failure of syneidetic action'.[97] This serves as important preparation for Kerkhoven's attempt to link not only the body and the soul, but biology and the divine in the search for a higher order. The overarching message is that science on its own is not sufficient to solve the ongoing human crisis. Moreover, this understanding of mental illness as part of a wider problem permits it to be explored in an open rather than judgmental way, which is crucial for the understanding of the character of Ganna.

Geliebter Wahn

Kerkhoven meets Bettina Herzog on the day of his great friend's funeral in Zurich and is thus left to carry on alone with his legacy. She confronts him

96 Jones, 'Kerkhoven', pp. 180–81.

97 Jones, 'Kerkhoven', p. 182.

with the case of her husband Alexander Herzog, that is, the writer in crisis. Before looking at Kerkhoven's cure, the story of the writer in crisis needs to be explored further, for it can also be understood as a reflection on the function of the text. After a long and successful career as a writer, Alexander Herzog now finds himself in a state he describes as: 'Mein ganzes Ich, der geistige, seelische und physische Teil, ist in einer heillosen Unordnung' (*JK*, p. 147). The reason for this crisis is the realization that his work, that is, his writing, has not brought about any change and that he is no longer in touch with the real world. In fact, he now considers his creation to be part of the 'Wahnwelt' and feels that his self has been taken away from him as he has lost all sense of reality, including a sense of time. Herzog has arrived at the conclusion that his writing is nothing but a form of escapism from a life that has long become unbearable. He has been living outside himself for a considerable time but eventually has to realize that it is not possible to 'lebendigen Leibes aus der Welt herauszukommen' (*JK*, p. 153). Wassermann thus confronts us with a fictional version of himself looking for his long-lost self in a piece of writing that has, among many others, brought about this loss in the first place. It can be understood as an altered attitude towards the idea of writing since Kerkhoven introduces the concept not as a form of escapism but as a 'Befreiungsakt. [...] eine seelische Selbstbefreiung' (*JK*, pp. 163–64). According to Kerkhoven, Herzog is befallen by a sick reality and has to find his way back into a different reality. We are thus presented with a fictional character who tries to be a little less fictional. In a similar vein, the novel as a whole can be understood as Wassermann's break with escapist writing and an attempt on his part to return to the reality of his own life.

The final outcome of 'Ganna oder die Wahnwelt' is that Herzog, with the help of Kerkhoven, comes to understand how the Ganna he describes in his text is his own mirror image. Even more importantly, she is at the same time part of his fictional or, as Kerkhoven calls it, sick reality. The Ganna he depicts is therefore no less deluded than Herzog himself. In other words, the Ganna we encounter in Herzog's account is a product of his own delusion. The destructive force therefore comes from within himself and is projected onto his first wife. As mentioned at the beginning of this chapter, the irrational is therefore born out of the rational, making it the source of our destruction. This result, which Kerkhoven arrives at towards the end of the novel, can already be traced throughout the 'Ganna' text; this is the aim of the analysis that follows.

To begin with it is important to comment briefly on the book's structure because it presents us with a novel-within-the-novel. Wassermann's concern with the depiction and depictability of character is thus extended to the form of the novel as a whole. In a manner hitherto unprecedented in his writing, Wassermann dedicates about a third of *Kerkhoven* to an account of Herzog's first marriage. Even though connected to the work's overall content, this interlude proves to be an interruption of the narrative flow and makes the reader aware of a change in structure. Following on from *Wahnschaffe* and its experimental form, Wassermann once again undertakes an intriguing experiment that allows his 'Romanpoetik' to be related to more general developments and innovations in modernist writing. Broch's *Schlafwandler* once again offers a fruitful point of comparison, with its inclusion of multiple narratives, poems and even essays, especially in the third volume. Exactly contemporary, Broch's trilogy has long been recognized as a cornerstone of German modernist writing and thus helps us to see Wassermann's writing in a less traditional light. Even though Broch's narrative is far more fragmented than *Kerkhoven*, the overall sense that an uninterrupted, linear narrative will no longer do justice to the world around them seems to be the same. Moreover, Broch also tries to capture several decades of life in the German-speaking world in his trilogy and arrives at a third book that is much more complex in terms of structure than the previous two.

Another meaning behind these complex structures is also the wish to combine thematically opposing narrative strands, namely literature and science or science and faith. In order to consider topics from these different angles at almost the same time, Broch intersperses his narrative in the third volume with philosophical reflections, that is, 'Der Zerfall der Werte' and the otherwise unrelated story 'Geschichte eines Heilsarmeemädchens in Berlin'. The 'Zerfall' allows Broch to go into deeper philosophical as well as scientific reflections to accompany and complement his novel, in this way offering an even fuller picture of the people and the period he aims to portray. In a similar vein, Wassermann presents the topic of 'Wahn' from various angles and chooses this unusual structure to do so. After taking a scientific and spiritual approach, Wassermann presents us with what could be termed 'the delusions of the everyday', that is, a highly personal account of the delusions we are all prone to fall victim to in our daily lives. The story of Alexander and Ganna, and the development the latter undergoes, are therefore to be perceived as symptomatic and as a mirror image for society as Wassermann views it, for not only are our actions shown to be frequently self-destructive, but this account can also be understood as a careful psychological exploration of the ways in which we create outsiders in order to make sense of our own world. As the following analysis will therefore also show, Ganna becomes Alexander's 'mad woman in the attic' so that he can continue to function in his world, making her an indispensable outsider in his universe. Their story thus becomes a powerful reminder of the mechanisms at work that seemingly allow us to distinguish between us and the Other.

In the first part of his book, entitled 'Spiegel der Jugend', Herzog portrays his time with Ganna up to their wedding day. He is already making it clear here that Ganna's reality is in conflict with that shared by most other people: 'Sie lebte in einer Sonderwelt, die eigens für sie gezimmert schien' (*JK*, p. 175). He entitles one of his paragraphs about her 'Sie dichtet sich ihre Welt' (*JK*, p. 178). The reasons he gives for her behaviour are most significant:

> [Sie] suchte vor allem einen Spiegel. Menschen konnten nicht ihr Spiegel sein, die Wirklichkeitswelt konnte es auch nicht sein, nur aus den Büchern kam ihr ein Wesen ihresgleichen entgegen, so wähnte sie, ein Dämmerwesen voll Begeisterung, Zutraulichkeit und Aufrichtigkeit. Das Bild entzückte sie, es war ja ihr eigenes Gedicht, ihre eigene Schöpfung, sie verliebte sich in es, es machte sie in ihren Augen wahr und gut (*JK*, pp. 178–79).

Ganna thus falls in love with her own fictional creation, which serves her as a mirror image. As a poet, Herzog becomes the perfect foil on to which she can project her vision. Ganna's concept of reality is mostly derived from books and Herzog becomes another character in her fictional world. It is most striking, however, that Herzog does the same with her; and on the day of their engagement he refuses to see what is in front of his eyes: '[Ich] sah nicht ein blaurot erhitztes Gesicht, eine schweißdurchnäßte Bluse, einen verworrenen, beinahe fieberkranken Blick; das zu sehen wäre mir widrig gewesen, es hätte mich abgestoßen für lange. Ich sah ein Geschöpf meiner eigenen Form und Vision' (*JK*, p. 189). Their subsequent failure to make each other conform to their respective realities and thus serve as mirroring images to each other will lead to the catastrophe Herzog describes in his book. This crisis will be accompanied by a loss of any sense of self or reality on Herzog's part, something already indicated in the depiction of his wedding day: 'Freilich hatte ich nicht die Empfindung von Wirklichkeit. Was war mir denn wirklich? Nicht einmal mein Hemd, nicht einmal meine Schreibfeder. Die beständige schweigende Übereinkunft mit jenen, die das bloß Scheinende als Wahres nahmen, war ungeheuer anstrengend' (*JK*, p. 208).

The second part of the Ganna section, entitled 'Das Zeitalter der Sicherheiten', is an illustration of an insight proclaimed by Herzog on its very first pages: 'Mir ahnt alsbald, daß ich sie formen müßte. Ich müßte ihr eine Gestalt geben, denn sie hat noch keine. Es hat lange, sehr lange gedauert, bis ich dahinterkam, daß man sie nicht formen konnte' (*JK*, pp. 211–12). This insight eventually compels Herzog to choose another path, namely that of fiction. In the course of their marriage he therefore creates a fictional Ganna that has nothing to do with the actual person. As a result he grows more and more estranged from the actual individual, an estrangement which finds expression in his numerous affairs with other women. As a consequence,

Ganna is equally obliged to start living in her own fiction, that of an intellectual marriage standing above erotic matters. However, according to Alexander this loss of reality extends beyond her marriage: '[V]om Leben hat sie keinen Dunst' (*JK*, p. 221). Ganna does not know how to talk to her servants or how to handle financial matters, an inability which plays a substantial part in her chaotic lifestyle. Alexander nevertheless talks himself into the delusion that Ganna is an indispensable part of himself. He is not ready to admit their whole marriage is based on 'Irrtum und Täuschung' (*JK*, p. 225); nor is he able to face the guilt of having married a woman he has never loved. As Ganna increasingly loses her self-control and shows signs of mental disturbance, he finds relief in creating an image of her as demonic and thus avoids a confrontation with reality:

> Manchmal schloß ich einfach die Augen, wenn ich sah, was zu sehen mich nicht freute. Ich bemühte mich, das Erlebnis Ganna als meine Bestimmung hinzunehmen. Je mehr die Wirklichkeit auf mir lastete, je mehr entlastete mich das Bild, das ich mir von Ganna schuf. Es war wie aus Erz, unzerstörbar für lange. Ein dämonischer Mensch, sagte ich mir (*JK*, p. 229).

For Herzog's sister-in-law Irmgard it shows that he knows nothing about reality when he simply accepts Ganna as an 'unbändige Natur' (*JK*, p. 232) instead of seeing beneath the surface. This indifference towards the actual person becomes most apparent in the context of his affairs, which she desperately tries to integrate into her fictional reality, while he never finds out how she actually feels about them: 'Was aber in ihrem tiefsten Innern dabei vorging, habe ich nie ganz erfahren können' (*JK*, p. 241). Instead, Herzog chooses to live in his 'Sonderwelt' (*JK*, p. 240), a word which he, not long previously, has used to describe Ganna's world. Despite all the predicaments, Ganna therefore remains a mirror image for him and a necessary one, too. This could also explain what he means by the alleged 'mystisches Band' (*JK*, p. 240) connecting the two and why divorce for a long time remains out of the question. In this context, Döblin therefore aptly refers to the 'Strindberghaften Verkrampfung zweier Menschen',[98] probably a reference to Strindberg's play *Totentanz*, which depicts a couple unable to separate despite their mutual hatred. In the play Alice says about her unfortunate marriage to Kurt: 'aber wir sind zusammengeschweißt und kommen nicht voneinander los! […] Jetzt kann nur noch der Tod uns trennen.'[99]

Alexander does not even shy away from idealizing his fictional construction as he dedicates one of his books to Ganna and even sends

98 Döblin, 'Letztes Buch', p. 521.

99 August Strindberg, *Totentanz*, trans. by Christel Hildebrandt (Stuttgart: Reclam, 2011), p. 29.

her wistful letters. The absurdity of the situation is further increased by his awareness of living with a fictional creation: 'Die Ganna in meinem Leben und die Ganna meiner Phantasie waren zwei grundverschiedene Wesen' (*JK*, p. 244). They are linked only by the strong sense of guilt he feels towards both of them. Since he finds himself unable to love Ganna, Herzog invents other ways of being connected to her:

> Ich erdichtete eine schier überweltliche Bindung an sie und übersah, daß der irdische Mensch Alexander Herzog keinen festen Boden mehr unter den Füßen hatte. Ich erhob Ganna zu einem Prinzip, zu einer Idee, sie und die Kinder waren eins, drei Herzen, [...] denen ich dienstbar zu sein hatte [...]. Das wußte Ganna (*JK*, p. 244).

The two characters therefore find themselves in the situation of denying each other their reality, one which leads them to lose control over each other's lives. At one point Ganna suffers a form of nervous breakdown and Alexander sees no other way of controlling her than to beat her up: 'Schlage auf sie ein wie ein Wirtshäusler. Wie ein Fuhrknecht. Ich' (*JK*, p. 264). This drastic climax to their inability to communicate or even reach each other marks the end of their life as a couple, for soon after Herzog meets the woman who will become his second wife, Bettina Merk. With the introduction of the Ganna section, Wassermann therefore adds another layer to his depiction of character. Although he has previously seemed concerned with the metamorphosis of one character and his or her individual response to it, he now explores the instability of the perception of character and the consequences this has for the observer.

Despite their separation and eventual divorce, Ganna and Herzog continue to depend on their delusions since without them their lives would be empty and insignificant. The final part of Herzog's manuscript, aptly entitled 'Das Zeitalter der Auflösung', therefore shows how they are both brought to the verge of destruction through their refusal to acknowledge each other's true realities. This inability to free themselves from their illusions, as well as their dependence on them, is expressed, for instance, when Herzog refers to Ganna's 'Ganna-Fiktionen, mit deren Hilfe sie sich immer eine Weile seelisch über Wasser hielt' (*JK*, p. 278); or when Herzog comes to the conclusion that 'Ganna richten [...] mich selber richten [hieß]' (*JK*, p. 287). As a consequence, Herzog finds it more than difficult to go through with a divorce which he experiences as a 'brutale[n] Eingriff in meine Existenz' (*JK*, p. 293). Herzog prefers to attribute this reluctance actually to leave Ganna to his general passivity and phlegm and thus proves himself to be unaware of the true reasons for his behaviour.

At the same time, however, he is clearly aware of Ganna's loss of reality and of her growing mental problems. This can be inferred from several passages in the text, for instance when he writes: 'Die Wirklichkeit war ihr unter den Füßen weggeglitten, doch sie bedurfte ihrer auch nicht mehr: Alles war so, wie sie es weltabgewandt imaginierte' (*JK*, p. 301). Another example is his description of how she would react to a given situation with various different personalities (*JK*, p. 295). Moreover, he also understands that most of their dilemma is caused by Ganna's increasingly desperate attempts to make her 'Wahnwelt' real, but he fails to understand that his own behaviour could be described in much the same way. In this respect their situation becomes comparable to that of Kerkhoven and Etzel, especially to Etzel's violent attempts to make people conform to his view of them. The only glimpse of an awareness of the fictionality of his situation can be found when Herzog is confronted with the peaceful divorce of Bettina and her first husband. He utters a rather curious line: 'Also, das ist möglich, so geht es unter wirklichen Menchen zu, war mein Gedanke' (*JK*, p. 299). However, the insight that he and Ganna are not 'wirkliche Menschen' does not come to Herzog through writing this text. Even though he claims that it felt liberating, he arrives at the rather sobering conclusion that his work is nevertheless nothing more than paper (*JK*, p. 387). On its own, the text is therefore denied a key function, namely that of a real impact on Herzog's life. Following the idea of a fusion, it will take the combination of the figure of the scientist and the literary text to open Herzog's eyes.

The final section of the novel, entitled 'Joseph und Marie oder die Glaubenswelt', deals with Herzog's struggle to overcome his delusion and the loss of Kerkhoven's manuscript. At the same time this leads to the fusion of their characters. As Mendelssohn has shown, the idea of the mirror image is taken a step further in *Kerkhoven* because eventually Kerkhoven and Herzog are no longer mirror images but merge to the point of becoming identical.[100] Both men have, albeit in different ways, dedicated their lives to the idea of delusion, a concept which also becomes their meeting point: 'Merkwürdig, daß wir uns so oft an einem Kreuzweg treffen. [...] In die Wahnwelt rüst' ich [Kerkhoven] seit Jahr und Tag meine Expeditionen aus' (*JK*, p. 412). Going back to the idea that for Wassermann the notion of 'Wahn' becomes a metaphor for describing the time and society in which he lives, Herzog in a similar vein becomes for Kerkhoven a 'sprechendes Instrument im Strom des Geschehens' (*JK*, p. 413). Kerkhoven therefore arrives at the important conclusion that Herzog's case is no exception but that he suffers from a 'zeitbedingte Erkrankung', namely the 'Einsturz des Identitätsbewußtseins' (*JK*, p. 421). Similarly, Ganna becomes for Kerkhoven the 'Zeitgebundene, der Zeit Entsprossene, Exponent der bürgerlichen Ära' (*JK*, p. 457). This would even allow a comparison between Ganna's individual downfall and that of her

100 Strindberg, *Totentanz*, p. 554.

class after the Great War.[101] It also enables another comparison between Ganna and Etzel since they are both described as the product of the seeming collapse of bourgeois paternal authority – Ganna's father was also an authoritarian patriarch. An understanding of Ganna's madness as 'zeittypisch' could be another indicator for a sympathetic reading of this character. If her madness is the product of the surrounding circumstances and the distressing times in which she lives, then it would not be justifiable to attribute any evil intentions to her behaviour. Leydecker is therefore right to conclude that 'these marriage crises [a recurring theme in Wassermann's works] become vehicles to convey Wassermann's ever sharper sense of a wider social, psychological and even metaphysical malaise, which becomes all-pervading by the last novel'.[102]

Herzog's identity crisis means he is unable to determine who he really is and that he has lost himself in a world he struggles to recognize. At times he is even unsure whether or not he really exists, which marks an unprecedented level of identity crisis in Wassermann's writing: Herzog's identity is not just unstable; rather, he cannot convince himself of his own existence and finds himself lost in fiction. This level of identity crisis can also be found with Broch and his narrator of the 'Geschichte eines Heilsarmeemädchens': '[M]ein Leben verdämmert hinter mir und ich weiß nicht, ob ich gelebt habe oder ob es mir erzählt worden ist, so sehr ist es in den fernen Meeren versunken'.[103] Wassermann's depiction of Herzog's identity crisis is therefore part of a bigger picture, namely that of the modern self having lost its grasp on reality.

In order to improve Herzog's situation, Kerkhoven needs to free him from his delusion, yet he soon realizes that the confession alone will not do the trick. Moreover, it is not a scientific method that will eventually provide the deciding insight but a vision. The reader would already be accustomed to the idea of a vision from the previously mentioned Imst case, which can be understood as another mirror image. On a train, Kerkhoven sees Ganna Herzog entering his compartment, ironically the only encounter they will ever have. Aware that he is confronted with a phantasm, Kerkhoven defeats it the moment he understands her true nature:

> Als er den Blick zu dem Gesicht der Frau erhob, sah er ein eigentümlich verblasenes Lächeln auf ihren Lippen, wie bei einem Kind, das schmollt, ja, dieses Lächeln gemahnte auf irgendeine Art an das eines wahnsinnigen Kindes; von diesem Augenblick an wich die alpdruckhafte Beklemmung von Kerkhoven, er atmete auf wie ein Mensch, der sich von einer leeren Drohung hat einschüchtern lassen (*JK*, p. 444).

101 On the stituation of the bourgeoisie after the war, see also Peukert, *Die Weimarer Republik*, p. 60.

102 Leydecker, 'The Case', p. 94.

103 Broch, *Schlafwandler*, p. 617.

The insights Kerkhoven gains during this encounter lead to a complete re-evaluation of the entire Ganna story. Hitherto this piece of 'autobiography' could be read as a realistic account of Herzog's divorce, only now he is revealed to be as deluded as his first wife, leaving the manuscript in an atmosphere of uncertainty. Kerkhoven therefore seems to speak for the reader when he says: 'Sie haben es fertiggebracht, mich vollständig mit Ganna und der Ganna-Atmosphäre zu durchtränken' (*JK*, p. 445).

As a result Kerkhoven now proposes a different cure: 'Ich werde Ihnen beweisen, daß das schauerlich Überlebensgroße, das hexenhaft Abstruse nur in ihrer Einbildung vorhanden ist, daß es keine Wirklichkeit besitzt, daß es nichts weiter ist als Wahn, Alexander Herzogs ureigenster, geliebter Wahn' (*JK*, p. 446). As it turns out, Ganna is nothing but a harmless, even pitiable, woman who suffers from some minor and rather ordinary mental problems.[104] Moreover, Kerkhoven claims that many of Ganna's actions are the result of 'korrespondierende Seelenbewegungen' (*JK*, p. 451), something which makes her even more the product of her husband's delusion. His destruction therefore comes from within. Wassermann thus not only radically changes the reader's perception of a text that initially seems like an act of revenge against his first wife. He also makes it questionable as to how much of it is actually true and thus skilfully plays with the idea of the reliability of text. To a certain extent, the reader is made to experience Herzog's own insecurity regarding the borders between fiction and reality for it simply becomes impossible for him to tell them apart: '[I]ch [habe] fast keine Gewißheiten. [...] Nicht einmal, ob ich wirklich *bin*, ist mir gewiß' (*JK*, p. 463).

The final aspect of the novel to be discussed is the loss of Kerkhoven's manuscript. The mirroring aspect of the fact that Herzog and Kerkhoven both write a book on the question of 'Wahn' is emphasized further in the final section. One day, Herzog happens to see Kerkhoven writing at his desk: 'Es war, als erblicke Alexander Herzog sich selbst in den edelsten, besten, hingegebensten Stunden seines Lebens' (*JK*, p. 482). In accordance with the idea of the two characters merging towards the end of the novel, Schneider-Handschin claims they become congruent to the extent that it becomes difficult to tell which of the two is speaking during their dialogues.[105] Herzog is supposed to take Kerkhoven's manuscript to Basel, where the latter wants to sell it to a publisher. However, Herzog forgets it on a train and it is lost forever, disappeared into nothingness. Despite his attempts to recover the text, it is as if 'sich das dickleibige Konvolut in

104 Schäfer has shown that this attempt to do Ganna justice is mirrored in the text's genesis, as Wassermann decided to leave out passages depicting Ganna at her most negative in his final manuscript (Schäfer, *Plaidoyer*, p. 194).

105 Schneider-Handschin, *Bild*, p. 144.

seine Bestandteile aufgelöst [hätte]' (*JK*, p. 505). This life's work was an attempt to establish a link between delusion, faith, biology and the divine and can never be rewritten because Kerkhoven suffers from a terminal illness that leaves him with only a few months to live. His reaction to the loss of the manuscript is therefore of interest because even though it upsets him there is also an element of deliberateness in this loss. It is the idea of the sacrifice that returns at the end of the novel. This becomes clear in a remark to Herzog, if we accept the characters' partial merging, which enables Herzog to receive telepathic orders from Kerkhoven: 'Sie haben in der Tat unschuldig eine Schuld auf sich geladen. Vielleicht nicht einmal so ganz unschuldig. Vielleicht ...' (*JK*, p. 520). Moreover, this ties in well with the consequences of the loss because it allows Kerkhoven a return to his local community. Hitherto Kerkhoven has led the life of an outsider as he was ostracized by the community he lived in on the basis of being a mysterious eccentric. With the loss of his manuscript he returns to the simple tasks of an ordinary doctor and suddenly enjoys great popularity among ordinary people. At the end of his life, Wassermann therefore seems to be willing to sacrifice the text that has been revealed to be the product of a delusion as well as essentially without consequences. Schäfer's interpretation of this loss as retrospectively diminishing the importance of the manuscript misses the significance of the idea of sacrifice.[106] In the end it is the simple deed that triumphs over the work of art and allows the outsider to return to his community; however, it comes at a high cost.

While this renunciation of the text certainly carries strong pessimistic connotations, the novel itself ends on a moment of optimism. Moreover, with the concluding scenes of *Kerkhoven* Wassermann comes full circle and ends where he began, namely with a child born from a Gentile mother and a Jewish father. In the last scene, Kerkhoven's stepdaughter Aleid, an otherwise minor character, gives birth to the child she initially wanted to abort, yet Kerkhoven teaches her to consider it an act of grace: '"Du mußt es als eine Gnade ansehen, Aleid," sagte Kerkhoven; "fühlst du, daß es die Gnade ist?" – "Ja ... ich fühls" war die Antwort, "ich fühls ..."' (*JK*, p. 526). In this final moment of his writing, Wassermann, in a highly symbolic manner, returns to the vision of a new-born child that will overcome the outsider status of his parents. Kerkhoven, the outsider by choice, is enabled to return to his community through a sacrifice. The outsiders by birth, however, in this case the woman and the Jew, still depend on a moment of grace to be freed from their status as outsiders.

106 Schäfer, *Plaidoyer*, p. 304.

CONCLUSION

This study has aimed to demonstrate new ways of looking at Wassermann and thus to have opened new routes for future Wassermann scholarship. The process of engaging with his work has revealed questions of wider significance than Romantic and Expressionist themes, the original purpose of this study. Rather than imposing a set of questions and theories from outside onto the work, I have therefore let it guide me towards its own set of thoughts and theories. This approach, even though lacking much of the usual or even expected theoretical framework, has allowed me to begin discovering what could be thought of as Wassermann's own vocabulary. In addition, and as a pre-requisite for this approach, the common assumptions about him as a person and a writer have been cast aside in order to take a fresh look. As a frequent victim of negative criticism Wassermann has proven to be a most valuable subject for demonstrating how fragile and actually irrelevant an author's reputation really is. I therefore hope I have given a fair account of Wassermann's works without being influenced by the negative reputation he holds among critics.

Used to the understanding of Wassermann as a writer more or less stuck in the forms and traditions of the nineteenth century, I never gave the idea of looking at his narrative techniques much thought. What was there to be found, after all, that was new and revelatory? It was only my lengthy engagement with *Wahnschaffe* that brought about the realization that there was something exciting about the ways in which Wassermann was 'doing' character. Keen to explore this aspect, I revisited his earlier works and began to see there was a traceable development. It soon became apparent that the concept of character increasingly took centre stage in Wassermann's portrayals of society. While it is of less importance in his earlier works, those written before the Great War, it becomes more and more pronounced in his later writing until eventually character and society are shown to crumble and fall apart. Moreover, this new interest in Wassermann's characters also paved the way to establishing a link between them and the author's attempts to portray German society at different historical stages. The idea of character as a mirror of the state in which society finds itself must be seen as one of the most important new insights into Wassermann's work. This link between his narrative technique and the critique of society he expresses in his novels has not been established so far, which is why it opens up a new space for discussion. Amongst other things it allows Wassermann's outsider figures to be seen in a new and altogether more productive light.

Regarding his outsider figures, the discovery of the role the homosexual man plays in Wassermann's writing is among the most significant. Given the continuous interest in this figure from his early novels up to the trilogy, it is clear by now that it goes far beyond any mere sensationalist concerns. Rather, it seems that Wassermann increasingly came to think of the place of the homosexual in society as one worth exploring alongside that of the Jew. It could even be said that after an initial interest in the status of woman as an outsider, as portrayed in *Renate Fuchs*, the concern with the figure of the homosexual would inevitably receive considerably more attention. So far no validation of this interest has been unearthed from the mass of Wassermann's unpublished fragments and letters; and no homoerotic fantasies have been recorded in his diaries. Given the strong interest in Wassermann's biography, also in connection with the interpretation of his works, this might at least in part account for the neglect of the figure of the homosexual in his writing up to the present day. The concern with Wassermann's biography, though certainly useful and indispensable in some respects, has therefore prevented some critics from considering these significant aspects of his writing. My research in this area is therefore just the beginning of what could be a starting point for further fruitful study. It would certainly be of interest to compare Wassermann's depictions of homosexuals to those of other writers of his time, thus adding another layer of relevance to his work.

The conscious move away from his biography also allowed a new way of looking at the Jew as an outsider figure in Wassermann's works. The plight of his Jewish figures has naturally been dwelt upon by critics and has sometimes lured them into making him a little bit more Jewish than he actually was. Wassermann's sense of his Jewish identity, similar to so many other cases, was largely triggered by the growing anti-Semitism around him. Wassermann himself drew this conclusion in *Mein Weg*: 'Genau betrachtet war man Jude nur dem Namen nach und durch die Feindseligkeit, Fremdheit oder Ablehnung der christlichen Umwelt'.[1] It would therefore be a mistake to regard Wassermann's work as being in close proximity to any significant Jewish thought or mythology, for his background remained that of an assimilated Jew with no clear religious pretensions, as his later quest for spirituality seems to belong to an altogether different category. However, his Jewish characters nevertheless add great interest to my argument because their function as counterparts in the construction of parallels has so far not been given much critical attention. Nonetheless, the discovery of the links and parallels between the outsiders portrayed by Wassermann offers further new insights. Moreover, it also helps us to see that Wassermann is not solely concerned with his own status in society but has,

1 Wassermann, 'Mein Weg', p. 41.

rather, developed an understanding of the trials and tribulations of the other Other. In this version, his Jewishness has therefore become a space in which communication with other outsiders is made possible.

Engaging with these outsider figures inevitably always includes a closer examination of the society around them. As we have seen in Wassermann's early novels, this leads to intriguing portrayals of Biedermeier and Wilhelmine Germany, establishing a clear link between those two key elements in Wassermann's writing. However, it is only in his later novels, in particular *Maurizius*, that we are finally confronted with a clear link between the figure of the outsider and the concept of character. Most notably with Warschauer, Wassermann has found a way of presenting the parallels between the different outsiders in one figure alone by using the technique of double-identities. Warschauer therefore embodies a twofold significance: not only does he combine the Jew and the homosexual man, and thus Wassermann's two most important outsider figures in one person, but he also loses control over his identity, making him the product of both the modern condition and the society around him. In the society Wassermann confronts us with in his later writing, character is no longer possible, which allows a connection between character, the outsider and Wassermann's depiction and critique of society. The trilogy therefore marks the point in Wassermann's writing when all these three elements are at last brought together in a meaningful way. 'Meaningful' here means there is a system to Wassermann's apparent madness or increasing lack of structure. Towards the end of his life chaos had become an inevitable part of Wassermann's everyday experience and therefore also found expression in his later writing. A different approach to Wassermann's 'bad' structure has proven most fruitful in the course of this thesis. What is more, the trilogy must be seen not only as a recapitulation of some of the concerns that occupied Wassermann throughout his life as a writer, but also as their fusion. The idea of fusion stands at the centre of *Kerkhoven* as well as characterizing the trilogy as a whole. These three novels are therefore indispensable in a discussion of the developments of Wassermann's writing, for it is here that they reach their climax.

I hope to have helped to restore Wassermann's standing as a major and accomplished novelist who was more than just a helpless amateur. On this basis, future research will, I hope, approach him with a more positive understanding, as there are many topics that still need addressing. Wassermann's relationship to Expressionism still deserves closer analysis, as does his relationship to Vienna, his 'Wahlheimat' of many years. Some of his lesser-known works, in particular his novellas, have not received enough attention. Wassermann's concern with the figure of the child and childhood offers another overarching topic for the analysis of his entire oeuvre. Finally, there is much archived material that has not yet been published, above all a wealth of his correspondence.

BIBLIOGRAPHY

Works by Jakob Wassermann

Aufruhr um den Junker Ernst (Berlin: Fischer, 1926)

Bula Matari: Das Leben Stanleys (Berlin: Fischer, 1932)

Caspar Hauser oder Die Trägheit des Herzens (Stuttgart & Leipzig: Deutsche Verlags-Anstalt, 1908; Munich: DTV, 1983)

Christian Wahnschaffe, 2 vols (Berlin: Fischer, 1920; Berlin: Fischer, 1932; Munich: DTV, 1989)

Christoph Columbus, der Don Quichote des Ozeans: Ein Porträt (Berlin: Fischer, 1929; Munich: DTV, 1992)

Etzel Andergast (Berlin: Fischer, 1931; Munich: DTV, 1988)

Der Fall Maurizius (Berlin: Fischer, 1928; Vienna and Munich: Langen Müller, 1981; Munich: DTV, 2007)

Geliebtes Herz ... Briefe, ed. by August Beranek (Vienna: Zwei Berge Verlag, 1948)

Die Geschichte der jungen Renate Fuchs (Berlin: Fischer, 1901; Berlin: Fischer, 1921)

Der goldene Spiegel: Erzählungen in einem Rahmen (Berlin: Fischer, 1911)

Hofmannsthal der Freund (Berlin: Fischer, 1930)

Jakob Wassermann. Deutscher und Jude. Reden und Schriften 1904–1933, ed. by Dierk Rodewald (Heidelberg: Lambert Schneider, 1984)

Joseph Kerkhovens dritte Existenz (Amsterdam: Querido, 1934; Munich: DTV, 1989)

Die Juden von Zirndorf (Paris, Leipzig and Munich: Albert Langen, 1897; Berlin: Fischer, 1906; Munich: DTV, 1996)

Laudin und die Seinen (Berlin: Fischer, 1925)

Lebensdienst. Gesammelte Studien, Erfahrungen und Reden aus drei Jahrzehnten (Leipzig & Zurich: Grethlein, 1928)

Mein Weg als Deutscher und Jude (Berlin: Fischer, 1922)

'Mein Weg als Deutscher und Jude', in *Jakob Wassermann. Deutscher und Jude. Reden und Schriften 1904–1933*, ed. by Dierk Rodewald (Heidelberg: Lambert Schneider, 1984), pp. 35–132

My First Wife, trans. by Michael Hofmann (London: Penguin, 2012)

'Rede an die Studentische Jugend über das Leben im Geiste: Zum Goethetag 1932', in *Die Neue Rundschau*, 43 (1932), 529–46

Die Schwestern (Berlin: Fischer, 1906)

Selbstbetrachtungen (Berlin: Fischer, 1933)
Der Wendekreis: Erste Folge (Berlin: Fischer, 1920)
Der Wendekreis: Ulrike Woytich, Dritte Folge (Berlin: Fischer, 1923)

Studies on Wassermann

Albanis, Elisabeth, 'Jakob Wassermann's Memorial to Walther Rathenau in *Etzel Andergast*', *German Life and Letters*, 50, (1997), 18–35

Appleton, Tom, 'Nachwort', in Jakob Wassermann, *Christoph Columbus: Der Don Quichote des Ozeans* (Munich: DTV, 1992), pp. 217–21

Bing, Siegmund, *Jakob Wassermann: Weg und Werk des Dichters* (Berlin: Fischer, 1933)

Blankenagel, John C., *The Writings of Jakob Wassermann* (Boston: Christopher, 1942)

Brandes, Georg, *Gestalten und Gedanken: Essays* (Munich: Langen, 1903)

Bullock, Marcus, 'Jakob Wassermann's novel *Der Fall Maurizius* presents the final expression of his views on the relationship of Germans and Jews', in *Yale Companion to Jewish Writing and Thought in German Culture, 1096–1996*, ed. by Sander L. Gilman and Jack Zipes (New Haven and London: Yale University Press, 1997), pp. 471–79

Choobak-Melle, Farsaneh, *Deutscher und Jude: Jakob Wassermann und das deutsch-jüdische Verhältnis im ersten Drittel des 20. Jahrhunderts* (Rudolstadt: Der Neue Morgen, 2012)

Classen, Isabelle, 'Wider die Todesstrafe: Über Vorlage und Fabel zum *Fall Maurizius*', in *Jakob Wassermann: Werk und Wirkung*, ed. by Rudolf Wolff (Bonn: Bouvier, 1987), pp. 33–46

Cölln, Jan, 'Von der Gewalt und Ohnmacht der Worte: Eine literarische Psychologie gestörter Kommunikation im Werk Jakob Wassermanns', in *Jakob Wassermann Deutscher – Jude – Literat*, ed. by Gunnar Och, Dirk Niefanger and Daniela F. Eisenstein (Göttingen: Wallstein, 2007), pp. 29–45

Döblin, Alfred, 'Jakob Wassermanns letztes Buch', in *Die Sammlung*, 10 (1933/34), 517–23

Elm, Theo, 'Kafkas Talmud, Wassermanns Kabbala: Gibt es ein "Jüdisches" Erzählen?', in *Deutscher – Jude – Literat*, ed. by Gunnar Och, Dirk Niefanger and Daniela F. Eisenstein (Göttingen: Wallstein, 2007), pp. 127–41

Feuchtwanger, Lion, 'Christian Wahnschaffe', in *Ein Buch nur für meine Freunde* (Frankfurt a.M.: Fischer, 1984), pp. 337–42

Garrin, Stephen H., *The Concept of Justice in Wassermann's Trilogy* (Bern: Peter Lang, 1979)

Goldmann, Walter, *Wassermann: Sein Kampf um Wahrheit* (Leipzig & Zurich: Grethlein, 1929)

Graf, Roman, '"Alles ist verdächtig": Zum Thema der "Homosexualität" in den Bearbeitungen der Kaspar-Hauser-Legende von Jakob Wassermann, Klaus Mann und Werner Herzog', in *Der imaginierte Findling*, ed. by Ulrich Struve (Heidelberg: Winter, 1995), pp. 103–22

Greissinger, Hermann, *'In die vierte Existenz vielleicht': Konzeptionen von 'Leben' und 'Nicht-Leben' im Werk von Jakob Wassermann und in den Erzähltexten der frühen Moderne* (Bern, Frankfurt a. M, New York: Peter Lang, 1986)

Heimann, Moritz, 'Zwei Romane', in *Die Neue Rundschau*, 9 (1898), 642–47

— 'Das jüngste Gericht im Roman', in *Die Neue Rundschau*, 30 (1919), 367–73

Heydenreich, Clemens, 'Trutzgesang im Zährental: Erzählen als Wider-Rede in Jakob Wassermanns *Der Aufruhr um den Junker Ernst*', in *Jakob Wassermann: Deutscher – Jude – Literat*, ed. by Gunnar Och, Dirk Niefanger and Daniela F. Eisenstein (Göttingen: Wallstein, 2007), pp. 157–80

Horch, Hans Otto, '"Verbrannt wird auf alle Fälle...": Juden und Judentum im Werk Jakob Wassermanns', in *Jakob Wassermann: Werk und Wirkung*, ed. by Rudolf Wolff (Bonn: Bouvier, 1987), pp. 124–54

— 'Deutschtum und Judentum: Eine unmögliche Synthese? Jakob Wassermann im Kontext der deutsch-jüdischen Literaturgeschichte', in *Jakob Wassermann: Deutscher – Jude – Literat*, ed. by Gunnar Och, Dirk Niefanger and Daniela F. Eisenstein (Göttingen: Wallstein, 2007), pp. 69–91

Jacobs, Jürgen, *Wilhelm Meister und seine Brüder: Untersuchungen zum deutschen Bildungsroman* (Munich: Fink, 1972)

Joeris, Christa, *Aspekte des Judentums im Werk Jakob Wassermanns* (Aachen: Shaker, 1996)

Jones, Geraint Vaughan, 'Jakob Wassermann's "Joseph Kerkhovens dritte Existenz": Its Philosophy and Structure', *German Life and Letters*, 3 (1949/1950), 169–85

Jütten, Elisabeth, *Diskurse über Gerechtigkeit im Werk Jakob Wassermanns* (Tübingen: Niemeyer, 2007)

Kahn, Lothar, *Mirrors of the Jewish Mind: a Gallery of Portraits of European Jewish Writers of Our Time* (New York and London: Thomas Yoseloff, 1968)

Karlstetter, Klaus, *Das Bild des Jugendlichen in der deutschsprachigen Erzählliteratur der Zeit zwischen dem Ersten Weltkrieg (1918) und der Diktatur (1933)* (Stockholm: Almquist & Wiksell, 1980)

Karlweis, Marta, *Jakob Wassermann: Bild, Kampf und Werk* (Amsterdam: Querido, 1935)

Koester, Rudolf, *Jakob Wassermann* (Berlin: Morgenbuch, 1996)

Kotulla, Theodor (director), 'Der Fall Maurizius', television mini-series, Germany: ZDF, 20 September 1981

Kovács, Kálmán, 'Ein Fall für zwei: Anthropologische Konzepte in Wassermanns *Caspar Hauser oder die Trägheit des Herzens* und in Peter Handkes *Kaspar*', in *Die Zeit und die Schrift*, ed. by K. F. Auckenthaler (Szeged: JATE, 1993), pp. 261–77

— *Kaspar-Hauser-Geschichten: Stationen der Rezeption* (Frankfurt a.M.: Peter Lang, 2000)

Kraft, Thomas, *Jakob Wassermann: Biografie* (Munich: DTV, 2008)

Kraske, Bernd M., '"Das stärkste jüdische Talent dieser Zeit...": Zur Rezeption Jakob Wassermanns in der völkischen Literaturgeschichtsschreibung', in *Jakob Wassermann: Werk und Wirkung*, ed. by Rudolf Wolff (Bonn: Bouvier, 1987), pp. 46–66

Krobb, Florian, *Die schöne Jüdin: Jüdische Frauengestalten in der deutschsprachigen Erzählliteratur vom 17. Jahrhundert bis zum Ersten Weltkrieg* (Tübingen: Niemeyer, 1993)

Landscheidt, Martina, 'Mutmaßungen über Waremme, Annäherung an Warschauer: Zu der jüdischen Doppelfigur Warschauer-Waremme in Jakob Wassermanns Roman Der Fall Maurizius', in *Jakob Wassermann: Werk und Wirkung*, ed. by Rudolf Wolff (Bonn: Bouvier), pp. 14–33

Leja, Gabriele, 'Jüdische Gestalten im erzählerischen Werk Jakob Wassermanns', in *Jakob Wassermann: Werk und Wirkung*, ed. by Rudolf Wolff (Bonn: Bouvier, 1987), pp. 66–98

Leydecker, Karl (ed.), 'The Case of Jakob Wassermann: Social, Legal, and Personal Crises in the Weimar Republic', in *German Novelists of the Weimar Republic - Intersections of Literature and Politics* (Rochester, NY: Camden House, 2006), pp. 85–101

Lindemann-Luiken, Heike, *Die Auswirkungen des Antisemitismus im ausgehenden 19. und beginnenden 20. Jahrhundert auf Leben und Werk Jakob Wassermanns* (Frankfurt a. M.: Peter Lang, 2005)

Mann, Thomas, 'Jakob Wassermanns "Caspar Hauser oder Die Trägheit des Herzens"', in *Gesammelte Werke* (Frankfurt a. M.: Fischer, 1960), II, pp. 553–55

Martini, Fritz, 'Die Utopie eines Messias in der Moderne', in *Zeit der Moderne: Zur Deutschen Literatur von der Jahrhundertwende bis zur Gegenwart*, ed. by Hans-Henrik Krummacher and others (Stuttgart: Alfred Kröner, 1984), pp. 461–85

May, Markus, 'Die Wunde Heine: Überlegungen zu einem Komplex jüdischer Selbstdeutung in Jakob Wassermanns *Mein Weg als Deutscher und Jude*', in *Jakob Wassermann: Deutscher - Jude - Literat*, ed. by Gunnar Och, Dirk Niefanger and Daniela F. Eisenstein (Göttingen: Wallstein, 2007), pp. 91–109

Mayer, Hans, 'Der Fall Wassermann', in *Literatur der Übergangszeit* (Berlin: Volk und Welt, 1949), pp. 177–82

Mendelssohn, Peter de, 'Nachwort', in *Der Fall Maurizius* (Vienna & Munich: Langen Müller, 1981), pp. 541–63

— 'Jakob Wassermanns letztes Werk', in *Joseph Kerkhovens Dritte Existenz* (Munich: DTV, 1989), pp. 531–59

Miller, Henry, *Maurizius Forever* (Michigan City, IN: Fridtjof-Karla Publications, 1959)

Müller-Kampel, Beatrix, 'Jakob Wassermann und die Autoren Jung-Wiens', in *Jakob Wassermann: Deutscher - Jude - Literat*, ed. by Gunnar Och, Dirk Niefanger and Daniela F. Eisenstein (Göttingen: Wallstein, 2007), pp. 45–69

— *Jakob Wassermann: Eine biographische Collage* (Vienna: Mandelbaum, 2007)

Neubauer, Martin, *Jakob Wassermann: Ein Schriftsteller im Urteil seiner Zeitgenossen* (Frankfurt a. M., Berlin: Lang, 1994)

Niefanger, Dirk, '"Das unbezwingliche Verlangen zu erzählen": Wassermanns Poetik des Narrativen', in *Deutscher - Jude - Literat*, ed. by Gunnar Och, Dirk Niefanger and Daniela F. Eisenstein (Göttingen: Wallstein, 2007), pp. 141–57

Och, Gunnar, 'Ahasver oder das andere Ich: Eine mythische Chiffre im Werk Jakob Wassermanns', in *Jakob Wassermann: Deutscher - Jude - Literat*, ed. by Gunnar Och, Dirk Niefanger and Daniela F. Eisenstein (Göttingen: Wallstein, 2007), pp. 109–27

Och, Gunnar, Dirk Niefänger and Daniela F. Eisenstein, eds., *Jakob Wassermann: Deutscher - Jude - Literat* (Göttingen: Wallstein, 2007)

Pazi, Margarita, 'Die Kraft des Intellekts: Jakob Wassermanns "Der Fall Maurizius"', in *Juden in der Weimarer Republik*, ed. by Julius H. Schoeps and Walter Grab (Stuttgart: Burg, 1986), pp. 61–88

Plöger, Nicole, 'Wassermann und die Münchner Moderne', in *Deutscher - Jude - Literat*, ed. by Gunnar Och, Dirk Niefanger and Daniela F. Eisenstein (Göttingen: Wallstein, 2007), pp. 15–29

— *Ästhet - Ankläger - Verkünder: Jakob Wassermanns literarische Anfänge (1890–1900)* (Würzburg: Ergon, 2007)

Poeschel, Erwin, 'Jakob Wassermann', in *Juden in der deutschen Literatur*, ed. by Gustav Krojanker (Berlin: Welt, 1922), pp. 76–101

Regensteiner, Henry, 'The obsessive personality in Jakob Wassermann's novel *Der Fall Maurizius*', *Literature and Psychology*, 14 (1964), 106–16

Reich-Ranicki, Marcel, 'Jakob Wassermann, der Bestsellerautor von gestern', *Jüdische Wochenzeitung*, 34 (1979), 7

Richter, Ruth, *Der Einfluss F. M. Dostojevskijs auf die Werke Jakob Wassermanns* (unpublished doctoral thesis, University of Bonn, 1951)

Robertson, Ritchie, *The 'Jewish Question' in German Literature 1749–1939: Emancipation and its Discontents* (Oxford: Oxford University Press, 1999)

— 'Schnitzler and Wassermann', in *Confrontations / Accommodations: German-Jewish Literary and Cultural Relations from Heine to Wassermann*, ed. by Mark H. Gelber (Tübingen: Niemeyer, 2004), pp. 249–63

Rodewald, Dierk (ed.), *Jakob Wassermann 1873–1934: Ein Weg als Deutscher und Jude* (Bonn: Bouvier, 1984)

— '*Der Fall Maurizius* – als Produktionsprozeß betrachtet', in *Deutscher – Jude – Literat*, ed. by Gunnar Och, Dirk Niefanger and Daniela F. Eisenstein (Göttingen: Wallstein, 2007), pp. 180–217

Roth, Joseph, 'Wassermanns letzter Roman', in *Werke*, 6 vols, ed. by Klaus Westermann (Cologne: Kiepenheuer & Witsch, 1991), III, pp. 553–57

Rychner, Max, 'Ein neuer Roman Jakob Wassermanns: "Christian Wahnschaffe"', *Neue Züricher Zeitung*, 140 (1919), p.1

Schäfer, Regina, *Plaidoyer für Ganna: Männer und Frauen in den Romanen Jakob Wassermanns* (Tübingen: Niemeyer, 1992)

Schlich, Jutta (ed.), '*Warum fliegen da so schwarze Würmer herum?*': *Das Kaspar-Hauser-Syndrom in Literatur und Film, Forschung und Lehre* (Würzburg: Königshausen & Neumann, 1999)

Schmitz-Emans, Monika, *Fragen nach Kaspar Hauser: Entwürfe des Menschen, der Sprache und der Darstellung* (Würzburg: Königshausen & Neumann, 2007)

Schneider-Handschin, Esther, *Das Bild des Bürgertums in Jakob Wassermanns 'Andergast-Trilogie'* (Bern: Peter Lang, 1990)

Schnetzler, Kaspar, *Der Fall Maurizius: Jakob Wassermanns Kunst des Erzählens* (Bern: Herbert Lang, 1968)

Sell, Anne-Liese, *Das metaphysisch-realistische Weltbild Jakob Wassermanns* (Bern: Paul Haupt, 1932)

Shaked, Gershon, 'Der Fall Wassermann', in *Die Macht der Identität: Essays über jüdische Schriftsteller* (Königstein: Athenäum, 1986), pp. 94–112

Stimilli, Davide, 'Findlinge: Franz Kafka und Jakob Wassermann', in *Deutsche Vierteljahrsschrift*, 73 (1999), 478–500

Theisz, R. D., 'Kaspar Hauser im zwanzigsten Jahrhundert: Der Außenseiter und die Gesellschaft', *German Quarterly*, 49 (1976), 168–80

Tiefenbacher, Herbert, *Textstrukturen des Entwicklungs- und Bildungsromans* (Königstein: Forum Academicum, 1982)

Voegeli, Walter, *Jakob Wassermann und die Trägheit des Herzens* (Winterthur: Keller, 1956)

Wolff, Rudolf, (ed.), *Jakob Wassermann: Werk und Wirkung* (Bonn: Bouvier, 1987)

Zuckerkandl, Victor, 'Jakob Wassermanns Essaybuch', *Die Neue Rundschau*, 40 (1929), 719–20

Other Primary Sources

Alighieri, Dante, *The Divine Comedy*, trans. by Dorothy L. Sayers (London: Penguin, 1949)

Andreas-Salomé, Lou, *Fenitschka: Eine Ausschweifung. Zwei Erzählungen*, ed. by Ernst Pfeiffer (Frankfurt a. M.: Ullstein, 1983)

— *Lebensrückblick*, ed. by Ernst Pfeiffer (Frankfurt a. M.: Insel, 1974)

Barlach, Ernst, *Der arme Vetter* (Stuttgart: Reclam, 1992)

Benjamin, Walter, 'Über einige Motive bei Baudelaire', in *Illuminationen*, ed. by Siegfried Unseld (Frankfurt a. M.: Suhrkamp, 1977), pp. 185–230

Bernstein, Elsa, *Dämmerung: Schauspiel in fünf Akten*, ed. by Susanne Kord (New York: The Modern Language Association of America, 2003)

Broch, Hermann, *Die Schlafwandler* (Frankfurt a.M.: Suhrkamp, 1994)

Brod, Max, *Jüdinnen* (Leipzig & Vienna: Kurt Wolff, 1915)

— *Über Franz Kafka* (Frankfurt a. M.: Fischer, 1974)

Daumer, Georg Friedrich, *Mitteilungen über Kaspar Hauser*, ed. by Peter Tradowsky (Dornach: Geering, 1983)

— *Kaspar Hauser: Sein Wesen, seine Unschuld*, ed. by Tradowsky (Dornach: Geering, 1984)

Dostojewski, Fjodor M., *Der Idiot*, trans. by E. K. Rahsin (Munich: Piper, 1954)

Feuchtwanger, Lion, *Jud Süß* (Berlin: Aufbau, 1991)

Feuerbach, Anselm von, *Kaspar Hauser oder Beispiel eines Verbrechens am Seelenleben Eines Menschen* (Stuttgart: Klett, 1984)

Feuerbach, Ludwig (ed.), 'Vorwort', in *Paul Johann Anselm Ritter von Feuerbachs Leben und Wirken* (Berlin: Akademie, 1976), pp. 1–19

Flake, Otto, *Die Stadt des Hirns* (Berlin: Fischer, 1919)

Flaubert, Gustave, *Trois Contes* (Paris: Gallimard, 1966)

Foucault, Michel, *Histoire de la sexualité. La volonté de savoir*, 3 vols (Paris: Gallimard, 1976), I

— *The Will to Knowledge: The History of Sexuality: Volume One*, trans. by Robert Hurley (London: Penguin, 1998)

Frenssen, Gustav, *Jörn Uhl* (Berlin: Grote, 1903)

Freud, Sigmund, 'Jenseits des Lustprinzips', in *Studienausgabe*, ed. by Alexander Mitscherlich and others (Frankfurt a.M.: Fischer, 1975), III, pp. 215–73

Hauptmann, Gerhart, *Der Narr in Christo Emanuel Quint* (Berlin: Fischer, 1910)

Hatzfeld, Adolf von, *Franziskus* (Berlin: Paul Cassirer, 1919)

Heine, Heinrich, *Historisch-kritische Gesamtausgabe der Werke*, ed. by Manfred Windfuhr and others (Hamburg: Hoffmann und Campe, 1973–1997), I (1975), *Buch der Lieder*, ed. by Pierre Grappin

Herzl, Theodor, *Der Judenstaat* (Zurich: Manesse, 1988)
Hesse, Hermann, 'Aus der Kindheit des heiligen Franz von Assisi', in *Legenden*, ed. by Volker Michels (Frankfurt a. M.: Suhrkamp, 1975), pp. 162–73
— *Sämtliche Werke*, ed. by Volker Michels, 21 vols (Frankfurt a.M.: Suhrkamp, 2001–2007)
Hofmannsthal, Hugo von, 'Das Schrifttum als geistiger Raum der Nation', in *Die Berührung der Sphären* (Berlin: Fischer, 1931), pp. 422–43
Horváth, Ödön von, *Der ewige Spießer*, ed. by Traugott Krischke (Frankfurt a.M: Suhrkamp, 2001)
Kafka, Franz, *Brief an den Vater* (Frankfurt a. M.: Fischer, 1999)
Kästner, Erich, *Fabian: Die Geschichte eines Moralisten* (Munich: DTV, 2011)
Kessler, Harry Graf, *Tagebücher 1918–1937*, ed. by Wolfgang Pfeiffer-Belli (Frankfurt a. M:Insel, 1996)
Key, Ellen, *Das Jahrhundert des Kindes*, trans. by Francis Maro (Weinheim & Basel: Beltz, 1992)
Lessing, Theodor, *Der jüdische Selbsthaß* (Munich: Matthes und Seitz, 1984)
Mann, Klaus, *Treffpunkt im Unendlichen* (Reinbek bei Hamburg: Rowohlt, 1981)
Mann, Thomas, *Tagebücher 1918–1921*, ed. by Peter de Mendelssohn (Frankfurt a. M.: Fischer, 1979)
— *Betrachtungen eines Unpolitischen* (Frankfurt a. M.: Fischer, 1983)
Marx, Karl, *Frühe Schriften I*, ed. by Hans Joachim Lieber and Peter Furth (Stuttgart: Cotta, 1962)
Mayer, Hans, *Außenseiter* (Frankfurt a. M.: Suhrkamp, 1975)
Merker, Johann Friedrich Karl, *Kaspar Hauser, nicht unwahrscheinlich ein Betrüger* (Berlin: August Rücker, 1830)
Musil, Robert, *Gesammelte Werke*, ed. by Adolf Frisé, 9 vols (Reinbek bei Hamburg: Rowohlt, 1978)
Pies, Hermann, *Die Wahrheit über Kaspar Hausers Auftauchen und erste Nürnberger Zeit* (Saarbrücken: Minerva, 1956)
Pinthus, Kurt (ed.), *Das Kinobuch* (Frankfurt a.M.: Fischer, 1983)
Polenz, Wilhelm von, *Der Büttnerbauer* (Berlin: Fontane, 1895)
Rilke, Rainer Maria, *Das Stundenbuch* (Wiesbaden: Insel, 1955)
Schnitzler, Arthur, *Tagebuch*, ed. by Peter Michael Braunwarth and Werner Welzig, 10 vols (Vienna: Verlag der Österreichischen Akademie der Wissenschaften, 1981–2000)
Simmel, Georg, *Das Abenteuer und andere Essays*, ed. by Christian Schärf (Frankfurt a. M.: Fischer, 2010)
Strindberg, August, *Totentanz*, trans. by Christel Hildebrandt (Stuttgart: Reclam, 2011)

Weininger, Otto, *Geschlecht und Charakter: Eine prinzipielle Untersuchung* (Berlin: Kiepenheuer, 1932)

Werfel, Franz, *Die schwarze Messe: Erzählungen*. ed. by Knut Beck (Frankfurt a. M.: Fischer, 1989)

— *Nicht der Mörder, der Ermordete ist schuldig: Eine Novelle* (Munich: Kurt Wolff, 1922)

General Secondary Literature

Barkhoff, Jürgen, *Magnetische Fiktionen: Literarisierung des Mesmerismus in der Romantik* (Stuttgart: Metzler, 1995)

Berglar, Peter, *Walther Rathenau: Seine Zeit, sein Werk, seine Persönlichkeit* (Bremen: Schünemann, 1970)

Biale, David, *Eros and the Jews: From Biblical Israel to Contemporary America* (New York: Basic Books, 1992)

Boa, Elizabeth, 'Aping and Parroting: Imitative Performance in Goethe's *Wahlverwandtschaften*', in *Performance and Performativity in German Cultural Studies*, ed. by Lucia Ruprecht and others (Bern: Peter Lang, 2003), pp. 21–41

— and Rachel Palfreyman, *Heimat: A German Dream. Regional Loyalties and National Identity in German Culture 1890–1990* (Oxford: Oxford University Press, 2000)

Burrow, J. W., *The Crisis of Reason: European Thought, 1848–1914* (New Haven, CT and London: Yale University Press, 2000)

Caminero-Santangelo, Marta, *The Madwoman Can't Speak, or, Why Insanity Is Not Subversive* (Ithaca, NY and London: Cornell University Press, 1998)

Figes, Orlando, *A People's Tragedy: The Russian Revolution, 1891–1924* (London: Pimlico, 1997)

Gay, Peter, *Weimar Culture: the Outsider as Insider* (London: Secker & Warburg, 1968)

— *Freud, Jews and other Germans: Masters and Victims in Modernist Culture* (New York: Oxford University Press, 1978)

Gerigk, Horst-Jürgen, *Ein Meister aus Russland: Beziehungsfelder der Wirkung Dostojewskijs* (Heidelberg: Universitätsverlag Winter, 2010)

Gilman, Sander L., *Freud, Race and Gender* (Princeton, NJ: Princeton University Press, 1993)

— *The Jew's Body* (New York and London: Routledge, 1991)

Göttsche, Dirk, *Zeit im Roman: Literarische Zeitreflexion und die Geschichte des Zeitromans im späten 18. und 19. Jahrhundert* (Munich: Fink, 2001)

Häfner, Heinz, *Ein König wird beseitigt: Ludwig II. von Bayern* (Munich: Beck, 2008)

Jennings, Michael, 'Towards Eschatology: The Development of Walter Benjamin's Theological Politics in the Early 1920s', in *Walter Benjamins Anthropologisches Denken*, ed. by Ben Morgan and others (Freiburg i.Br., Berlin, Vienna: Rombach, 2012), pp. 41–59

Jørgensen, Johannes, *Saint Francis of Assisi: A Biography*, trans. by T. O'Conor Sloane (New York etc.: Longmans, Green, 1912)

Joll, James, 'Prophet ohne Wirkung', in Walther Rathenau, *Tagebuch 1907–1922*, ed. by Hartmut Pogge von Strandmann (Düsseldorf: Droste, 1967), pp. 15–55

Jones, James W., *'We of the Third Sex': Literary Representations of Homosexuality in Wilhelmine Germany*, German Life and Civilization (New York: Peter Lang, 1990)

Kringelbach, Morten L., *The Pleasure Center: Trust your Animal Instincts* (New York: Oxford University Press, 2009)

Lethen, Helmut, *Verhaltenslehren der Kälte: Lebensversuche zwischen den Kriegen* (Frankfurt a. M.: Suhrkamp, 1994)

Midgley, David, *Writing Weimar: Critical Realism in German Literature 1918–1933* (Oxford: Oxford University Press, 2000)

Neumann, Helga and Manfred Neumann, *Maximilian Harden (1861–1927): Ein unerschrockener deutsch-jüdischer Kritiker und Publizist* (Würzburg: Königshausen & Neumann, 2003)

Nygren, Anders, *Agape and Eros: A Study of the Christian Idea of Love*, trans. by A. G. Herbert, 3 vols (London: Society for Promoting Christian Knowledge, 1932)

Peukert, Detlev J. K., *Die Weimarer Republik: Krisenjahre der klassischen Moderne* (Frankfurt a. M.: Suhrkamp, 1987)

Prickett, David, 'Envisioning the Homosexual: Gender Performance, Photography, and the Modernist Homosexual Aesthetic', in *Performance and Performativity in German Cultural Studies*, ed. by Lucia Ruprecht and others (Bern: Peter Lang, 2003), pp. 177–201

Robertson, Ritchie, 'Historicizing Weininger: The Nineteenth-Century German Image of the Feminized Jew', in *Modernity, Culture, and 'the Jew'*, ed. by Bryan Cheyette and Laura Marcus (Cambridge: Polity Press, 1998), pp. 23–39

— 'Modernism and the Self 1890–1924', in *Philosophy and German Literature 1700–1990*, ed. by Nicholas Saul (Cambridge: Cambridge University Press, 2002), pp. 150–97

Sagarra, Eda, *Tradition and Revolution: German Literature and Society 1830–1890* (London: Weidenfeld & Nicolson, 1971)

Scholem, Gershom, *Sabbatai Sevi: the Mythical Messiah* (Princeton, NJ: Princeton University Press, 1973)

Schönfeld, Christiane (ed.), *Commodities of Desire: The Prostitute in Modern German Literature* (Rochester, NY: Camden House, 2000)

Segal, Naomi, *The Banal Object: Theme and Thematics in Proust, Rilke, Hofmannsthal, and Sartre* (London: Institute of Germanic Studies, 1981)

Service, Robert, *Trotsky: a Biography* (Basingstoke and Oxford: Pan, 2010)

Tatar, Maria, *Lustmord: Sexual Murder in Weimar Germany* (Princeton, NJ: Princeton University Press, 1995)

Tradowsky, Peter 'Einleitung', in G. F. Daumer, *Kaspar Hauser: Sein Wesen, seine Unschuld*, ed. by Peter Tradowsky (Dornach: Geering, 1984), pp. 3–11

Webber, Andrew J., *The Doppelgänger. Double Visions in German Literature* (Oxford: Clarendon Press, 1996)

Wegner, M., 'Europäische Romanentwicklung im 20. Jahrhundert und F. M. Dostojewskij', *Zeitschrift für Slawistik*, 21 (1976), 500–12

Wilson, Daniel W., *Goethe. Männer. Knaben*, trans. by Angela Steidele (Berlin: Insel, 2012)

Young, Harry F., *Maximilian Harden, Censor Germaniae: The Critic in Opposition from Bismarck to the Rise of Nazism* (The Hague: Martinus Nijhoff, 1959)

INDEX

www.ingramcontent.com/pod-product-compliance
Lightning Source LLC
LaVergne TN
LVHW022051300826
846742LV00002B/2